The Second Centering Book

More Awareness Activities for Children and Adults to Relax the Body and Mind

GAY HENDRICKS

and

THOMAS B. ROBERTS

PRENTICE HALL PRESS

NEW YORK   LONDON   TORONTO   SYDNEY   TOKYO

Prentice Hall Press
Gulf+Western Building
One Gulf+Western Plaza
New York, New York 10023

Copyright © 1977 by Simon & Schuster Inc.

PRENTICE HALL PRESS and colophon are registered trademarks of Simon & Schuster Inc.

Library of Congress Cataloging-in-Publication Data

Hendricks, Gay.
    The second centering book: more awareness activities for children and adults for relaxing the body and mind / Gay Hendricks and Thomas B. Roberts.
        p. cm.
    Bibliography: p.
    ISBN 0-13-798448-0
    1. Affective education. 2. Self-actualization (Psychology) 3. Movement education. I. Roberts, Thomas B. II. Title.
LB1072.H47   1989
371.3'07'8—dc19   89-3545
                                                               CIP

Text illustrations by Nancy Hendrick

Manufactured in the United States of America

10 9 8 7 6 5 4 3 2 1

With love and thanks to

CTR for your encouragement
of my interests and hobbies,
and especially for the good desserts

TER for your example of karma yoga,
and especially your interest in words
and help with writing

DWR for being such a worthy example
to look up to, and especially
for the good visits with your family
and your old bathrobe

—Tom

To my daughter, Amanda
For kids everywhere

—Gay

Contents

2

Centering

in Physical Education 27

3

Teaching with Fantasy 35

4

Working with Dreams 51

5

Meditating, Relaxing, Energizing   55

6

Building Intuition
by Frances Vaughan Clark   73

7

Centering in Feeling
and Communication
by Lynn C. Elliott   87

8

Parapsychology:
Exploring the Mind 157

Preface

An Expanded View
of Centering

In writing the first *Centering Book,* our aim was
to meet a need for something that had been too long
ignored in education: activities for the nonverbal, intuitive, and creative part of children. We were concerned with the development of *being,* because we felt
that education's emphasis was too much on doing and
thinking. Parents, teachers, and others apparently shared
that concern, because *The Centering Book* was received
very warmly. No sooner was the book off the press, however, than we began to collect new activities and broaden
our scope and understanding of what was involved in
being centered.

Two points quickly became clear. First, the concept of centeredness expands into verbal areas as well as the nonverbal. There is a way of being centered in our communications and values that is as important as our mental and physical sense of centeredness. So, we found ourselves putting energy into the verbal areas, discovering and developing techniques for communicating from a centered place. Second, several of the reviews of *The Centering Book* mentioned that the book would have been more effective if the activities had been better integrated into the standard curriculum. So, in this volume we have given examples to show how centering activities can be integrated with science, math, or English lessons. In addition, many physical educators found centering activities useful; we have therefore included a section on centering for coaches in this book. Our expanded view of centering reaches also into intuition, ESP, and fantasy, as well as meditation, relaxation, and mind/body integration.

The world is changing rapidly. There are many ideas now current that radically affect the way we live our lives. Some of these ideas are:

- The value of ecological awareness and kindness to the earth
- Honesty in communication
- The value of quiet and solitude
- The value of open, honest relationships in which deepest feelings and fantasies are shared

- The value of meditation
- The value of taking care of our bodies (for example, nutrition, jogging, yoga, Tai Chi, relaxation)
- The joy of movement
- The value of intuition
- Personal responsibility (for example: we are responsible for our thoughts, our feelings, and the creation of our reality)
- The awareness that our way of being (centered vs. scattered, relaxed vs. tense) profoundly affects our doing

The authors are deeply grateful to all those who embrace and disseminate these kinds of ideas. It is our belief that a radical change in personal consciousness is necessary to change the course of humanity. We also believe that to open children to these new ways of seeing the world is to make a loving and profound contribution to the betterment of our world. To expand awareness together with children is liberating, interesting, and a great deal of fun.

We believe that one of the most important developments of the last few years is the accelerating expansion of transpersonal psychology and education. It appears that this expansion is part of a larger transition in our culture. Introductory psychology textbooks are including chapters on altered states of consciousness. The Association for Transpersonal Psychology's membership is expanding consistently, college and university courses in consciousness, eastern psychologies, parapsychology and transpersonal psychology are springing up. Much of this growth in academic psychology is being forced by students who are pushing their departments to consider consciousness as a subject of academic inquiry. Popular books by Ornstein, Tart, Grof, and others who explore transpersonal domains are opening doors to new paradigms in psychology.

Psychologists who are familiar with Abraham Maslow's work on humanistic psychology are discovering that his later work is taking them beyond humanistic psychology and beyond self-actualization. In the "Preface" to the second edition of *Toward a Psychology of Being*, Maslow states that he sees the development of transpersonal psychology as "going beyond humanness, identity, self-actualization, and the like." His hierachy of needs (see facing page), which is so familiar to students and teachers, ends up with transcendence as a need above self-actualization.

The consciousness revolution in psychology is permeating education, too. This book is part of it. Teachers, administrators, and parents who are concerned with optimum learning are introducing transpersonal techniques into the classroom. These techniques not only help improve student learning of traditional subject matter, they also improve morale and open new vistas of learning. The readings listed in the Transpersonal Treasure Map at the end of this book illustrate these techniques and

MASLOW'S NEEDS HIERARCHY

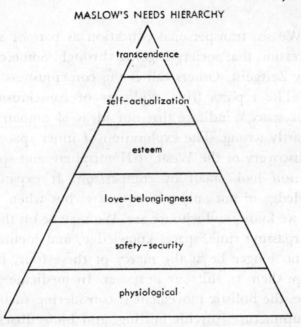

transcendence

self-actualization

esteem

love-belongingness

safety-security

physiological

document the benefits. As the dates of bibliographic items show, interest in transpersonal approaches to learning is growing. Often, schools that are ready to adopt new ways of teaching hesitate because they expect the parents will not understand what is going on. On their part, parents wonder why the schools keep doing the same old things in the same old ways. Meanwhile, the children are learning less than they could. If you are a parent who is interested in bettering your children's schools, you might lend this book to the teachers or principal. One of the advantages of transpersonal teaching is that it makes teachers' jobs easier because the students enjoy these methods. In addition, the methods enhance learning.

We see transpersonal education as part of a larger progression that society is going through. Some call this a new Zeitgeist. Others call it the consciousness revolution. The reports from explorers of consciousness, or "inner space," indicate that our ideas of human nature are vastly wrong. The exploration of inner space makes the discovery of the Western Hemisphere and space exploration look small by comparison. It expands our knowledge of not only *where* we are, but when we are; what we know, and who we are. We may be on the verge of surpassing time, space, knowledge, and identity. We may no longer be at the mercy of these four, but can change them to suit our purposes. In medicine, for example, the holistic movement is considering such things as acupuncture, psychic healing, and biofeedback as legitimate concerns. A Council of Nurse-Healers has formed, which teaches such things as "therapeutic touch"; this seems to be a sort of mental or psychic healing which has been measured to effect hemoglobin levels.

In religion, there is increased interest in those transpersonal experiences which religions spring from and which nourish ongoing faith. After being neglected for years, mysticism, healing, and phenomena that do not fit into our scientific way of viewing the world are again beginning to be taken seriously by scientists. Transpersonal psychology recognizes mystical experiences as legitimate and normal. In a sense this is enlarging the domain of psychology to include behaviors that had

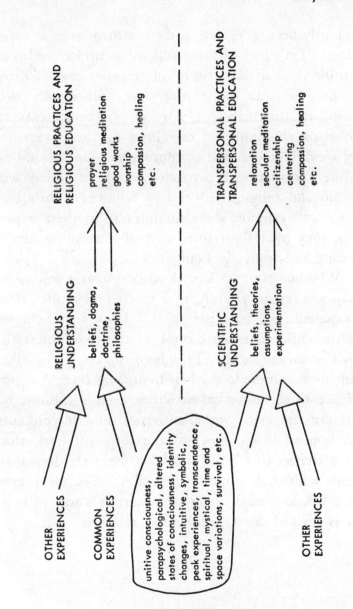

OTHER
EXPERIENCES

COMMON
EXPERIENCES

unitive consciousness,
parapsychological, altered
states of consciousness, identity
changes, intuitive, symbolic,
peak experiences, transcendence,
spiritual, mystical, time and
space variations, survival, etc.

OTHER
EXPERIENCES

RELIGIOUS
UNDERSTANDING

beliefs, dogma,
doctrine,
philosophies

RELIGIOUS PRACTICES AND
RELIGIOUS EDUCATION

prayer
religious meditation
good works
worship
compassion, healing
etc.

SCIENTIFIC
UNDERSTANDING

beliefs, theories,
assumptions,
experimentation

TRANSPERSONAL PRACTICES AND
TRANSPERSONAL EDUCATION

relaxation
secular meditation
citizenship
centering
compassion, healing
etc.

previously been relegated to the occult or seen as superstitious. "Let's look at these and try to understand them scientifically," is the attitude of transpersonal researchers. Because this information has traditionally been studied in the realm of religion, religious texts are studied for the light they can throw on these areas. But they are only one source of information. One should not confuse transpersonal psychology and education with religion and religious education, however. While both science and religion share an interest in these experiences, they offer their own ways of examining, understanding and applying them.

Whether you work with children as a counselor, group worker, or advisor, as a teacher or principal, or as a parent, the exercises in this book will help you and the children explore some of the most interesting activities in the world. This book makes an excellent companion volume to the first *Centering Book*. You will find plenty of nonverbal activities in this volume, but there are also many verbal activities (how to communicate, how to listen, how to take responsibility), along with activities that build intuition, help children make friends with their minds and bodies, relax them, energize them, and teach them that there is a way of being that is relaxed, alert, whole, and *centered*.

Children of a future age
Reading this impassioned page,
Know that in a former time
The use of mind was thought a crime

—After WILLIAM BLAKE,
with thanks and apologies

In one of C. S. Lewis's books for children there is a conversation about a star. "In our world," a boy says, "a star is a huge ball of flaming gas.' He is answered "Even in your world, my son, that is not what a star is but only what it is made of."

—from *Books with Men Behind Them*
by EDMUND FULLER

The Second
Centering Book

1
Centering Body and Mind

In this section we will explore new ways of centering the body and mind. We will present exercises to do with small groups or an entire class, and we will suggest ways to integrate centering activities into the standard curriculum.

Growing up is a complex and sometimes painful process. Children occupy a relatively powerless place in society, and are easily buffeted about by the actions and emotions sweeping around them. Anything we as parents and teachers can do to give children sources of internal stability will benefit them greatly. The centering activities in this section were selected because they are key processes that can help children move through their rapidly changing worlds with a greater sense of self.

The exercises in this chapter should be done in the order in which they are presented. They have been arranged to create a developmental flow in the participants' experience. Also, it is important to preface the activities by discussing some of the information contained in the introductions to several of the exercises. This will help the participants form a cognitive framework for a fuller appreciation of the activities.

#1: The Centered Mind

Age Range: Third grade to adult

This experience teaches a very valuable lesson. The "message" is that being in the here and now is a liberating (and often rare) experience.

Several points of information should be discussed with the participants.

1. Most of us spend a great deal of time doing one thing, such as walking, while thinking of something else, like replaying yesterday's argument or fantasizing about tonight's dinner.

2. It can be an interesting experience to watch where our minds take us.

3. It can be a very interesting experience to be centered in the here and now, e.g., just walking. Being

in the here and now can have a very special effect on our actions.

4. Explain that there are several things our minds often do to take us out of the here and now: memories (things that happened in the past), fantasies (things that never happened, or might happen in the future), and talk (our own voices and the voices of others talking to us).

Requirements: A piece of paper and a pencil for each person, and something on which to focus, such as a flower, a vase, a candle, or the second hand of a clock. Have participants make three columns on their paper, labeled Memory, Fantasy, and Talk.

INSTRUCTIONS

"Let's sit comfortably, letting our bodies and minds relax."

Pause 5 seconds

"Let your eyes focus softly on the (clock, candle). Relax your eyes, just let them be windows, receiving the sight in front of them.

Pause 5 seconds

"We spend a lot of time thinking about the future, remembering things from the past, talking to ourselves. Let's keep track of where our minds take us for a while, by making a mark in the column whenever we find our minds somewhere else. If we're fantasizing about the future or thinking something that probably would never happen, make a mark under Fantasy, then just gently return to focusing on the (object).

"If you're thinking about the past, put a mark under Memory. If you find yourself talking to yourself or hearing other people's voices, then mark under Talk and bring yourself easily back to the (object). See how many of each you can spot."

Continue for 3 to 4 minutes,
longer for subsequent repetitions

"Now let your mind just go wherever it wants for a few moments, just relax and let go."

Pause 10 seconds

"And gently return your attention to the people around you."

DISCUSSION

An interesting discussion can emerge from the preceding experience. Here are some questions that can stimulate the discussion. Of course, there are no "right" answers to these questions.

- Why do some people have mostly memories, while others have more talk or fantasies?
- Did anything besides these three types of thoughts occur (like music)?
- Can fantasies cause us any problems? How about memories? Talk?
- What makes us leave the here and now and have fantasies, memories, and talk?
- What would it be like if we didn't do this?

#2: The Labeling Game

Age Range: Third grade to adult

This exercise makes use of the same information as #1, but approaches the task in a slightly different way.

Nothing is required; everything is done internally. It would be good first to review the concepts (memory, fantasy, talk) explored in #1.

INSTRUCTIONS

"Sit comfortably, take a deep breath, and let your body go. Let yourself go and be as relaxed as you will let yourself be."

Pause 5 seconds

"Gently let your eyes close . . . just let them relax in the darkness."

Pause 5 seconds

"Begin watching your thoughts as they go through your mind. Every time you spot one that's a memory, say 'Memory, memory,' to yourself, and just gently return to watching. Do the same for fantasies and talk. If you find yourself having a fantasy or listening to talk, just say, 'Fantasy, fantasy' or 'Talking, talking,' and go back to watching. Label each thought in this way. If something else happens (like hearing music) label that, too. If you're not sure what it is, just say, 'Thinking, thinking.' "

Continue for 3-4 minutes at first, working up to about 10 minutes

DISCUSSION

How can labeling the events in our minds be useful in helping us be happier? (Sample answer: If we label something, we are less likely to be afraid of it.)

#3: Going Deeper into the Mind and Body

Age Range: Third grade to adult

Here are several additions to the previous two exercises. These instructions will deepen the participants' understanding of their minds and bodies. Since these instructions build on the first two activities, it would be good to review the basic ideas from the previous exercises, especially if a week or so has elapsed since they were practiced. Ideally, exercises #1, #2, and those in

#3 should be done on successive days over the period of a week.

INSTRUCTIONS

"Sit comfortably, take a good, deep breath, and let your body and mind relax. Let your system settle down gently."

Pause 5-10 seconds

"Recently we've been exploring our minds by watching our thoughts and gently labeling them. When we see a memory, we say in our minds, 'Memory, memory,' and when we see a fantasy we say, 'Fantasy, fantasy.' When we hear ourselves talking to ourselves, we say, 'Talking, talking.' Now let's add to that a new type of naming and labeling. As you relax and go inside, notice the rising and falling of your breath. Just pay attention to it in a gentle, nonpossessive way, and when you feel your breath come in, say to yourself, 'Rising, rising,' and when your breath goes out say, 'Falling, falling.' When your mind wanders, which it will, see where it goes, make a mental note, such as 'Talking, talking,' or 'Thinking, thinking,' then return to your breath, 'Rising, rising' and 'Falling, falling.' Now close your eyes and begin."

Continue for 5-10 minutes

(For Another Day)

"Sit gently and let your body relax."

Pause 5-10 seconds

"Remember how you named and labeled your breathing and your thoughts by saying to yourself 'Rising, rising,' 'Falling, falling,' and 'Memory, memory,' 'Fantasy, fantasy,' or 'Talking, talking.' Today we'll do all of that plus some new types of awareness. Sometimes we have feelings inside of us. Sometimes all we notice about them is that they are pleasant or unpleasant. Sometimes we notice that the feeling is some particular emotion like anger, fear, sadness, or happiness. During today's exploring, see if you have any feelings in your bodies like the ones I've just mentioned. If you feel a pleasant feeling, say to yourself, 'Pleasant, pleasant.' If you feel an unpleasant feeling, say to yoursely, 'Unpleasant, unpleasant.' If you feel scared, say, 'Scared, scared' or 'Fear, fear.' If you feel anger, say 'Anger, anger.' If sadness comes up, simply make a mental note that says, 'Sadness, sadness.' Do the same with happiness. When you're not feeling anything, continue to follow your breathing, 'Rising, rising,' and 'Falling, falling.' "

Continue for 5-10 minutes

(For Another Day)

"Now we've learned how to name and label thinking, breathing, and feeling. Today you should do all of these, plus something new. When you are seeing, hearing, touching, tasting, or smelling, you are using your senses. So, when you find yourself concentrating on one of these, label it 'Sensing, sensing.' If you're aware of one specific sense, like seeing or hearing, say to yourself, 'Seeing, seeing' or 'Hearing, hearing.' Do the same with tasting, smelling, and touching. When you're not aware of any senses, note your breathing, 'Rising, rising,' 'Falling, falling,' and your thoughts and feelings."

Continue for 5-10 minutes

Comments: Other experiences will emerge during the practice of these techniques: tension, boredom, sleep, anxiety, bliss, nothing, etc. Simply note these experiences with whatever label seems appropriate, "Boredom, boredom," "Tension, tension." These techniques are drawn from the Vipassana (Insight) meditation practices of

Ceylon (now Sri Lanka) and Burma. For a lovely exposition of these techniques, readers are urged to read Joseph Goldstein's *The Experience of Insight.*

Integrating #1, #2, and #3
into the Curriculum

Almost any classroom experience can be turned into an experience in centering the mind. For example, one teacher uses the preceding techniques with her eleventh grade class as part of what she calls "math meditation." She has the class members track their memories, fantasies, and talk while she is presenting math lessons. This makes use of the normal tendency of the mind to wander away from the task at hand. By helping the students be aware of the meanderings of their minds, this teacher is turning a mundane experience into an exercise in self-discovery.

A major benefit to be gained from centering the mind is to know that our thoughts are just thoughts. Sometimes we take our fantasies, memories, and talk so seriously that we become just as frightened, sad, or angry about something that we create in our minds as we do about a real event. It helps to be able to get a perspective on our thoughts so that we can treat them as what they are: our own creations, with only as much reality as we are willing to give them.

#4: Centering Body and Mind

Age Range: All ages

This is an exercise that integrates the mind and the body. It begins by helping the body achieve total relaxation, then uses the power of the mind to bring a serenity to the entire organism. The exercise is best done lying down.

INSTRUCTIONS

"Find a spot where your body feels most comfortable. Let your legs lie flat and relaxed on the floor. Settle your back onto the floor, letting your whole body feel completely supported by the floor."

Pause 5 seconds

"Now close your eyes and let your eyes relax, letting them sink back into your head, feeling rested and relaxed. Give your eyes total permission to relax."

Pause 5 seconds

"And now let your cheeks relax, along with your mouth and jaw, just letting them relax and be easy."

Pause 5 seconds

"And now relax your tongue . . ."

Pause 5 seconds

"And your neck . . ."

Pause 5 seconds

"Give your tongue and your neck complete permission to relax."

Pause 5 seconds

"Let the soothing feeling of relaxation fill your head

and neck. Your mind stays alert, your head, eyes, cheeks, and neck relax deeply."

Pause 5 seconds

"Find any tension in your stomach, give your attention to it, then let it go, just giving in and relaxing your stomach."

Pause 5 seconds

"Relax down in your pelvic area . . . letting your buttocks feel completely supported by the floor, giving in and relaxing throughout your body."

Pause 5 seconds

"And now give your legs permission to relax and feel supported by the floor. Let your thighs and your calves go, and feel the deep feeling of relaxation soak into your legs."

Pause 5 seconds

"And let your feet and toes relax . . . just give in and let all of the tension go . . . now feeling your whole body supported by the floor."

Pause 5 seconds

"Relax your eyes and sense a little spot of energy way down in your stomach beneath your navel. Breathe down to that spot and feel it grow."

Pause 5 seconds

"There is a spot in our bodies that is the center, the place that is the balance point for our whole being. Find that spot down in your stomach and breathe to it . . . feeling it awaken so that you'll always be able to find it."

Pause 10 seconds

"Take a finger and place it gently on the spot . . . breathing down to that spot, awakening that spot of energy in you."

Pause 10 seconds

"Now take everything in your mind and send it all down to your center . . . just be your center . . . breathing in and out, feeling the center of your body . . ."

Pause 10 seconds

"And now I'll count back from 10 to 1, and when

I hit 1 you'll feel rested and very alert. 10, 9, 8, 7, let your toes and fingers wiggle . . . 6, 5, 4, feel awareness returning to your body . . . 3, 2, open your eyes, and 1, sit up, rested and alert."

#5: Standing Centered

Age Range: First grade to adult

Our goal is to be centered in all our actions: sitting, standing, moving. This activity is designed to help us learn to stand on our own two feet, centered and grounded.

INSTRUCTIONS

"Find a spot to stand in that feels comfortable, letting your eyes close and your body relax. Let your eyes relax in your head . . . letting your ears take over for a while. Unlock your knees and relax your legs . . . Relax your stomach . . . your chest . . . your shoulders."

Pause 5 seconds

"Let your body rock from side to side, shifting your weight from one side to the other . . . Keep rocking slower and slower until you find the spot where you are perfectly balanced and centered."

Pause until everyone is still

"And now rock front and back until you find the place where your weight is right over your arches, heels and toes sharing your weight equally."

Pause until everyone comes to rest

"Now pretend you have a body inside you that no one can see . . . let it rock side to side until it becomes centered, too . . . then front to back."

Pause 10 seconds

"And now take your mind and imagine letting it sink down to your center."

Pause 5 seconds

"Enjoy the feeling of being perfectly balanced, relaxed, and centered, realizing that you can return to that feeling whenever you need to feel relaxed and at peace with yourself."

Pause 5 seconds

"And now let your attention come back to the people around you."

Integrating #4 and #5 into the Curriculum

Of course #4 and #5, like all the centering activities, are useful by themselves as personal growth activities. However, these two activities have broad usefulness when integrated into the standard curriculum. Here are several suggestions:

- Use #4 or #5 to get students calmed down before a test, before lunch, or after recess.
- Use #5 as a prelude to giving oral reports.
- (Parents) Use #4 at bedtime when children are too wound up to go to sleep.

- Have children shoot free throws before and after #5. Their scores usually go up after they've learned to stand centered.
- Have them take each other's pulse before and after #4, tying the activity in with a science or physiology lesson.

#6: Moving Centered

Age Range: First grade to adult

This activity can be a memorable experience. Sometimes participants become so centered and relaxed that they feel as if they're floating. It can be done in a gymnasium, or outdoors on a pleasant day. The only requirement is a large, open space in which to walk.

INSTRUCTIONS

"Let's begin by walking easily . . . getting the feel of our bodies in motion."

Pause 10 seconds

"Get the feel of how your feet touch the ground . . . how your arms feel . . . how your legs move."

Pause 15 seconds

"Now let your neck relax and your head just sit on your shoulders. Let it relax there, completely supported as you move along. Relax your eyes and let them see softly."

Pause 10 seconds

"Now relax your shoulders . . . just let them go."

Pause 10 seconds

"And now relax your chest, giving in and letting all the tension go."

Pause 10 seconds

"Now relax your stomach . . . just let all the tension go from it."

Pause 10 seconds

"With every step you take, relax the whole upper

half of your body . . . check each part . . . head . . . shoulders . . . chest . . . stomach . . . let each part go, completely relaxing it."

Pause 10 seconds

"And now completely relax your pelvis and thighs . . . letting each step take you deeper into relaxation. If you find one area tensing up, just relax it again."

Pause 15 seconds

"As you walk along, completely relaxed, you can imagine a ray of light coming out of your center . . . imagine it pulling you gently along, making each step you take sure and centered."

Pause 15 seconds

"Anytime you need to feel centered while you are moving, just relax all of your body, let all the unnecessary tension go from it . . . then let yourself just move along, effortlessly and relaxed."

Pause 10 seconds

"Now come to a rest at your own speed, pausing for a moment to enjoy a feeling of peaceful stillness inside."

Integrating #6
into the Curriculum

There are many times in the school day when the centered walk can be useful. It can help when quiet walking is required, as on a trip to the library during classtime. Often teachers rely on injunctions ("BE QUIET") to cue children to walk quietly; #6 is an alternative way to achieve the goal of quiet walking while teaching a set of skills that can be used throughout life.

Another possibility is to take a Polaroid shot of someone walking in a normal, hurried way. The photo will usually reveal a very *uncentered* posture. The head will be straining forward, shoulders will be hunched up, hips locked back. Compare this with a Polaroid picture of someone walking during #6. The snapshot will reveal a straight, flowing relaxed posture. Students can act out the two postures, comparing them for straightness, muscle tension, and to see which way of being feels best. This type of experience can be integrated with information on health, physiology, or anatomy.

#7: Centering in Relationship

Age Range: Fifth grade to adult

Most of our lives are spent in relationship to each other. Therefore, the truest test of our centeredness is whether we can maintain it while relating to others. This is difficult because other people make demands on us, give us occasion to be angry, frightened, and sad, and do things that almost seem calculated to pull us off-center. However, when we can relate to each other in clear, direct ways, there is a boundless joy available in relationships.

The following activity is designed for staying centered while doing things which people usually find difficult in relationships.

There are several points of information that can be useful to participants in this activity.

1. Most of us have difficulty staying centered in stressful situations, and interpersonal relationships can contain some of our most stressful times.

2. One way to tell if people are afraid and uncentered is if they lose eye contact with us.

3. If we can stay centered and maintain contact with each other while we are communicating, our relationships will have more depth and clarity.

INSTRUCTIONS

"Find a partner and stand facing her/him. Let your eyes close and your body relax. Start with your head, letting all the tension drain out of your mind and your eyes."

Pause 5 seconds

"Now relax your shoulders . . . letting your arms hang loosely at your sides."

Pause 5 seconds

"And now take a deep breath . . . and relax your chest as you exhale . . . let your shoulders and chest feel loose and free."

Pause 5 seconds

"And now relax your pelvis and legs, giving in and letting all the tension go. Let your body feel relaxed, balanced, and centered. Check to make sure your weight is balanced on both feet . . . side to side, front to back."

Pause 5 seconds

"Now open your eyes and make eye contact with your partner."

Pause 10 seconds

"Check your body to see if any part tensed up, or if you became unbalanced. If you become tense or un-balanced, just relax that part of you and go back to making eye contact. If your mind wanders, see where it went, then go back to making eye contact."

Pause 1-2 minutes

"And now keep making eye contact as you totally relax your shoulders . . . your chest . . . your stomach . . your pelvis . . . your legs."

(*Optional:* Have the participants do Exercise #2 [The Labeling Game] while continuing to make eye contact.)

Pause 15 seconds

"Now close your eyes again and feel as centered as you can . . . and when you're ready, open your eyes and return your attention to the people around you."

DISCUSSION

- Why is it hard to make eye contact without giggling, tensing, or becoming uncentered?
- Where did minds wander during this activity? Why?
- Why are eyes called the "windows to the soul"?
- Is it possible to make your eyes look frightened? Angry? Sad? Joyful? Can it be done just with the eyes (without raising eyebrows, etc.)?
- What happens to our bodies when we make our eyes look angry? Scared? Sad? Joyful?

2

Centering
in Physical Education

There is a revolution underway in physical education, and it is one of the brightest hopes for change in our schools. For many years physical education plodded along, relying mainly on calisthenics and choose-sides competitive sports. The problem was that many sports —softball is a good example—are not generally lifetime sports (that is, they do not teach skills which encourage the individual to exercise throughout life) and they involve long periods of inactivity punctuated by short bursts of action. Much of the rest of physical education was, like calisthenics, downright boring to students. Then came a new generation of educators who saw the potential for mind-body development inherent in this subject.

Now, new ideas are pouring into physical education so fast that it's difficult to keep up with them. Prominent among these are lifelong sports, movement education, and centering activities. Lifelong sports are those which can be practiced throughout life, by the lawyer, the laborer, and the office worker. These include hiking, jogging, bowling, and tennis, among many others.

Books such as Mike Spino's *The Innerspaces of Running* and Fred Rohe's *The Zen of Running*, for example, explore new approaches to running.

Movement education is a trend in physical education which emphasizes the process of movement. Here students explore the *processes* involved in throwing, stretching, jumping, and running. The joy of movement is the focus.

Centering activities have recently begun to make an impact on physical education. Among the activities which have been found useful are fantasy, relaxation, meditation, and body awareness.

Fantasy is the use of the natural ability of mental imagery to enhance performance or personal growth. The applications to sports are almost limitless. For example, the U.S. Olympic ski team used the services of psychologist Richard Suinn, who is with the Department of Psychology at Colorado State University in Fort Collins. Suinn, an expert in the use of fantasy in athletics, helped the members of the team prepare for and compete in the 1976 games at Innsbruck. Using a process he called visuomotor behavior rehearsal, Suinn had the skiers practice imagining their ski runs, with particular emphasis on mentally correcting mistakes they had made in the actual runs. Skiers found that rehearsing the runs mentally had a positive effect on subsequent performance. This finding draws upon a sizeable body of research on mental practice over the past 30 or 40 years. The main findings of this research is that mental practice, under certain conditions with certain sports, can be as effective as physical practice. In the case of the ski team, the mental practice was conducted in conjunction with relaxation training, so there may also have been a relaxation effect enhancing the fantasy technique.

Fantasy is particularly useful in sports involving fine discrimination, such as diving, archery, basketball, and tennis. The heavy body-contact sports are probably less amenable to mental imagery, since it is brawn more than finesse that counts most. For all sports the process is basically the same. The players attain a relaxed state, using one of the many relaxation techniques available in this book and elsewhere, then imagine themselves engaging in successful performances of the target behavior. The process can be done alone or with the help of a coach or assistant. Here is part of a session in which a coach was working with a group of beginning tennis players.

> [The players were lying on the floor, relaxed, with their eyes closed] Picture Tom (the pro) serving the ball in slow motion. Watch him throw the ball in the air . . . watch his body stretch . . . see the

way his eye never leaves the ball. Watch him as he connects with the ball and it rockets into the far corner of the court.

(Pause)

Now imagine your racket is in your hand. Feel the grip and the heft of it. Feel how perfectly balanced it is, like an extension of your arm. Feel the ball in your other hand. Sense the energy in your racket arm that you're going to transfer to the ball. Stand poised and balanced. Now imagine throwing the ball into the air in slow motion. Your body stretched, the racket arm moves and you connect, sending the energy into the ball, firing it into the other court.

Fantasy can also be used to correct habitual mistakes. For example, a common problem in golf, lifting the head, can be corrected by having the golfer mentally rehearse the swing while keeping his head down.

Perhaps there is no sport that cannot use fantasy as a tool.

Relaxation ties in very closely with fantasy because the latter is often enhanced when the body and mind are relaxed. Relaxation can be used before or after any sport activity. When used before, it counters anxiety and allows space for the creative and intuitive parts of us to work. When used after play, it allows tense, contracted muscles to relax while giving time for the person to process the performance, whether it is a gym-class soccer game or an Olympic dive; in addition, other teachers sometimes complain if students come to their class "wound up" after physical education; a brief period of relaxation at the end of gym class gives an opportunity for bodies to quiet down.

There are many approaches to *meditation,* and many explanations for its effects. For our purposes here, we will consider it as a mental relaxation technique, although there are other benefits of meditation practice that are beyond the scope of this book. (For longer discussions of meditation, see Robert Ornstein's *The Psychology of Consciousness* and Naranjo and Ornstein's *The Psychology of Meditation.*) Mental relaxation is a beneficial tool in all athletic endeavors, since there is no sport that cannot be enhanced by a centered, focused mind. It is easy to see how precision sports like billiards or archery would benefit from a calm mind, but even the players of the most physically demanding sports, such as football, are turning to meditation as a way of attaining peak mental concentration. Joe Namath, Bill Walton, and Willie Stargell are some of the well-known meditators from various sports.

Once a journalist found Jim Brown, then a star at Syracuse University, sitting alone in the empty stadium the morning of an important game. The journalist asked Brown what he was thinking about.

"Football," he said.

"What specifically? Your footwork? Your blockers?"
"No," he said, "Football. The word *football.*"

This interchange happened long before the current meditation boom in the United States; it is likely that Brown had never even heard of meditation. But he was clearly meditating, although the *mantra* he was repeating in his mind was certainly no magic Sanskrit incantation.

Body awareness activities have many uses in physical education. In movement education, one of the major goals is simply to increase awareness, on the principle that we will be less likely to neglect or abuse the beautiful machines that are our bodies if we are keenly aware of their functioning. Another goal of increased awareness is to free more of the body's potential. Most of us get stuck in repetitive patterns of movement which become rigid and self-limiting; many movement education activities dissolve old patterns so that increased freedom results.

Stretching is one of the more widely used body awareness techniques. Activities that systematically stretch the various muscle groups are nearly indispensable in a comprehensive approach to physical education. Stretching is used before sports as a warm-up, and after playing as a way of relaxing contracted muscles. (An excellent book called *Stretching,* by Bob Anderson, is available for $7 from Stretching, P.O. Box 1002, Englewood, Colorado 80110.) Other body awareness activities are breathing, centering, yoga, Tai Chi, and Feldenkrais exercises.

The latter are thousands of ingenious and effortless movements designed by Dr. Moshe Feldenkrais, a contemporary Israeli movement master, and author of *Awareness Through Movement* and *Body and Mature Behavior*. The exercises have the effect of increasing the range of the body's movement while building awareness and literally resculpting the body's structure.

Beyond all techniques, there is an attitude that we can bring to physical education which can transform us and our students. We can see the mind and the body as one, and we can bring to the gym and field the same high goals we have for the mind in the academic classroom: to be free, to be creative, to fulfill its potential, to be always striving for improvement. In the classroom we want students to appreciate the joy of learning; in physical education we can teach and celebrate the joy of movement itself.

Lucy Graff, a talented teacher of physical education in Colorado, began using many centering activities in her classes. The activities were greeted at first with wariness (and a fair share of giggles), then with relish as the students began to develop a new perception of themselves and their bodies. At the end of the year Lucy received a number of cards thanking her for the new awarenesses she had given the students. One of the cards said simply, "I love you—stay centered."

3

Teaching with Fantasy

Using fantasy journeys is one of the most fun-filled ways to teach, and one of the most efficient. Fantasy journeys speed students' intellectual development and build their creativity while helping you teach the subject matter. There are also counseling fantasy techniques; although counselors may want to use the techniques from this chapter, the focus here is on the classroom uses of fantasy.

Research has shown that fantasy journeys not only help students develop their creative abilities, but they also help with intellectual tasks. How can this be? Most adult thought is abstract, that is, it is about things that cannot be seen and about ideas, generalizations, and abstract concepts like "democracy" or "gravity." It is important for children to learn how to think about things they can't see, and fantasy journeys train and develop this ability to conceptualize. All planning about future events and memory of past ones also relies on the ability to think of things that can't be perceived, and, in fact, most science deals with abstractions too—frictionless surface, pure chemicals, center of gravity.

"Don't we have too much fantasy?" one might ask. This question usually is based on the assumption that children should learn about reality. It's true, they should. And the ability to fantasize *is* a real human ability. Neglecting it is to neglect a part of reality. Moreover, a way to learn to control fantasy is consciously to practice it. The self-control results as a person consciously fantasizes, then consciously stops. When people can either fantasize or not as it is appropriate, they are no longer at the mercy of their fantasies, but rather they are putting fantasy to work for them. So by exercising your students' abilities to fantasize, you are laying the groundwork for later cognitive growth, bringing fantasy under control, and improving creative problem solving.

In this chapter we will take you on a fantasy journey about writing fantasy journeys of your own. After a few directions on set and setting (your expectations and the place you're in), we'll give you a fantasy journey to do. We recommend you get together with a small group of people and have one of them read the fantasy journey aloud to you rather than read it silently to yourself.

Set and Setting

The way you approach a fantasy journey is your *set*. Psychologists, medical researchers, and others are now realizing that the person's set of expectations is a major influence on what actually does happen. First, it will be helpful if you feel relaxed and at ease. You might want to use the exercises in Chapters 1 and 5. When doing fantasy work with your class, both physical and mental relaxation is almost always a good way to begin, too.

Second, approach the fantasy journey as fun. Practically everyone enjoys doing them. Anything you might think up is all right. There are no wrong answers. After the fantasy journey is over, you may edit it and decide whether or not to use it.

Third, you may come up with ideas that are not at all applicable to the fantasy at hand. Don't be surprised if a solution to a different problem pops into your head. One of the main benefits of fantasy journeys is that ideas can come out of the blue. The skill of finding one thing while looking for another, called *serendipity*, is a basic way to solve problems and is recom-

mended by such diverse thinkers as Arthur Koestler and
B. F. Skinner. If you find that your attention has wandered, don't get upset about it. Just pick up the leader's
or teacher's voice and follow it.

It's okay to fall asleep during a fantasy journey. Research is beginning to show that even when people are
unconscious, part of their mind picks up what is going
on. It is best to remain awake, but don't let falling asleep
bother you, as long as you are not disturbing others.

In a fantasy journey anything is possible. *Everything
is possible.* Don't allow yourself to stop your imagination
with thoughts like "That doesn't fit in" or "How can
that be?" Don't limit yourself to your past experience or
to what's logical. One moment you might be at a beach
sunning and the next skiing down a mountain in your
bathing suit. If that bothers you, imagine ski boots and
a parka. Or imagine a new kind of snow that doesn't
melt in 80-degree heat. You can even be two places at
once, see something from several perspectives, or even
be two, three, or more characters in your fantasies.
If an inconsistency comes, let it. You can learn first
to tolerate inconsistencies, then to enjoy them, finally to
imagine your own. They can add a spice of humor to your
fantasy life. You can be in cold outer space and see
a fragrant, blue rose drift by. The world we have experienced with our senses and the world of logic should not
place limits on fantasy.

Finally, feel comfortable. You may want to lie down on the floor or find a comfortable chair to sit in. Loosen any tight clothes. Make sure you won't have to interrupt your fantasy trip for a trip to the bathroom. It usually is most restful to keep arms, legs, and ankles in an uncrossed position. But if you do become sore or tired, by all means move to a more comfortable position. Don't let an uncomfortable body distract your mind.

The *setting* is the location you are in for a fantasy journey. Basically the room should be comfortable with as few distractions as possible, conducive to letting the mind wander. In most classrooms this means closing the windows and doors to keep out noise, and turning off the lights. Before starting, give the students the right set. Also, tell them that if there is an announcement over the speaker or any other interruption, to let it come and go as if it were a radio or television commercial. They can listen if it pertains to them; otherwise let it go by. If there is noise from outside the room, a relaxation period will help people to adjust to it.

In using fantasy journeys for teaching, your first step is to decide what content you want to teach. Then design a fantasy journey for it. After you take the fantasy journey, the last part of this chapter will show you how to turn it into a class lesson.

A Fantasy-Journey
Fantasy Journey

This fantasy journey is written to help you write your own fantasy journeys for teaching. It will help you generate ideas. The fantasy journeys you use in class are likely to be more specific in the script than this one is because you will want to teach some specific information. Fantasy journeys which are used to stimulate creativity usually are less specific about the adventures than those designed for teaching.

We recommend you get together with a small group of others who want to use fantasy teaching. One of you is the leader and reads the fantasy. The others lie on the floor or otherwise make themselves comfortable. It sometimes helps to go through the fantasy journey several times in one session. We recommend taking the journey, followed by a relaxed discussion and sharing period, then the journey followed by another sharing session. You may even want to do a third round. A different person can serve as leader each time. You can stick with the same topic or you may want to switch each time. It's convenient to have a piece of paper and pen nearby to jot down one or two key words or a visual symbol-reminder as you go along. We recommend you try to use your memory, but if you find yourself saying, "I know I had a good idea, but I can't remember it," then use the pen. You don't want to stir up your verbal-analytic abilities during the journey. Any writing should be done with as little commotion as possible so as not to bother your fellow journeyers.

Are you all ready to go?

- How's your set?
  Relaxed?
  Playful attitude?
  Open to all possibilities?
  Noncritical?
  Comfortable?
- How's your setting?
  Quiet?
  Dimly lighted?
  Fewest possible distractions?

If each person has learned how to relax deeply, then give several minutes for them to relax. If the participants have not learned a relaxation technique, try one of the techniques you have already learned, but hold the wake-up instructions for after the fantasy journey.

Now that you're comfortable, relaxed, and ready, the leader starts:

"This fantasy trip is composed of two parts, first

selecting a topic, then questions and directions to stimulate your ideas for writing your own fantasy journeys. If the telephone rings or if some other kind of distraction occurs, I'll take care of it. Just remain relaxed and let ideas flow through your mind." (Short pause)

"In the first part of the fantasy journey we will select our topics. Think back through all the subjects, units, and topics you teach. As you do this, try to look at them in a detached, objective way." (Long pause)

"Pretend these units are all file folders, student papers, classroom equipment, magazine clippings, and so forth spread out before you in a large field. Visualize all these papers, pieces of equipment, and articles all spread out." (Short pause) "They cover a lot of area, don't they?" (Short pause)

"Imagine that you can float over them. You waft here and there looking down at them." (Short pause) "You might notice that there are lots of words, numbers, formulas, forms, and symbols there." (Short pause) "Probably not too many pictures." (Short pause)

"Continue floating over your papers, and as you do so, one of them will rise and float up to you." (Pause)

"Examine the paper, folder, or piece of equipment as if you have no idea what it is . . . you have never seen it before." (Pause)

"You may write your fantasy journey on this topic if you like. Don't be surprised if this is a topic you didn't expect to write your fantasy trip on today." (Short pause) "You can let it float back down to the field and wait for another topic to float up, or you can keep it." (Pause) "Now you and your topic have selected each other. You and your topic are floating away from the field to a favorite, quiet place. It might be a beach, a garden, a favorite room, any place that is restful and where you like being." (Pause)

"Feel how good it is to be there." (Short pause) "What's this? Your topic has changed. It's no longer a piece of paper or equipment. It's changed into your favorite food. You look at it. Can you feel your mouth watering?" (Short pause) "Go ahead. Eat it." (Pause)

"You're digesting it now, it's going through your whole body." (Pause) "As it spreads it makes you feel relaxed and happy. From your stomach it spreads down into your abdomen and hips. Into your legs and down into your feet and toes. It expands, making your lungs feel nourished and warm. They breathe naturally and easily. It goes into your shoulders and down your arms to your wrists and fingers. The feeling flows up your neck and into your head." (Short pause) "It's good brain food. Now that your favorite food is nourishing your whole body, it will feed your imagination. The food was really the transformed paper from back on the field, so it will help you imagine things about that topic. The topic that floated up to you is food for fantasy consciousness. It makes you feel at ease and alert, relaxed and aware, and ready to see whatever ideas and images pop up." (Short pause)

"Some of the situations and directions that follow

might have to be changed to fit your topic. Go ahead and change them. If a different instruction comes into your mind, go ahead and follow it.

"Suppose you were seeing or experiencing your topic for the first time and had no idea what it was." (Short pause) "At first you can't imagine what this strange thing is. See it with 'fresh eyes,' full of wonder, and curiosity. Observe it closely." (Long pause)

"Now suppose your size changes as you explore it. You might want to be gigantic or minute, like an insect, bacteria, or subatomic particle, or even smaller." (Long pause)

"What if you actually were the topic? How would you feel about yourself?" (Long pause)

"Imagine what your physical sensations could be." (Long pause)

"Remember to experience with all your senses. Sight, touch, smell, taste, sound. You can have X-ray vision if you want. You can have 'X-ray touch' and feel the inside of things. Also 'X-ray' smell, taste, and sound. If you are observing people, you can know what's going on inside their minds and bodies if you want to. Use all your senses and make up more if you'd like to." (Long pause)

"What are your emotions? How do other things and people feel about you?" (Long pause)

"Why are you important? What do you give to mankind and to other objects or activities?" (Long pause)

"If you were the object or activity, how would you

experience the teacher and class that is learning about you? How does it feel to be studied?" (Long pause)

"What if time were going very fast, or very slowly? How would you experience your topic? You can move backwards and forwards in time as fast and as far as you want." (Long pause)

"Suppose you started to hear colors or feel sounds when you regarded your topic. What would they be like? What if smell or touch became sound?" (Long pause)

"Suppose you were part of what you are studying. How do you relate to the whole? How do you contribute to it? How does it contribute to you? How does the whole relate to a larger whole?" (Long pause)

(Notes to Leader: If you think of other image-raising directions or idea-provoking questions, try them. If your group is familiar with relaxation techniques, you can let them bring themselves back. If not, try the wake-up exercises at the end of any relaxation exercises from this book or *The Centering Book.* Don't be in too much of a hurry, as it is better to take a bit more time than a bit too little.)

"Keep all those ideas and images in mind."

"Now it's time to come back." (Short pause) "Bring yourself back gently and slowly and keep in mind those ideas and images that you have thought of. You might want to make a note or two on your pad of paper." (Wait until writing has ceased or slowed down)

"Now let's share what we've got."

During the discussion time following a fantasy journey, it helps to keep the lights low, perhaps using a candle or two if it's dark. Keep the pace and feeling relaxed because people will still be getting ideas and will want to consider them or jot them down. Any sharing should be completely voluntary.

Teaching Hints

The preceding fantasy journey is to help you stimulate your imagination to build your own fantasy journeys. It is not one that you are likely to use in your classroom, except for helping your students write their own journeys. Most teachers report that it is best to use a fantasy journey as a lead-in to a new topic. It provides students with experiences that they can then attach to the written assignment, class lecture, or other word- and symbol-based instruction. Students have the easiest time learning something they have had experience with. But many things are beyond direct experience, so fantasy experience can substitute for actual sensory experience.

When students experience fantasy journeys before they read about the material, they will not be able to use their knowledge of the subject to screen out the imagery.

During a fantasy journey inside the bloodstream, for example, their imaginations will work better if they mentally see the white blood cells fighting off an infection before they are told about this in class or before they read about it. Otherwise they can dismiss the fantasy by recognizing and labeling it: "Oh, it's the white blood cells." Don't allow them to turn off their minds, because they'll miss important things you want to get across.

This brings up another hint in using fantasy: When presenting something new, don't call it by its name until late in the journey, or not at all. Not-naming is an important key to getting people to pay attention. Instead of saying that the white cells are attacking an infection, for example, describe the cells, the infection, and the battle between them as if two monster hoards were fighting. You might want to say what they are later, or you might want to leave the students' curiosity open to see when they are able to connect the fantasy with the class work or reading later on.

After you use fantasy journeys a few times, some students will want to write their own. This can also be a fun-filled way of teaching, because creating a fantasy journey requires a knowledge of the topic. It is wise to ask the student to tell you the fantasy before leading the rest of the class, so you can make sure it is factually accurate.

Students can also be asked to write a brief fantasy as a homework assignment, class discussion, or test item. When studying chemistry, for example, what would an oxygen atom go through when becoming water? Dialogue and brief scenes give practice in writing skills, exercise creativity, and require knowledge of the topic or situation. Some students really take to writing them, and writing a fantasy journey can keep a gifted or creative student busy learning without just repeating work that he already knows.

Psychologists are finding that our brains work in at least two fashions. The left hemisphere is calculating, linear, and uses language, formulas, and mathlike symbols. The right hemispehre is better at visual-spatial knowledge, thinking in images and pictures, and perhaps is even in contact with the unconscious and intuition. The best thinking seems to integrate the two ways of knowing. By providing fantasies and our usual verbal information, we give students experience in combining these two modes of thinking and knowing.

When you organize a lesson plan, note those things that you want to stress, for example a barter economic system. What aspects of barter do you want to emphasize? These are the items to be sure to include in your fantasy journey. If you want students to learn that there is no money, then a fantasy journey to a barter system can repeatedly point out that the people are buying things without money, that they are trading, or that your student in the fantasy tries to buy something but they don't know what money is and will trade only for the intrinsic worth of the pictures on the bills. Here again, you would not mention "barter," but would describe what is going on and have the students participate in it.

If you were trying to emphasize the crystaline structure of a certain type of rock, you could have the students shrink to atomic size and walk through the crystal, or slide down the faces. They might note that the crystal's molecules are well organized, like a city on a grid pattern. The rule is: Have the students participate with the ideas or objects you're teaching them.

A picture variation that can be fun is to have students look at an illustration (perhaps in one of their textbooks) and be led on a fantasy journey into the picture. There are several ways to do this. They can look first; then you tell them to remember the picture and lead them into it. This is a good way to get them to pay attention to the aspects of the picture you want to emphasize. You can have a slide ready to show them as a visual stimulus either before the fantasy journey or during it. If your students are lying on the floor and you can manage it, you can project the picture on the ceiling. If you do this, practice beforehand, as most slide projectors are not made to project upward. You'll have to make sure the slide doesn't fall out. Usually one picture is best for overhead projection because gravity-fed slide cassettes can be a problem. If you have students look at a picture during a fantasy trip, be sure to tell them when to open their eyes and when to close them again.

Remember that we are talking about the use of

fantasy journeys as part of classroom instruction, so the follow-up is important. Don't let your fantasy trip be an isolated part of your class. During the discussion you can ask if anyone experienced the parts of the journey you wanted to call attention to, the absence of money or the regular structure of the crystal in the examples above. Students can also write stories and poetry, or draw, based on their fantasy experiences. Movement and music can incorporate fantasy experiences, too. If your lecture or the readings give the same information in a verbal form, the fantasy journey can act as a preorganizer, in effect, getting their minds ready for the verbal presentation of the same material.

Finally, when you invent a good fantasy story, share it with others: the faculty where you teach, people from other schools, and teachers across the nation. Teaching journals are always interested in spreading the word about techniques that are fun and that work. Pick your favorite teacher's journal and send it in. The *Journal of Humanistic and Transpersonal Education* is a new source that is particularly open to this type of exercise (P.O. Box 575, Amherst, Massachusetts 01002). Or, send it to the authors of this book. If we get enough good ones, we'll have the makings of a teacher-written book of fantasy journeys.

4

Working with Dreams

The last few years have seen a tremendous increase in interest in dreams; this interest has been matched by an explosion of books that offer suggestions about working with dreams. In this section we will present a list of ideas for using dreams in the classroom.

1. Remember dreams.

   Dream recall is aided by a number of things, but probably most by suggestion ("Tonight I will remember at least one dream . . .") and by sharing them. Somehow the act of becoming interested in dreams often brings about greater recall. Practically all good dream books have a section on ways to remember dreams.

2. Share dreams with another person or a small group.

3. Keep a dream diary or journal.

4. Use dreams for writing projects.

5. Use dreams for art projects.

6. Act dreams out.

   Dreams make great classroom dramas. The dreamer can be the director or one of the actors. If the dream contains music, so much the better.

7. Try to figure out what dreams symbols mean.

8. Bring dreams to completion.

   The Senoi, a primitive people in Malaysia, have a ritual dreamwork which revolves around learning to finish dreams. Dream books by Ann Faraday, as well as the first *Centering Book*, all contain detailed instructions on Senoi-style dreamwork.

9. Role-play the various parts of dreams.

   Often the meaning of a dream will become clear if the dreamer takes the parts of a dream and role-plays them. Reversing the roles is also fun and useful.

10. Work with the idea that all parts of the dream represent different parts of the dreamer.

11. Paraphrase dreams.

12. Relate dreams to the recent events of daily life.

13. Use dreams to understand your inner needs, values, emotions, desires, creative urges, conflicts.

    An example of how a dream can point the way toward an unconscious conflict happened one day when the 9-year-old daughter of one of the authors (GH) was out walking the dog with her dad. She began describing a dream she'd had the night before in which she had thought someone had stolen all of the model horses that belonged to a friend of hers. When her father asked her what she thought the dream meant, she thought for a while, then laughed. "It's because I'm jealous of all her horses," she said.

14. Look for themes in dreams.

Some of the themes common to dreams are flying, losing things, trying to get away from something, failure, examinations.

15. Look for guidance in dreams.

People often can receive answers to perplexing problems by asking that an answer be revealed through their dreams. Even complex mathematical problems have been solved in dreams!

16. Look for psychic phenomena in dreams.

There is some evidence for the occurrence of psychic phenomena in dreams. Two types of phenomena that have been studied are telepathy and precognition.

Readers who wish to investigate a particular dream technique in depth will want to build their own dream library. Here are several books that would be essential to such a library: Ann Faraday, *The Dream Game* and *Dream Power;* Patricia Garfield, *Creative Dreaming;* and Wilson Van Dusen, *The Natural Depth in Man.*

5

Meditating, Relaxing, Energizing

We might think of human energy as being like the ocean, ebbing and flowing with a pulsation old as time itself. There is a time to let energy flow out, to be active, and there is a time to let it flow in, to be receptive. It is important to keep this balance in our lives, for if we lose equilibrium we can become drained of energy and even drain others of theirs. For example, many professions such as teaching, parenting, and doctoring require much outflow of energy. There is a great deal of giving involved in these jobs. If our teachers, parents, and doctors do not take time to receive energy from others and the Universe, they can become uncentered, eventually feeling dissatisfaction and sometimes despair. Similarly, there are people who receive from others constantly, but seldom give. No matter what direction the imbalance is in, a more centered stance is possible through learning how to use energy wisely.

The activities in this section show how to fill yourself with energy from your own wellspring, so that you can give without draining yourself, and receive without draining others. All of the following activities can and should be used to enhance the standard curriculum, as well as to teach important skills which facilitate personal growth. So, use these activities before a test, after recess, between subjects, anytime the mind and body can benefit from a quick calming experience.

Breath Awareness Relaxation

Age range: Fifth grade to adult

Have everyone find a space and lie down on their backs. Ask them to wiggle a little to get comfortable.

INSTRUCTIONS

"Let your eyes gently close, feeling them relax in the darkness. Let your body begin to settle down, one part at a time. Let your head and neck relax . . . then your chest . . . your stomach . . . your buttocks . . . your legs. Now gently let your right hand come up to rest on your stomach. Feel the rise and fall of your stomach as your breath flows in and out of your body."

Pause 10 seconds

"Now place your left hand on your chest, feeling the rise and fall as your breath flows in and out of your chest. Compare your hands to see which moves first and which moves more. Listen to your breath flowing in and out of your body."

Pause 15 seconds

"Now let the breath come in through your nose and flow out through your mouth. As you let it flow out through your mouth, make a smooth blowing sound that only you can hear. Make a sound as soft as a gentle wind. In through the nose, through the mouth."

Pause 20 seconds

"And now after you exhale through your mouth, pause a few moments until your breath naturally comes back in through your nose by itself. Don't hold your breath forcefully, just gently pause until it flows in spontaneously."

Pause 20-60 seconds

"During the pause, listen to your body, to what is going on inside it."

Pause 30 seconds

"And now let your breathing go back to normal again, enjoying the feeling of relaxed alertness you feel inside. When I count backwards to 1, sit up feeling refreshed and calm. 10-9-8-7-6-5-4-3-2-1."

DISCUSSION

- Why did a philosopher say "Breath is Life?"
- What are some ways breath is like life?
- What happens to our breathing when we get angry? Scared? Excited?
- Why does our breathing change when we have feelings?
- (For a science lesson) What happens to our bodies when we breathe?
- How can being tense affect our breathing?

The Relaxing Cloud

Age Range: All ages

Here is a pleasant process that can quickly bring about a restful state of relaxation.

INSTRUCTIONS

"Let's begin by lying down on the floor, on your back, finding a good spot and letting your body move around until it feels comfortable."

Pause 5-10 seconds

"Now chooose a spot on the ceiling to look at. Just let your eyes softly focus on that spot as the rest of the room just fades away."

Pause 5-10 seconds

"Continue letting your eyes get softer and softer

until they close, feeling warm and relaxed. As your mind relaxes and floats along, imagine that you are lying outside, watching clouds float by above in the sky. Watch them peacefully and lazily float along, easy and graceful."

Pause 5 seconds

"Now find a place in your body which is very relaxed."

Pause 5 seconds

"Imagine that area surrounded by a warm, fuzzy cloud of relaxation. Let that area be supported inside the cloud, very relaxed, very warm."

Pause 5 seconds

"Now let the cloud expand through other parts of you . . . until all of you is floating along inside this beautiful, warm cloud."

Pause 1-2 minutes

"And now it's time to come back to the people around you. Count backwards from 10 down to 1 [provide the count for younger children], and when you come to 1 sit up, feeling peaceful and alert."

Inside to Outside

Age Range: Second grade to adult

This process follows the natural tendency of the mind to move from outside to inside so that eventually the center is discovered. It can be done lying down or seated with heads down.

INSTRUCTIONS

"Let's begin by closing our eyes and letting our ears take over. Listen very carefully to all the sounds you can hear, inside and outside the room."

Pause 10-15 seconds

"Now become aware of all the things touching you, like the desk, the floor and your clothes . . . feel the way your clothes touch your skin."

Pause 10-15 seconds

"And now become aware of the inside of your skin, how your bones and the inside of your body touch your skin."

Pause 10-15 seconds

"And now be aware of where the very center of your body is, the place that's the very center of you."

Pause 10 seconds

"And when you're ready, come back and become aware of the room around you, and sit up, feeling rested and alert."

Earth Meditation

Age Range: All ages

Here is a way of soaking up energy directly from the earth. It can be done standing up or lying down.

INSTRUCTIONS

"Close your eyes and find a way of (standing, lying down) that feels balanced and centered. Give your eyes and ears a rest, and let your attention go inside you. Take a moment to be aware of your body."

Pause 10 seconds

"Now imagine that the earth is a big ball of energy that you can draw upon to make yourself feel strong and good. You can imagine that energy humming and buzzing, or you could imagine it warm or glowing. Relax your feet now and imagine that energy beginning to come into your feet."

Pause 5 seconds

"Now relax your ankles and let it come up toward your legs."

Pause 5 seconds

"Let your legs, ankles, and feet feel the energy pouring up through them from the earth."

Pause 10 seconds

"And now let the energy flow on up through your pelvis . . . letting everything below your waist feel that energy from the earth."

Pause 5 seconds

"Now let the energy flow up through your stomach . . . your chest . . . your throat."

Pause 5 seconds

"And now let it come up through your eyes, on up through the top of your head. Feel that flow from the earth on up through the top of your head."

Pause 10 seconds

"Whenever you need to 'charge your batteries,' just feel that flow of energy come up through your feet into your body. It's there whenever you need it. Now, let your attention come back to the room and feel rested and refreshed."

Energizing and Grounding

Age Range: All ages

These two activities, which can be done in less than a minute, are ideal for a short break since they are both energizing yet calming. The first posture flexes the body backward and allows breathing to deepen, while the second flexes the spine forward and brings a sense of well-being to the person.

INSTRUCTIONS

"Stand with your feet about shoulder width apart . . . then turn your toes slightly inward. Relax your knees and unlock them. Put your fists on your hips, and arch your body back so your chest opens up. Look the world straight in the eyes and breathe deeply." (Optional: Have them say "ahhh" on the exhale.) "Make your body a gentle arch."

Continue for about 10 deep breaths

"And now roll your body forward until your fingertips touch lightly on the ground for balance. Let your weight stay on your legs, remembering to keep your knees relaxed. Relax your neck, shoulders, and stomach."

Continue for about 15-20 seconds

"Now roll back up to a standing position."

Still Waters of the Mind

Age Range: All ages

This is an exquisitely simple meditation that teaches us to watch the waves of our minds until we come to the still point within us all. It is best done lying down.

INSTRUCTIONS

"Find a space on the floor where you can lie down and feel comfortable. Let your body relax so that it feels supported by the floor and let all the tension drain out of you so you can be peaceful yet very alert."

Pause 5-10 seconds

"And now let your mind relax and picture yourself floating along on a raft on a lake . . . feel the gentle ripples of the water flowing under you . . . feel the water supporting you. Whenever thoughts go through your mind just pretend they are ripples on the lake, then go back to just floating on the lake again. Let your thoughts be ripples."

Pause 1-2 minutes

"Now let your lake be perfectly still . . . let all the ripples become still and peaceful."

Pause 10-15 seconds

"Then let your mind become active again, and sit up, feeling rested and alert."

Soaring

Age Range: All ages

This is an energizing activity that can lift us free from all the tension we store in our bodies. It is done standing up.

INSTRUCTIONS

"Find a place to stand where you can stretch out your arms without touching anyone else. Stand with your feet about shoulder width apart . . . and find a way to stand that's relaxed and balanced."

Pause until people get centered

"And now take a deep breath and raise your arms to shoulder height. Breathe deeply in and out as you stretch your arms out as far as they'll go."

Pause 4-5 breaths

"Now with each in-breath raise your arms above your head, and with each out-breath lower them to your sides."

Pause 4-5 breaths

(*Optional:* "Now say 'Ahhh . . .'")

Light Meditation

Age Range: Third grade to adult

Here is a beautiful meditation that can put children in touch with the natural light within them. It is done lying down.

INSTRUCTIONS

"Let your eyes close and your body wiggle around until it has found a place to relax and be easy. Notice the breath coming in and out of you . . . follow its path in and out of your body."

Pause 10-20 seconds

"Now feel your toes . . . let them disappear into light . . . feel your feet . . . let your feet disappear into light. Feel your ankles and let them disappear into light . . . feel your legs and feel them disappear into light . . . feel your buttocks and feel them disappear into light . . . feel your stomach and let it disappear into light . . . feel your chest and feel it disappear into light . . . feel your shoulders and feel them disappear into light . . . feel your face and feel it disappear into light . . . feel your head disappear into light . . . feel your mind disappear into light. Let all of you disappear into light. . . ."

Pause 10 seconds

"Let the light shine through you and all around you so that everyone else is bathed in your light."

Pause 10 seconds

"And when you want to feel beautiful and bright, just relax and let the light shine through you."

Rag Doll

Age Range: All ages

Sometimes when we are tense it feels good to collapse like a loose rag doll. This activity can be done in a chair or sitting on the floor.

INSTRUCTIONS

"Sit with your back straight and your legs apart a little. Now let yourself collapse like a rag doll, letting your head and arms fall into your lap. Close your eyes and listen to your breathing. Let each breath relax you more, so you keep relaxing into your lap."

Pause 10 seconds

"Imagine that your eyes are soft and relaxed, so loose that you aren't putting any effort into them. Let your mouth and jaw relax, so relaxed that your whole face becomes warm and heavy. Then let your arms relax and be warm and heavy."

Pause 10 seconds

"Remember what being relaxed feels like, so that next time you are feeling tense or scattered, you can relax like a rag doll. And now we'll count backwards to 1, and when we hit 1 you'll feel rested and alert. 10–9–8–7–6–5–4–3–2–1, sit up, feeling relaxed and alert.

6

Building Intuition

Part of being centered means to be in the process of developing and using our full potentials. Human beings are complicated and have vast untapped potential. We are intellectual, rational beings, but we also have social, emotional, spiritual, psychic, and intuitive potentials, to name just a few. Intuition is important, because it represents one of our most basic processes—how we know things. We are most familiar with the rational, logical way of knowing about ourselves and the world. The rational mode is important and receives much attention in school. The intuitive mode is just as important, but it receives substantially less attention. We think this situation is unfortunate because it de-

"Intuition," by Frances Vaughan Clark. © 1977 by Frances Vaughan Clark.

73

prives children of a valid and useful way of knowing things. In addition, some children who may not be adept at the logical, intellectual way of knowing may be much more at ease with intuition.

To extend the concept of centering into the area of intuition, we asked Frances Clark to write a chapter for this book. Frances is particularly well qualified for the task. The current president of the Association for Transpersonal Psychology, she is a well-known teacher and writer in the area of intuition. Not only has she taught classes on intuition for a number of years, but she has also appeared on radio and TV. A Phi Beta Kappa at Stanford, Frances received her doctorate from the California School of Professional Psychology. In addition to her strong intellectual credentials, she is a warm, intuitive, and actualizing person.

Here Frances introduces us to some very interesting experiences and information designed to expand our awareness of intuition.

Intuition is a way of knowing associated with the right side of the brain. Often, when we know something inutitively, we cannot explain how we know it, but we feel sure about it. Intuition takes the mind beyond logical thought into areas of creativity both in scientific discovery and artistic inspiration. Everyone has intuition, but some people have learned to use it more than others.

You can all learn to expand the use of intuition by following three basic steps:

1. Quieting the mind. Learn to sit quietly without thinking. Any form of meditation training is useful in quieting the mind.
2. Focusing attention. When the mind is quiet, you can focus your attention on anything—any person, situation, or problem that you would like to consider intuitively.
3. Receptive attitude. After focusing your attention, simply stop trying to do anything. Be receptive to whatever comes into your awareness, regardless of whether it seems to be relevant or not. Don't try to change anything or judge anything. Simply notice whatever you are aware of.

In order to find out if your intuitive hunches are accurate, it is important to check them out. You will learn quickly if you are not afraid of being wrong. Forget the mistakes and remember the successes. Soon you will become more aware of the feelings, sensations, and thoughts which indicate accurate intuitive insights.

Intuition may come into your awareness in the form of physical sensations, feelings, ideas, or images. Or it may be independent of these familiar ways of knowing, and simply be a sense of certainty, of knowing that you know something.

Pure intuition is a way of seeing into the nature of reality. It is not knowing *about* something, it is knowing something as if that thing were a part of you. For example, if you want to use your intuition to get a sense of what another person is like, instead of noticing what they look like or what they do, you might imagine what it would feel like to be that person.

Intuitive experiences are usually associated with increased or new awareness. Often they are intense experiences which are felt to be total, involving the whole of one's being. Persons reporting such experience often refer to a sense of being guided or directed by something other than reason. Such experiences are frequently unexpected and yet marked by a sense of clarity and a feeling that the experience is "right" or appropriate for the individual at that particular time. Spontaneous intuitive experiences can occur when a person is active either physically or mentally, but in training oneself to be receptive to these intuitive insights, the methods outlined here are particularly useful.

Tuning-In

You can begin the process of tuning in to your intuition right now by taking a few minutes to quiet your mind, to tune into your present awareness of sensations, feelings, and thoughts, then to reflect for about five or ten minutes on your own life and your own experience of intuition. How does intuition operate in your life? What experiences have you had that you would consider intuitive? What type of intuition is most readily available to you? What type of intuition would you particularly like to develop further? Reflect on how you have treated your intuitive abilities up to this point in your life. How important do you think intuition has been for you up to now?

Remember to maintain a nonjudgmental, conscious awareness of whatever comes into your mind in response to these questions. The important thing is for you to increase your awareness of how intuition already is working in your life. You can start only from where you are, not from where you would like to be. It is also useful to write down any significant intuitive experience that may come to mind as a result of this exercise. Your experience will be unlike anyone else's. There is no way your experience can be right or wrong, it is simply your experience, and this is your opportunity to begin to pay attention to it. As soon as you do give it your attention, it will emerge more clearly into your conscious awareness. Attention is the psychic energy which can activate your intuitive ability.

Intuition Meditation

A good exercise for developing intuition by way of mediation is simply to mediate on the word, "intuition." When you are sitting quietly relaxed, simply hold the word intuition in your awareness. You may visualize the word written out before you, or you may simply repeat the word to yourself as a mantra, or continuing sound. Initially many extraneous thoughts and feelings are likely to intrude. When you realize that your attention has wandered to something else, simply bring it back gently to the word "intuition."

Many associations and unexpected insights may also appear spontaneously during such meditation, and you may wish to write down some of them after the meditation period is over. It is usually best to begin with brief periods of concentration, five minutes or less, in order to avoid fatigue and the resistance which is likely to be generated if you push yourself too hard. Again, the key to amplifying your awareness of intuition is attention.

One person reported her experience with meditating on intuition as follows:

I began to listen to myself for the first time.

I realized that there were many layers to my awareness and I could get in touch with much deeper levels of myself. Superficial conflicts lost their importance and I found it easier to make decisions. It was as though I had gotten in touch with some inner guide, or sense of knowing. I no longer felt agitated and confused, but somehow more trusting of life itself as a process. The idea of allowing more of my experience to come into my conscious awareness without having to *do* anything to change it helped me learn to accept myself as I am.

Associations

Another way of working with the word "intuition" is to write down any associations you may have to the word. Associations should be brief; one or two words are enough. There is no need for explanation or amplification. The word "intuition" should be written between each association. If you were to work on it for five minutes, you might write something like this:

*Intuition knowing intuition seeing intuition
feeling intuition understanding intuition
consciousness intuition growing intuition space*

*intuition timeless intuition expansion intuition
roots intuition flowing intuition universal
intuition beyond intuition transcendence intuition
spiritual intuition earthbound intuition rebirth
intuition circle intuition natural intuition colors
intuition light intuition clear intuition stars
intuition deeper intuition centering intuition
letting go intuition trust intuition love intuition
letting be intuition acceptance intuition energy
intuition giving intuition receiving intuition
allowing intuition movement intuition creating
intuition expectation intuition living
intuition . . .*

If you keep going, allowing yourself to repeat words as they occur to you, and allowing yourself to be blank, or write the word "blank" when you feel it, you can get beyond the superficial associations and get closer to what the word really means to you. As you uncover some of the deeper meanings which are already there for you, you not only increase your understanding of intuition, you also clear away a lot of preconceptions once they are out in the open.

The same type of exercise may be done orally, with a partner. If you are working with another person, ask your partner to simply repeat the word for you, allowing you to give your associations between repetitions. If you are silent for a few moments, your partner should simply repeat the word, pausing long enough between repetitions to allow you to give your association. After five or ten minutes, depending on how long you want to work, switch roles. It is interesting to see how much people differ in their responses to a word which is familiar to all of us, and it is also interesting to note what associations you may have in common with your partner. Obviously the person who speaks first has an advantage, starting with a clean slate. The person who speaks second will have to allow for all the words he or she just heard, but will no doubt have fresh associations to add.

Images

Once you have worked on verbal associations for some time (you will know intuitively how long is long enough for you), you may want to work on eliciting images of intuition. Simply think of an image that would visually portray the essence of intuition for you. One person saw a chalice, another a crystal ball, another a triangle of light. You may get something in a flash, or you may not. If you do, you may want to draw it or make a note of it. If you do not get anything, don't be discouraged. Spontaneous visual images associated with intuition are most likely to occur when your mind is quiet and your body relaxed. Give yourself plenty of time and remember to be receptive to anything that comes to mind, without judging or interpreting it.

The capacity to observe inner imagery in a receptive, noninterfering way can give you information about your inner reality and subjective emotional states, as well as intuitive insights about external reality. The question which arises at this point is always, "How do I know if what I see is true?" The obvious way to find out if your images reflect a realistic view or a subjectively distorted one is to get to know your own imagery. Checking it out whenever you can will enable you to learn to discern when you are seeing clearly and when your perception is distorted by your own fears or desires.

The following exercise is particularly useful for evoking a flow of inner images, and can also be good practice in observing the images without interpretation. By working with a partner you have the added advantages of being able to check the accuracy of your perceptions and to give each other feedback about your feeling responses to the images that come to mind.

Sitting opposite your partner, preferably someone you do not know, take a few minutes to become centered and quiet. Close your eyes and be aware of your breathing, and notice any physical sensations that are present for you at this moment. Be aware of any feelings that are present, and notice the thoughts that are going through your mind. Be aware of how it feels to be you at this moment, and what your energy field feels like. If you were to visualize an energy field surrounding your body, what would it be like? Give yourself a few minutes of silence to be fully aware of your experience right now.

Open your eyes now and give your partner your full attention. Without talking, simply look at your partner and notice how you feel being with this person. In a receptive mode, simply allow this person into your awareness. Close your eyes again and see if you can get a clear picture of your partner in your mind's eye. If some details are not clear, open your eyes again and fill them in. Look at your partner long enough and carefully enough to get in your mind a clear picture of what he or she looks like.

For the remainder of this exercise your eyes can be either open or closed. Do not try to make anything happen. Simply notice what images come to mind when you are given a suggestion. If nothing comes to mind, that is okay. Do not try to interpret or judge your images as they appear; simply notice them and let them be.

The teacher or group leader can ask the following questions while the partners remain in contact:

- If this person were an animal, what type of animal would it be?
- If this person were a plant, what type of plant would it be?
- If this person were a landscape, what would it be?

- If this person were a body of water, what would it be? How deep? How clear? What temperature? How much movement?
- If this person were a light, what color and intensity would it be?
- If this person were a geometrical symbol, what would it be?
- If this person were a type of music, what would it be?
- If this person were a tool, what would it be?
- If this person were a character in history, who would it be?
- Can you visualize your partner as a little child? As a very old person?
- How do you experience your partner's energy field?
- What is the energy field like between you—the energy field in which you both participate?

Take a few minutes of silence now simply to be quiet and receptive to any images that may emerge spontaneously as you continue to focus your attention on your partner.

Take as much time as you want to share with your partner the images which emerged for you. You can share any feelings you have about the images, but it's usually better not to interpret them.

You may have found that during this exercise some images just popped into your mind without any effort on your part, while others seemed more difficult, and you began thinking about what image would be appropriate. You may also have noticed that if an image appeared spontaneously and you did not like it, you tried to reject it and get something else. The first image may have been so persistent that it would not go away, or you may have managed to erase it and substitute something you liked better. The first image is the best one to work with. If you did not like it, you were probably interpreting it. Give yourself the opportunity simply to observe the images as they are, rather than trying to decide whether they are what you think they should be.

Working with a friend or a partner, sharing images and talking about how intuition works for you, is good practice for developing intuition. But the essential work goes on inside your own mind. When you learn to be receptive to your thoughts, feelings, sensations, and images, you can discover that you know more than you thought you did about what you need for your personal growth and development. There is no pattern that fits everybody. Some people need to work on developing concentration, others need to learn to let go. Some people need to get in touch with their feelings and own them, others need to disidentify from them and decide not to get caught in emotional turmoil. You know better than anyone else what really is going on inside you, but if you are out of touch or unaware of your own subjective state, you are likely to feel confused and anxious about making choices and decisions which will affect your life. Expanding your intuitive awareness allows you to get in touch with what is true for you. The more conscious you are of your intuitive choices, the more you will be able to make the choices which are truly satisfying to you.

Begin NOW. How does it feel to be you at this moment?

7

Centering in Feeling and Communication

Being centered extends into the areas of feeling and communication. As children become harmoniously balanced in the nonverbal realm through the preceding activities, it makes sense to introduce them to a way of communicating with themselves and others that makes use of the principles of centering. Language is one of the remarkable aspects of being human. As the famous linguist B. L. Whorf said, "Language is the best show man puts on!" However, language can be used both to help us and hinder us in our development. For example, if one child is angry at another, language can be used to say, "I'm angry at you," stating the feeling clearly without blaming the other person, or it could be used to say, "You're a stupid jerk," thus pointing a finger in blame. So, language can be used as a means to communicate meaningfully, and it can be used to make matters *worse: it can either enhance or retard our centeredness.*

Because we wanted to expand centering activities into verbal areas, we asked a talented children's therapist, Lynn C. Elliott, to contribute a chapter on communication, exploring such areas as feelings and responsibility. Lynn has helped many children to become more centered through getting in touch with their feelings, communicating effectively, and taking responsibility for themselves. Here Lynn explains these concepts and describes activities for developing verbal centering skills in children.

Responsibility

A first step in becoming responsible for ourselves is figuring out what we want and need. Needs can be defined as those biological and psychological conditions whose gratification is necessary to maintain us within the limits required for our survival and actualization of our potential. Maslow, in the second edition of *Toward a Psychology of Being,* has identified the following needs: physiological (hunger, thirst, sex), safety, love, esteem, self-actualization and transcendence, and arranged these in a hierarchy to indicate that if a lower need, such as the need for safety, hasn't been satisfied, we will not be able to satisfy the higher needs of love, esteem, self-actualization and transcendence. If our needs aren't met, we will, at best, be off-balanced, not centered, and hindered in the fulfillment of our potentials. At worst, our very survival is threatened if our needs go unmet for long periods of time.

Wants, on the other hand, are things or conditions we desire or would like to have but that we can survive without, although getting what we want is important to our self-fulfillment. For instance, we want a particular job because it pays well, offers an opportunity to do what we have been trained for, and has an opportunity for advancement. We will survive without it (and get another job), and we may settle for a job which satisfies less of our potential and desires.

Passivity, which can generally be defined as ineffectiveness in getting wants and needs met, is the opposite of responsibility. When we are passive, we do not take the time and energy to figure out what we want or need. Instead, we wait until other people or situations determine what happens. This passive approach obviously decreases the chances that our wants and needs will be met, although we do get something out of being passive. (A general rule is that people get *something* out of their actions, or else they wouldn't persist in them. Very often, however, what we get out of our actions is reinforcement of a negative self-concept or a negative view of life. For instance, a passive person may be reinforcing his notion that he can't have what he wants no matter what he does.)

One of the most common payoffs for passivity is that we get to disown or deny any responsibility for our behavior and life situation. After all, we didn't do anything, but look what has happened! Another very common payoff for passivity is the "poor me" or "ain't it awful" game. For more information on this and other games see Eric Berne's *Games People Play*. When we don't get what we want or need because we've been passive and allowed others to determine what happens, it is very easy to bemoan our situation and say, "Ain't it awful that this has happened to me." Yet another advantage of being passive is that we do not have to invest ourselves in anything; we do not have to *risk* wanting or needing anything, so if we don't get it, we are not in pain.

Many children learn early in life that they can't have what they want because their parents decide what they get; or they may learn that "there isn't enough to go around" (this situation arises when the parents set up a competitive situation where only one person can get her/his wants and needs met), and so it is much safer *not* to want or need, and maybe they will get something. Thus, people maintain their passivity because it provides the illusion of safety.

For many people, passivity was a survival mode adopted in childhood to deal with just such competitive situations as described above. Especially in the situation where a parent is competing with a child to get his or her needs and wants met, it would be very dangerous for the child to win: "Mommy will leave" or "Mommy won't love me" are probably the two most common fantasies or fears a child has in such a situation. So, in order to keep Mommy around and keep her love, the child decides to take care of her by being passive and not asking for his or her needs and wants to be met.

In the latter example, it makes sense for a child to decide to be passive because he is dealing with his own survival ("if Mommy leaves, who will take care of me?"). The problem is that the feelings and behaviors that we learn as children persist into adulthood, even when the reasons for those actions no longer exist. As adults, we are no longer in the position of being dependent upon a parent for our survival, and we can develop many alternative ways of acting to get our needs met. However, most of us continue to operate on what we learned as children. Often, we go about recreating childhood situations in adult life; thus, we continually reinforce our original passive position. Also, we tend to generalize what we learn in childhood. That is, we believe that since we had to be passive with Mother and Father, we must behave the same way with everyone. Such a situation is often seen in marriage where wives and husbands believe they must be passive with each other to keep their partners in the relationship.

Thus, it is very important to learn as children that even if we are required to be passive at home, it is all right for us to determine our wants and needs and to be effective about getting them with other people. We need to learn that there are alternative ways of behaving.

Following are some exercises and strategies for helping children to become responsible and effective at getting their wants and needs met.

Owning Behavior, Thoughts, Feelings

Age Range: Kindergarten to adult

An important part of becoming responsible for ourselves is "owning" what we do, what we think, and what we feel. Often, when expressing our opinions or feelings, we speak in general, universal terms such as, "When you say something stupid, you feel embarrassed," or "People get angry when they're insulted." In both cases, it is more than likely that the speaker is really talking about him or herself. The speaker could own these statements by using "I": "When I say something stupid, I feel embarrassed."

Owning feelings and thoughts by the use of "I"

statements also gives others information about us. Conversely, we can use universal, general language to avoid closeness and intimacy, and even avoid ourselves and how we feel. When we say, "People . . ." or "You . . ." we are usually expressing our opinion or feeling, yet we may not even realize that because we are projecting onto others. Thus, we can use language to stay remote and removed from ourselves and others, or we can own our feelings and thoughts and maintain contact with ourselves and others.

STRATEGIES

Throughout the following exercises, encourage children to use "I" statements when they are expressing their feelings and thoughts. When you hear children say "people" or "you" or "we" you can ask them whether they really mean "I," whether they are really expressing something they feel or think, and ask them to restate what they have said and own that using an "I" statement. Another way to confront this is illustrated in the following example: A child says, "When someone calls you a name, you feel angry and want to hit them." (This child is obviously expressing how *he* feels). You can say,

"Who feels that way?" and he will probably say, "I do!" or you could say, "Is that how *you* feel?"

Taking Responsibility

Age Range: Second grade to adult

This exercise is designed to help children take responsibility for themselves and their behavior, to create an awareness about their responsibility and ability to choose how they behave, and to confront their passivity.

INSTRUCTIONS

"I want everyone to get into small groups of four or five." (With younger children, you may want to make the groups larger and have an adult in each group.) "I want all of you to make a list of the things you have to do. Some of the things that might be on your list are, 'I have to make my bed every morning.' 'I have to go to bed at 8:30.' 'I have to go to school.' Write down as many things that you have to do that you can think of."

Pause while they make their lists

"Now I want you to read some of the things on your list to the other children in your group, and as you do that, say, 'I choose to . . .' instead of 'I have to . . .' for each of the things that you read. I want you to do this even though you may think you really do have to do these things. Try saying, 'I choose to . . .' even though you may not agree."

As they are doing this in their groups, circulate among them and make sure they are saying "I choose to. . . ."

DISCUSSION

Many, if not all of the children, will probably argue that they *don't* choose to do the things on their list; their parents "make" them, etc. You can discuss how their parents "make" them do these things. This will probably lead into a discussion of the consequences of not doing the things on their list. For instance, a child may say that if she doesn't make her bed every morning, her mother gets angry. Or, another child may say that if he doesn't go to bed at 8:30 on school nights, his mother makes him go to bed early on the weekends. You can reflect that what it sounds like is that they choose to do these things because there are negative consequences if they don't. They *could* choose not to do these things and face the consequences.

This can lead into a discussion of the alternatives available to them. It is important that they realize that they do have a choice about what they do, that only rarely does someone really make them do something. In some cases they may discover that there is an alternative they prefer and decide to change their behavior. In other cases, they may decide that they choose to do something because if they don't they face a worse consequence. They may also decide that they really want to do something different and need to talk with a parent or someone else to negotiate that. For instance, a child may decide that he wants to stay up until 9:00 instead of 8:30 so he can see the end of TV shows. He may decide to go home and talk with his mother about this to see if she is willing to let him do that. Whether or not his mother is willing to let him do that or not, the important thing is that he is taking responsibility for his behavior and feelings by figuring out what he wants and asking for that.

Discuss how realizing that we choose to act the way we do allows us to take responsibility for ourselves, which then enables us to decide how we *want* to act: whether we want to change or to continue doing what we've been doing. This realization gives us a lot of power over ourselves.

Figuring Out What You Want:
Looking at Alternatives

Age Range: Second grade to adult

This exercise can be used in conjunction with the preceding one, or separately when one or more children are having difficulty figuring out what they want.

One of the ways that we maintain passivity is to believe there are no alternatives to the ways we think, feel, or behave. *There are always alternatives:* some of them may make sense, and others may not be possible or realistic. It is important to realize we have choices and the power to change what we do. The following exercise is designed to help children look at the alternatives and decide how they want to act, feel, or think.

INSTRUCTIONS

"Think of all the things you could do instead of . . . (depending on when and how you do this exercise, you may want to have them list alternatives to one of the things on their 'have to do' list, or alternatives to a specific behavior a child is feeling 'stuck' in). What else could you do besides. . . ?"

Often children will claim they can't think of anything. Give them permission to think: "You can think and figure out some other things you could do. I can think of several." Don't do their thinking for them: give them time to think for themselves. After they have come up with a couple of alternatives, you could suggest a few others. At this point in the exercise, it's all right for them to list alternatives which are impossible. Later, you will help them discard the unrealistic ones.

After they have come up with several alternatives, ask them, "Are all of your alternatives possible ones? Which ones aren't possible? Why? Of the alternatives that are possible, which one do you like the best?"

If they have difficulty deciding between alternatives, have them rate each alternative on a scale of 1 to 10: 10 being "like the most"; 1 being "like the least." They can then eliminate the choices that they rated 5 and below and choose between those left based on which they like the most and which makes the most sense as being possible.

A variation of this exercise which is helpful when a child is having difficulty deciding between two choices is to divide a piece of paper into two columns and list the Pros of an action on one side and the Cons on the other. When they are trying to decide between two courses of action, they can list why they want to do one of them (what they get out of it, what needs of theirs will be met, etc.) on one side of the paper, and why they want to do the other on the other side. Often, just doing this exercise immediately clarifies what they want to do. However, if they still have difficulty deciding, they can again rate each thing they have written down, discarding those rated 5 and below.

Conflict Resolution:
Being Afraid to Act

Age Range: Fifth grade to adult

When individuals experience conflict (for instance, wanting to do something but being afraid to do it) it is helpful to externalize the two parts of the conflict so that they can look at and fully experience both sides. Sometimes when they keep a conflict inside themselves, in their thoughts and feelings, they just go around and around, unable to decide, or they only partially experience the two sides of the conflict, so they stay "stuck." The following exercises are ways to externalize a conflict and experience both sides of it fully.

INSTRUCTIONS

A situation in which you might use the following approach is: A child wants to stand up to another child who has been teasing him, but he is afraid to do so because the other child is bigger.

You may need to help the child clarify the conflict. After he has described it, you can reflect: "It sounds as if you feel angry at _____ for teasing you, yet you're afraid to stand up to him. Is that right?" Or, "So, you're angry on the one hand about being teased, and afraid to stand up to him because he's bigger than you." Help the child also clarify what he is afraid the other child will do: "What are you afraid he'll do?"

Figuring Out
What You Want to Do
in the Classroom

Age Range: All primary grades

Children experience feelings of powerlessness in school and adopt a passive attitude because they are too seldom allowed or invited to take an active part in decision making about the activities they do there. With feelings of powerlessness often go feelings of anger and an attitude of passive resistance. In this situation, it is easy for children to blame adults for what they do or don't like. Often, they have never thought about what they want; they know only what they don't want in opposition to what the teacher plans.

The following exercise is designed to give children an active part in choosing at least some of what they do in school. This exercise requires that the children have some free time set aside daily or during some part of each week.

INSTRUCTIONS

"I want each one of you to write down two to five activities you would like to do during your free time." (With your young children, have them make suggestions while you list them on the blackboard.) "Think about what *you* would like to do with your free time. Remember some of the activities we've done before that you've liked, and think about other things you would like to do that we may have never done before."

Collect all of their lists. Read each of the activities they have listed out loud to the class and discuss each one. You may not be willing to let them do all of their suggested activities, or you may have some concerns about messes or safety. In this case, ask the child who suggested the activity to identify him or herself. If you are not willing to allow the activity, give your reasons and ask the child if he or she has another suggestion. If you have some concerns about the activity, state those, and ask the children if they are willing to comply with what you want. (Example: A child wants to fingerpaint. You are concerned about the children getting paint on their clothes and messing the room. You could say, "I'm willing to let you fingerpaint if you will wear smocks and agree to clean up the paints and table when you're done. Are you willing to do that?" Ask the children to respond to your question. Don't assume they agree.)

After you have negotiated what activities they want and you're willing to allow, have the children make up a Menu book of the activities. This can be an enjoyable art project for them. The Menu book will contain all the activities available for them to do during their free time. The children can then go to this book and decide what they want to do. Any safety or clean-up requirements that you have agreed upon should be listed with each activity. Encourage the children to make additions and revisions of the book. You may find that some activity just didn't work out; if you want to eliminate it, explain your reasons and encourage the children to think of alternatives.

Asking for What You Want

Age Range: First grade to adult

It is important for people to learn how to *ask* for what they want, instead of manipulating, controlling, being competitive, or going without. Asking directly for what we want greatly increases our chances of getting it, and we can learn to do this without suffering ourselves or hurting someone else.

It is often a frightening thing to do, because we have been taught (or we believe) that the only way to get our wants met is through roundabout means (manipulating, lying, acting helpless, being "tough," etc.). When we ask straightforwardly, we are risking being honest and letting the other person know how we feel, and we also take the risk that the other person will say "no." You may find that the children (or adults) you are working with will ask for superficial things from each other at first. However, as they find out that this is safe and that it works, they will begin to risk more and ask for what is really important to them. Especially with children, it will be helpful if you set an example by asking each child for something that you want from them at the beginning of this exercise.

INSTRUCTIONS

"I want all of you to get into small groups (five or six)." (You may want to assign children to groups.) "We're going to do an exercise to help you think about and ask each other for what you want from each other. Sometimes, we want something from someone, want to do something with them, or want them to change something about how they act, but we don't ask them for that. Maybe we're afraid, or we don't think they'll listen, or maybe we don't think we have the right to ask them for what we want. Sometimes we do things to try to make people do what we want; sometimes we are sneaky and try to trick them into doing what we want; and sometimes we just go without what we want.

"Right now, we're going to practice *asking* each other directly for what we want. Take a few minutes, and think about what you want from or with each person in your group. As you do this, think about how you want the person to act."

If it is at all possible, it would be helpful if you or another adult could be in each group to model how to ask for what you want. If this isn't feasible, you can illustrate in front of the entire class or group by asking several children for what you want from them. It is important that you be very specific in your requests. For example, "I want you to be nicer. Will you do that?" does not define what you want the person to *do,* and furthermore your definition of "nicer" is likely to be different from the other person's definition. Instead, you could say, "I want you to talk to me and tell me how you feel and ask me for what you want, instead of giving me dirty looks, not talking to me, and slamming the door. Will you do that?" This gives the other person specific information about what you're asking and provides both of you with a common definition.

Be sure to give the children permission to say "no" when they are asked if they will do something. When a child does respond "no" to another child, encourage the second child to think of something else he or she wants.

This exercise can also be done with the children asking *you* for what they want from you or what they want different in the classroom. This will help the children become involved in the class and allow them to take responsibility for getting what they want. As you do this exercise, use the same format as in the preceding exercise: Have the children state what they want and ask if you will do that; then you respond "yes" or "no," giving reasons if you are not willing. Again, encourage them to think of alternatives if you say "no."

DISCUSSION

Ask the children how they felt as they did this exercise. Was it frightening? Did someone say "no" to what they asked for? How did they feel about that? Did they think of another alternative?

Discuss why it is important to figure out what we want: "Sometimes we feel angry at someone, or afraid, or unhappy about something and it is important to figure out what we want as a result of those feelings. If we don't figure out what we want and ask for that, we will probably just stay angry, or afraid, and nothing will change to make us feel better."

Also discuss the importance of responding honestly when someone asks you to do something. If we say "yes" to someone's request of us, even when we aren't really willing to do it, the chances are we won't do it anyway. It is better to be honest with someone than to say what we think they want to hear. If we say "no," then the other person can think of something else he or she wants from us. If we are dishonest and say "yes," then the other person is counting on us and will be angry if we don't do as we agreed, which just creates problems between us.

Asking for what you want isn't magical; it doesn't guarantee that you will get what you want, although it greatly increases your chances. We don't get what we want all the time, but it is important that we learn how to be as effective as we can be at figuring out what we want and asking for it so that we can get what we want most of the time.

Choosing to Be Where You Are

Age Range: First grade to adult

When we are being passive, feeling bad, not being effective about solving a problem, being confused, feeling frightened or angry or sad, it is important to admit it and make that a choice. Examples: "I choose to sit here and not be effective in my thinking," "I choose to feel miserable right now." Doing this counteracts our tendency to feel "poor me," be a victim, or blame everybody and everything else. It also reminds us that we are in control of ourselves and that we choose to feel and do as we do. Another advantage of choosing to be where we are is that, often, when we realize we are choosing to be uncomfortable, and realize we have control over that, we choose to do something else more effective.

It is useful to have children verbalize that they choose to be where they are. You will also find that they are very resistant to doing so. It is much more comfortable to place the blame elsewhere. When they *choose* to be unhappy, they are more uncomfortable about their feelings and will be more likely to choose and feel differently.

Passivity Confrontation

Age Range: Kindergarten to adult

When we are passive, we are not thinking or acting effectively to solve a problem. When children are being passive, "being confused" or rebellious, having a temper tantrum, acting out to get attention, or otherwise not figuring out what they want or need, an effective way to confront this type of behavior is to have them stand in a corner (or put them in a time-out area). Doing this removes the attention or reinforcement they are getting for being passive, and when they are faced with having to stare into a corner until they think effectively, it is surprising how quickly they will figure out what they need or want.

When you put children in the corner, you should explain that they are not thinking and they are being sent to the corner to think and figure out what they want or need. They may come out when they have this figured out. It is important that the child stand facing the corner, hands at sides, not playing with things or otherwise fidgeting. (Fidgeting and agitating are also forms of passivity that are used to avoid thinking.)

This is not a form of punishment and should not be used as such. It is a technique to confront passivity and help children think effectively. If you should find yourself using this technique in an angry or punitive way, it might be useful to put yourself in the corner to think about what you want and need.

Victims and Villains

Age Range: Fourth grade to adult

Taking responsibility for ourselves requires that we give up our favorite villains: our parents, teachers, siblings. We must give up playing Victim. Sometimes it is true that someone acts cruelly or unfairly, but it is *our* choice as to how we respond. We do not have to feel bad when someone is mean to us. We do not have to feel angry when someone cheats us. We do not have to feel frightened when someone threatens us; and we do not have to make others into villains who "make" us do things. When we make someone into a villain, we disown our responsibility in the situation.

INSTRUCTIONS

This is an exercise designed to help children give up the Victim position and to stop making others into villains.

Have the children get into groups of three. "Remember a situation in which you were a Victim, a situation in which bad things happened to you. In your groups, take turns and describe that situation. As you describe it, stay in Victim and describe what the other people did to you. The others in your group are to make sure you stay in Victim and make everything the other person's fault." Allow all of the children to do this in their groups.

"Now, I want you to describe the same situation, but this time *you* are to take full responsibility for what happened. Use 'I' statements and describe what *you* did to create the situation and your bad feelings." Children (and adults) may have difficulty doing this, but encourage them to do it anyway.

"As you are doing this, think about *why* you created this situation. What did you get out of the situation? What did you get out of your bad feelings of being a Victim? What did you get out of making someone else the villain or bad guy? What opportunity did it give you to work on some aspect of yourself?" (Example: A child describes a situation in which he got blamed for something his sister did. As he does this exercise, he realizes that he kept quiet, felt bad and angry, and did not try to tell his parents what really happened. The situation gave him an opportunity to work on standing up for himself and to give up his investment in being a Victim.) "What could you have done differently to not end up feeling like a Victim?"

DISCUSSION

Discuss the exercise with the children. How did they feel when they took full responsibility for what happened in their situation? Did they learn something about themselves? Did they have trouble taking full responsibility for the situation? If necessary help them to see what they did or didn't do to create their situation, and help them think about what they could have done differently.

Passivity

Schiff (1975) has identified four specific passive behaviors:

1. *Doing nothing:* Instead of energy being used for action, it is used to inhibit response.
2. *Agitation:* Repetitive, non-goal-directed behavior we engage in instead of dealing effectively with a problem. Examples: foot-tapping, beard-stroking, smoking, picking lint. Agitation is an outlet for the energy that could be used to solve the problem.
3. *Overadaptation:* Doing, feeling, or thinking as someone else wants us to (or as we imagine they want us to) instead of identifying what *we* want or what *our* goals are. Example: Johnny is reaching for the cookie jar. His mother walks in looking stern. Johnny leaves the kitchen without getting a cookie because he imagines his mother is angry and doesn't want him to have a cookie. In fact, Johnny's mother may have looked stern for any number of reasons.
4. *Incapacitation or violence:* The discharge of energy we build up while being passive, during which we

do not think and do not take responsibility for our behavior. Examples of incapacitation: asthma, fainting, migraines. Examples of violence: physical assault, destruction of property.

Following are some strategies for confronting and dealing with these passive behaviors and an exercise to help children recognize and understand overadaptation.

Confronting Agitation

Age Range: Kindergarten to adult

Children do a lot of agitating. Much of what we label "hyperactivity" is extreme or escalated agitation and is often the product of much anxiety and anger. Agitation represents an outlet of the energy produced by feelings, and unresolved problems. We do not think as effectively when we agitate as when we channel all of our energy into figuring out what we need to do.

Confront agitation as you see it. (Children very readily understand what agitation is if you simply identify fidgeting, picking at things, tapping, etc. as agitations and explain that we agitate instead of feeling or thinking or doing.) Ask the child to stop agitating and to think about what he wants or needs. If the child is very agitated or persists in agitating, you can use the passivity confrontation technique of standing him or her in the corner.

Mind Reading:
Confronting Overadaptation

Age Range: Third grade to adult

A lot of overadapting is based on a belief that we can read minds and know what someone else is thinking and wanting us to do. It is true that we get many nonverbal clues from people's tone of voice, facial expressions, body posture, gestures, etc. and that we can often very accurately figure out what they feel. Sometimes we misinterpret, though, and even if we are accurate, we cannot know *why* they are feeling a certain way (although, again, we may be able to guess somewhat accurately).

When we overadapt we do or feel what we think someone else wants us to, regardless of whether that makes sense and regardless of what *we* want or need to do. Thus, overadapting usually results in behavior that is ineffective, inappropriate, and sometimes destructive.

INSTRUCTIONS

This can be presented to the children as a game in which they are going to try to read minds. Have each child pick another child in the room and try to figure out either how the other child is feeling at that moment, what the child is thinking, or what he or she wants them to do. Have them write down their mind readings. After they have done this, have them talk to the other child and find out if they were right or wrong.

DISCUSSION

Discuss whether people can really read minds. What kind of clues do we get from them that tell us something about their feelings or thougths? How do we guess about what someone wants or expects from us? Are we always right? How could we find out if we're right? Encourage them to think of times when they have tried to read their parents' or other people's minds. What kinds of things do they do because they think someone else wants them to? Does it work to try to do what we think someone else wants us to do?

"Sometimes we're right, sometimes we're wrong. When we pick up clues from people, we can check those out to find out if we're right or wrong, rather than guessing." (Example: "I'm thinking that you're angry because I'm making noise and that you want me to be quiet. Is that right?") "Once we're clear about the messages people are sending us, we can decide whether we are willing to do what they want and decide what *we* want to do. Sometimes others want us to do things that aren't good for us, don't make sense, or aren't things that we like to do. Can you think of examples of when someone wanted you to do something that wouldn't have been good for you, or would have gotten you into trouble?"

"What can you do when your mother or father or teacher wants you to do something you don't want to do?" (Encourage the children to come up with alternatives.) "One of the things you can do is to ask them for their reasons for wanting you to do that. Sometimes those reasons make sense. Other times, they don't have very good reasons and you might be able to discuss why you don't want to do what they have asked. You can tell them your reasons for not wanting to do what they've asked and suggest an alternative. (Example: Your mother wants you to go to bed. You want to stay up to watch a particular TV show. You can ask your Mother why she wants you to go to bed. She may say, 'So you'll be able to get up in the morning.' You can tell her that you want to watch this show for a half hour and that you promise to get up right away in the morning.) People do and feel and think things for reasons, and it is important that we know those reasons so that we can decide what *we* feel and think and want based upon information and facts. It is also important that we figure out what *we* want and not just do what others want us to do."

Other Forms of Passivity

Passivity can also be expressed in confusion, as when a child says, "I don't know" or "I can't. . . ." More often than not, confusion is used as an excuse for not thinking. Except in the case of factual information, the response, "I don't know" is rarely true. Children, in particular, use this response when they don't want to talk about or think about something, when they're frightened, or when they don't understand what has been asked. The statement, "I can't" is also seldom true, because "can't" implies an inability, and most people *can* do what they choose to. "I can't" is often used to mean "I don't want to" or "I'm not willing to." All of the above excuses are ways to avoid dealing with a situation or a problem.

These more subtle forms of passivity will be immediately observable if you take the time to listen to those around you and, for that matter, yourself. It is important to use language that accurately reflects reality. The child who is allowed to use confusion, "I don't know," and "I can't" as ways to avoid responsibility comes to believe that he really *is* stupid, or really can't control himself or think effectively to solve problems.

Following are some ways to confront such passivities. (It is appropriate to confront children as young as four or five years old.)

When children say, "I don't know" (unless they are being asked to recall information), tell them they can think and figure that out.

> ADULT: "What do you want to do with your free time today?"
>
> CHILD: "I don't know."
>
> ADULT: "You can think about that and decide what you want to do."
>
> CHILD: "I don't know!" (whining)
>
> ADULT: "Well, you're the only one who can figure out what you want to do. How about your doing that?"

When children seem not to want to talk about a subject and say, "I don't know," give them permission to be straightforward about not wanting to talk about it.

> ADULT: "How do you feel about the fight you and your father had?"

CHILD: "I don't know."
ADULT: "I don't believe that you don't know. If you don't want to talk about it, that's okay, and you can say, "I don't want to talk about it.""
CHILD: "I don't want to talk about it."

When children say, "I can't" or "I couldn't" about behavior which is in their control (which includes almost all behavior unless they are handicapped, retarded, or physically coerced to do something), confront that and give them the information that they *can* or *could,* but choose or chose not to.

CHILD: "When Jimmy calls me names, I just can't control my temper!"
ADULT: "It isn't true that you *can't* control your temper. You can if you decide you want to. You are in control of what you do."
CHILD: "Well, he just makes me so angry . . ."
ADULT: "I understand that you get very angry when he calls you names, and you are in control of what you do about that."

Confusion used as a way to avoid thinking or dealing with a problem can be confronted similarly. The child may choose to stay confused, but he should be clear that that is his *choice,* over which he has control.

CHILD: "I'm so confused I can't think!"

ADULT: "You can unconfuse yourself and figure out what you need to do."

CHILD: "I don't know."

ADULT: "You can figure that out."

CHILD: "No I can't. I'm too confused."

ADULT: "Well, you can choose to stay confused or you can do whatever you need to do to get unconfused. If you need to have more information to get unconfused, you can ask for that."

Discounting

Discounting is the mechanism by which passivity is maintained. Discounting occurs when we deny or minimize some aspect of ourselves (self-discount), some aspect of others, or some aspect of the situation. The child who does not raise his hand to ask a question because he thinks he'll sound stupid is discounting himself. Interrupting someone is a discount of that person. Bringing up an important subject to discuss with your husband when he is tired and falling asleep is a discount of the situation.

When we discount, we are being passive, because in

one way or another we are disowning the problem, our behavior, or feelings and avoid dealing with that effectively to get our needs met. When we discount ourselves, we avoid acting. When we discount others, we avoid dealing with them directly and equally. When we discount situations, we avoid dealing with reality and give ourselves an excuse for maintaining passive, irresponsible behavior.

The opposite of discounting is accounting or being accountable. We are accounting when we give attention to and act on all relevant aspects of ourselves, others, and situations.

Exercise in Discounting

Age Range: Fifth grade to adult

INSTRUCTIONS

Explain what discounting is, using the definitions above. Give the children examples of each kind of discount (thinking that we are stupid, that we don't have a right to ask for or do something, putting ourselves down, are self-discounts; interrupting, calling people names, acting as if we're more important than they are, are discounts of others; ignoring what is going on in a situation, such as asking to play when a serious discussion is going on, or asking your mother to take you somewhere when you know she is tired, are discounts of the situation.)

Have the children get into small groups of about six. Everyone is to do everything they can think of to discount everyone else interrupt, ignore each other, put down and criticize what the other says, etc.

DISCUSSION

Discuss how the children felt as they did this. How did they feel when they were discounted? How did they feel discounting others? Did they like discounting or being discounted? What are some situations at home or school or with friends when they've felt discounted?

What can they do when someone discounts them? (Probably the most effective way to handle being discounted is to confront the person who is discounting, state how you feel about being discounted, and ask them for what you want different. Example: "I'm angry because I feel discounted by you when you interrupt me. I want you to listen to me and wait until I've finished talking before you talk. Will you do that?") If someone continues to discount us even when we've confronted them, what can we do?

Discounting and Accepting Strokes

Age Range: Fifth grade to adult

Stroke is another word for attention. There are negative and positive strokes and they may be verbal, nonverbal, and physical. Examples of positive strokes are saying nice things to someone, praising him or her, acknowledging an accomplishment, giving someone a hug, smiling warmly at someone.

One of the most common ways we discount, give up personal power or deny ourselves access to it, is by discounting the positive strokes we get. When someone says to us, "You really did a good job," and we say, "Oh, it was nothing," we have discounted their stroke by belittling what we did. When someone says, "I really think you're neat!" and we think to ourselves, "He doesn't really mean that" or "No, I'm not," we have discounted that stroke. We could accept those strokes by saying,

"Thank you" and believing that the person means what he or she says and by stopping any disparaging, self-deprecating thoughts or statements.

The following exercise will give children an opportunity to experience what it is like to discount all strokes and then to accept all strokes.

INSTRUCTIONS

Have the children get into groups of about six. "Another way in which we discount is to discount the strokes we get." (Give an example of discounting a stroke.) "We are going to do an exercise in which, first, we discount all the strokes we get, and then we accept all the strokes we get. Each of you is to give a positive stroke to everyone else in your group. Find at least one thing that you like about each person and give them a positive stroke for that. Some examples might be, "I think your hair is pretty," or "I think you're really smart," or "I like you." As each of you receives a stroke you are to discount it, deny it, and not accept it, as for example, "Oh, my hair is dirty today," or "I'm not really smart. I just act that way."

Allow every child in each group to give strokes to everyone else in the group as they discount the strokes.

DISCUSSION

How did you feel as you gave strokes? Was it hard or scary? How did you feel when your strokes were discounted? How did you feel as you discounted the strokes you got? Do you ever discount the strokes you get at home, at school, or with your friends? Do you know of others who discount strokes? Why do you think we sometimes discount the strokes we get? (We are embarrassed, or don't think it's right for us to accept strokes, or we may think we have to be perfect, feeling if we haven't done something exactly right that we did not do well at all.)

INSTRUCTIONS

Now, have the children get into different groups. Do the same exercise, each child giving positive strokes to everyone else in the group, but this time they are to accept all strokes. This may be more difficult than discounting them. "As you receive a stroke, be as open and accepting as you can be. If you find yourself arguing with what the person has said to you, or putting yourself down in your own mind, accept that you have those thoughts and accept the stroke anyway. You can accept strokes by simply saying, 'Thank you,' or smiling and nodding at the person, and take a few seconds to love and appreciate yourself for who you are."

DISCUSSION

How did you feel as you accepted all the strokes that you got? Was it hard to accept some strokes? Did you find yourself wanting to argue with or deny the strokes? How did you feel as you gave strokes? What differences were there between discounting strokes and accepting them? Do you usually accept the strokes others give you, or do you discount them?

Regaining Personal Power

Feelings of powerlessness are engendered in us as children by what Steiner (1974) calls the Rescue Game.

This game is based on the belief that people can't really be helped and can't help themselves. It is clearly different from the situation of someone needing help, asking for it, and someone else offering help. The Rescue Game is based on discounting: the "I can't help myself" position is a self-discount; the "People can't be helped or help themselves" position is a discount of others. When we operate from these assumptions, the Rescue Game is inevitable.

The three roles of the Rescue Game are Rescuer, Persecutor, and Victim. Karpman (1968) arranged these roles into a triangle (called the Karpman Triangle or Drama Triangle) to show how people switch back and forth between roles and to show the interaction among the roles:

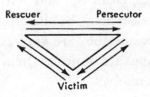

The Victim's position is: "I am helpless and can't help myself; try to help me." The Rescuer's position matches the Victim's: "You are helpless and can't help yourself; but I'll try to help you." The Persecutor's position is: "You are helpless and it's your own fault." As we play the Rescue Game it is common to move around the triangle and change roles as the game progresses. However, most of us have our favorite role. For instance, the nurse's favorite role may be Rescuer, although she may play Victim with a Doctor she works with.

Training in powerlessness and the Rescue Game occurs primarily in the family. We train children to feel powerless when we rob them of the potential power they have. Children are forced into a Victim position by parents acting either as Persecutors who oppress them or as Rescuers who do for them what they can do for themselves. An eight-year-old girl, for instance, could learn to get up by herself, dress, make her bed, cook her breakfast, make her lunch, wash her dishes, and go to school. However, most parents prevent eight-year-olds from using their capabilities to a full extent, so most of them are awakened by their mothers who then feed them, make their lunches, clean up, and tell them when to go to school. In this situation, the children are Victims who are Persecuted because they are kept powerless and then Rescued when things are done for them which they could have done for themselves.

As children grow older and begin to acquire power separate from their parents, they often begin to express their anger and resentment at being Victimized. The more extensive the Victimization has been (the more complete the parents' Rescuing and Persecution), the more severe the child's retaliation will be, and he or she may become the parents' Persecutor. The child may retaliate by stealing, getting arrested, by flunking out of school, by getting suspended. The more the child has been Victimized, the more that child will play the Rescue Game as an adult.

The more powerless we feel, the more we don't think, don't act effectively, don't work, don't enjoy ourselves, don't understand or deal with the world, and don't love. Some of us feel completely powerless, others only at certain times, but most of us play the Rescue Game to some extent. It is very commonly carried on in the classroom. For instance, the teacher who allows the children no freedom of choice about their activities (and, thereby, also teaches them not to be responsible) is both Persecuting and Rescuing them.

Following are some exercises and strategies to help children regain their power and stop the Rescue Game.

Acting Out the Rescue Game

Age Range: Third grade through junior high

INSTRUCTIONS

"We're going to act out something called the Rescue Game. It takes three people to play this game, so I need

three volunteers who would like to do some play-acting."
Explain each role: "One of the roles is the Persecutor or
bad guy. He or she is mean, picks on the Victim, and
thinks the Victim is helpless. Another role is the Victim.
He or she acts helpless, like a poor thing who can't take
care of him or herself. The other role is the Rescuer.
He or she acts like the good guy who takes care of the
Victim and solves the Victim's problem." (Be sure to
indicate that the Rescuer is really not a good guy, but
acts as if he is. Make very clear the problems caused by
Rescuers.)

Describe a situation in which there is a Persecutor,
Rescuer, and Victim. Example situation: Teacher (Persecutor) blames child (Victim) for something he or she
didn't do. The Victim acts helpless and guilty and doesn't
even try to tell the teacher what really happened. Another child (Rescuer) jumps in and explains what happened, saving the Victim from being in trouble.

Have the children act their roles in the situation.

DISCUSSION

Discuss how they felt as they played these roles. Do
they ever act this way in real life? Which role do they

usually play? Do they ever see other people playing these roles?

INSTRUCTIONS

Now, have them act out the same situation again, but this time all three players think, take care of themselves, ask for what they want, own their own behavior. Help monitor so they don't slip back into the Rescue Game.

DISCUSSION

Discuss the difference in the way the players acted this time. How did they feel while being effective, thinking for themselves, and taking care of themselves?

Rescuing

Age Range: Fifth grade to adult

INSTRUCTIONS

Have the children get into groups of about six. Ask for one volunteer in each group to play the role of Victim. The others will be Rescuers who are going to try to help the Victim solve a problem. The Victim is to present a problem to the group, either a made-up problem or a real one. After the Victim explains the problem, the Rescuers are to come up with all the suggestions they can think of for solving the problem. The Victim is to respond to each suggestion by saying, "Yes, but . . ." and then giving reasons why that suggestion can't possibly work, or why he or she can't possibly do what is suggested.

Allow them to do this for 10-15 minutes or until the Rescuers are thoroughly frustrated and angry.

DISCUSSION

Discuss what happened. How did the Rescuers feel as they worked so hard to try to solve the Victim's problem, only to have the Victim discount all suggestions? Have they ever experienced something like this in real life? Is it possible to solve someone else's problem, especially when they aren't doing anything to solve it themselves?

Strategies for Stopping the Rescue Game

Age Range: Kindergarten to adult

You will now be able to observe the children in your class playing Victim or Rescuer or Persecutor. When a child gets into Victim, confront that ("You're playing Victim" or "You're acting as though you were helpless") and say, perhaps, "I want you to think and figure out what you need to do to take care of yourself, or to solve the problem." If the child continues in Victim ("Yes, but . . ." or continues to pout, etc.) tell the child again that he or she can think and figure out what he/she needs to do to take care of him/herself, and that you will not talk to him/her or allow him/her to continue an activity until he/she decides to be effective. You may also use the corner or time-out if the child continues in Victim.

Don't Rescue children by letting them off easily, before they have put energy into thinking effectively and solving the problem. Ask them what they have figured out that they need or want to do. Praise them a lot for thinking effectively and taking care of themselves, and reflect the fact that they *can* think and take care of themselves.

Some children always seem to be getting hurt or picked on by other children. Chances are, such children are playing Victim and setting up situations so that they are ultimately justified in that position. You can use several strategies for confronting and stopping this. You can gather the facts of what happens from the children involved and find out what the one child is doing to set himself or herself up as the Victim; then confront that, refuse to give attention (comfort or defense) to that child for being in Victim, and insist that the child ask straight for what he or she wants. (Children who habitually play Victim are usually seeking attention, as well as reinforcing their notion that they are helpless, and you can insist that they *ask* for the attention they want.) Another way to handle the habitual Victim is to refuse to take part in the argument or fight, or give any attention to the children involved; sit them down together and have them solve the problem between them. If you do this, the children need to know how to problem-solve cooperatively, i.e., stating how they feel, asking for what they want, and negotiating that.

Children frequently Rescue each other. They answer questions for each other, try to "help" each other by solving each other's problems, do things for each other when they haven't been asked. Again, confront this as you see it occurring: "You're rescuing . . ." or "Don't Rescue; she can figure that out for herself."

Be aware of your own Rescuing. Children will often escalate a problem or behave in other ways to get someone else to solve the problem for them. You rob children of their power by Rescuing, and in order to Rescue you must have a Victim. While it often takes more time to allow children to think for themselves, you will help them regain the personal power they have given up if you insist and believe they can think effectively and take care of themselves.

Feelings

Feelings are an important part of us which we too often deny, repress, or intellectualize. Becoming aware of how we feel is a necessary part of being responsible for ourselves. Feelings reflect a need, a loss, or satiation and are a form of energy which can be used to help us act effectively to take care of ourselves.

Feelings are a direct experience of reality (as opposed to thoughts, which are a translation or analysis of our experience) and give us important information about what we need to do, what we want, or how we need to change. Anger is the feeling we have when our wants and needs have not been met. Fear is the feeling we have when we anticipate that our wants and needs will not be met or when we are presented with a problem that we don't know how to solve. Sadness is the feeling of loss; and happiness is the feeling we have when we have what we want and need. Thus, the feelings of anger, fear and sadness indicate a need or lack and provide the energy to act effectively to get what we need.

One of the ways that we stop ourselves from experiencing our feelings is through body tensions and blocks. When we begin to feel afraid, we may tense our stomach muscles to stop the feeling, or hunch our shoulders up in a position of protectiveness. When we feel angry, we may tighten our shoulder and neck muscles, or clamp our jaws together, or grind our teeth. (This kind of tension also often produces headaches.) When we feel sad we may tighten our facial muscles or stomach muscles to stop ourselves from crying.

We learn such chronic muscular tension when we do not have permission to feel our feelings and when we think we must stop ourselves from feeling. Another way we stop ourselves from feeling is by not breathing deeply and completely. When frightened, we may breathe only in our chests. Breath is energy and should flow freely throughout our bodies. When we develop chronic muscular tensions, we create blocks in our bodies so that we do not breathe deeply and freely. Such blocks inhibit or stop feelings, and thus we lose a valuable source of information about our wants and needs.

The way past or beyond a feeling is through it. We do not "get rid" of feelings except by experiencing them fully and accepting them. Burying, blocking, denying, and repressing feelings only serve to store those feelings, and instead of getting rid of them, we end up holding onto them. We can get through feelings by breathing into them, relaxing into them, and letting ourselves feel what we feel. By doing this, we integrate our feelings and energize ourselves to take whatever action is necessary.

How Do Feelings Feel?

Age Range: All primary grades

Because many of us are not given permission to feel and express our feelings, we are not always clear about how we feel, what the difference between feelings is, or how to express how we feel in a direct way. Following are some exercises to help children clarify the different feelings and learn how to express feelings straightforwardly.

INSTRUCTIONS

Have the children take turns acting out or miming the different feelings: anger, fear, sadness, happiness, excitement. Have the other children figure out which feeling is being acted out.

Have each child pick a partner and take turns being angry, frightened, sad, and so on. Have them do this nonverbally.

What Do Feelings Look Like?

Age Range: All primary grades

INSTRUCTIONS

Have the children draw a picture of each feeling. These pictures may have people in them or faces, or they may be more abstract representations (example: a picture of a hurricane or storm for anger). Ask the children to share their pictures with the class and identify what feeling each represents. If they have drawn abstract pictures, you might ask them what their pictures mean to them. Why did they draw that particular picture? (A child may say, "I feel all stormy inside when I'm angry.)

(For very young children, you may want to provide empty faces on which they put expressions.)

What Do Feelings Sound Like?

Age Range: All primary grades

INSTRUCTIONS

Have the children make angry noises, scared noises, sad noises, happy noises, excited noises. You can do this individually or with the whole class. This activity can also be used as an effective outlet for the children to vent some of their feelings.

What Are Feelings About?

Age Range: First grade through junior high

INSTRUCTIONS

Ask the children what they get angry about, what they get frightened about, what they get sad about, and so forth. Take one feeling at a time. You may want to write what they say on the board, or just talk about it. Guide them so they don't confuse feelings (i.e., talk about something frightening and say they were angry).

As you do this with each feeling, summarize what is common to all of them: what they all get angry about, what they get frightened about, etc. (Example: "It sounds as if all of you feel scared when you think something bad might happen.) With older children, ask them to discuss what seems to be common: when do we feel angry, scared, etc.?

This exercise will help children to distinguish between feelings and become more clear about the differences between feelings.

Where Do We Feel Feelings?

Age Range: Third grade through high school

Although people differ as to where in their bodies they feel feelings, some are commonly felt in certain parts of the body. For instance, many people experience fear in their stomachs; anger in their shoulders, neck, and jaw; sadness as a tightness in the chest or a lump in the throat. Everyone has some unique experiences with feelings. One fourteen-year-old boy described feeling tingly all over when he felt scared and said it felt like he *had* to do something.

INSTRUCTIONS

Ask the children where in their bodies they feel angry, frightened, sad, etc. Take one feeling at a time. The younger the children are, the more you will probably need to provide examples of where one feels certain feelings.

DISCUSSION

Discuss what they do with those feelings in their bodies. Do they let themselves feel those feelings? Do they stop themselves from feeling or do something so they won't feel that way? Do they ignore those feelings? What do they think happens when they stop or ignore the feelings they have?

"We all have feelings and all feelings are okay. Feelings are there to tell us that we need or want something and they provide us with the energy we need to act to get what we need. It is important to let ourselves feel our feelings. When we stop them, or block them, or ignore them, they don't go away. The way to get out of feeling the way we do is to let ourselves feel what we feel *completely*, accept and love ourselves for feeling that way, and then do whatever it is that we need to do so that we don't feel that way again in that situation."

Expressing Feelings Directly
and Effectively

Age Range: First grade to adult

Most of us have not been taught to express feelings directly. We learn either to stop our feelings or to express them in roundabout, ineffective ways. For instance, when we feel angry at someone, we may attack them verbally, trying to make them feel bad. This only makes matters worse. The other person will become defensive, may verbally attack us back, and it is very unlikely that they will change what they've been doing, so we will probably end up getting angry with them again about the same thing. Instead, we could be straightforward about how we're feeling, own the feeling ("I'm angry!"), tell them why we're angry, and ask them to change or do something different so that we don't stay angry or get angry again.

It is often very easy to figure out how someone is feeling, even though they don't tell us. When someone stomps in the room, slams the door, and throws his books down on the table, it isn't difficult to discern that he is probably angry. However, while it might be clear to an observer that he is angry, the person himself may not be aware of that feeling, or he may be focusing so intently on what someone else did to "make" him angry that he is not owning how he feels—at any rate, he is not acting effectively to get what he needs.

INSTRUCTIONS

You can help children own their feelings and express them directly by simply asking, "How do you feel?" or "What are you feeling right now?" The most direct way to express a feeling is simply, "I'm angry!" or "I'm really scared." Such statements also reflect ownership of the feeling by the use of "I." When expressing to someone how we feel, it is also important to give them information about why we feel the way we do. Then we can ask for what we want different. Example: "I'm angry because you're late, and what I want is for you to be on time when you say you will be. Will you do that?" Using the format below helps focus our attention on figuring out how we feel, why, and what we want different.

I'm (feeling) _____
because (reasons why) _____
and I want (what you want different, or what you
    want from the other). _____
Will you do that? (asking for what you want)

Distinguishing Between
Feeling and Thinking

Age Range: Kindergarten through junior high

There is a difference between feelings and thoughts. As was discussed earlier, feelings are a direct experience while thoughts are intellectualized translations of experience and much more removed from our actual experience. While most of us would probably claim to know the difference between feeling and thinking, we use language to obscure this difference. How many times have you heard someone say, "I really feel we should do that"? (This is a thought, not a feeling.) Or, "I feel that you're lying to me." (This is also a thought.) When we use the word "feel" indiscriminately, as in the above examples, we confuse the difference between feelings and thoughts and make it harder to be in touch with real feelings.

In general, the phrase "I feel" should be followed by words such as angry, sad, frightened, happy, and excited. In learning to distinguish feeling from thinking, it may be helpful to realize that if "I feel . . ." is not followed by one of these basic feelings, what is being expressed is probably a thought.

INSTRUCTIONS

"We have feelings and we have thoughts, and there is a difference between the two. Feelings are angry, scared, sad, happy, and excited. Thoughts are what we think *about* feelings, our opinions, our conclusions, what we understand or figure out about what we see and experience. Sometimes we say, "I feel . . ." when what we are talking about is a thought, not a feeling." (Give examples.)

"As we talk about things in class, I want you to talk about how you feel or what you think, and see if you can tell the difference. As we do this, I want you to say, "I feel . . ." or "I think. . . ."

This exercise can be built into any discussion you have in the classroom, or you can create a discussion for this purpose.

Integrating Feelings

Age Range: Third grade to adult

We learn to stop our breathing and tense our bodies against feelings because we do not have permission to have feelings. Through what our parents say and do, we learn whether or not it's right to have feelings, and which ones are all right to have. Some of us have permission to be frightened, but not angry; or we may have permission to be angry, but not frightened; and some of us don't have permission to feel at all. We learn chronic muscular tensions in order to control our feelings, and we develop fantasies about what will happen if we let ourselves feel. For instance, people who don't have permission to be angry often have the fantasy that if they allow themselves to get angry, they will kill or destroy. These fantasies often develop because we have held back feeling for so long that we imagine a feeling is overwhelming. We are often not consciously aware of such fantasies; yet we use them to scare ourselves and remain passive. Once we become conscious of such fantasies and verbalize them, we can see whether they make any sense and are likely to come true. Doing this usually makes them less frightening so that we are more likely to allow ourselves to feel what we feel.

In order to integrate feelings and make them a part of us, we must allow ourselves to experience them fully. To do this, we have to give up our chronic muscular tensions, relax, breathe into the feeling, and accept the feeling as natural. It is important to give children permission to feel what they feel, without guilt, and to encourage them to accept and love themselves for feeling the way they do. This will help them integrate their feelings and get through them.

INSTRUCTIONS

"All of us have feelings. Sometimes we feel angry; sometimes we feel scared; sometimes we feel sad, and sometimes we feel happy. It's okay to feel what we feel. Sometimes we think we're not supposed to feel certain feelings, and we tense our bodies to stop feeling, or we don't breathe deeply, or we have scary thoughts (or fantasies) about something bad happening if we let ourselves feel. We're going to do an exercise to help us feel our feelings.

"We can't feel tense and relaxed at the same time, so let's take a few minutes and get relaxed. Find yourself a place when you can be comfortable." (If at all possible, it would be best if the children could lie on their backs.) "Close your eyes and take a couple of deep breaths. Put your hands on your stomach, and see if you can breathe all the way down into your stomach so that your hand rises." (Pause about 30 seconds) "Now put your hands on your chests and breathe deeply into your chests, making your hands rise." (Pause about 30 seconds)

"Now, just breathe normally again. Take a little journey through your body and find any tense places you have. Start at your feet, go up through your legs, your stomach, your chest, your arms, your shoulders, your back, your neck, and your face. If you find a tense place, breathe into it, and relax." (Pause about 1 minute)

"Now that you are relaxed and comfortable, imagine that you are angry with your mother or father, or remember a time recently when you felt angry at one of them. As you feel angry, stay relaxed. If you tense up your shoulders or stomach, relax them. Be aware of what you think as you feel angry." (Pause about 10 seconds) "You're very angry. Imagine what you say and do. Tell them how angry you are. Let yourself feel angry and breathe deeply into that angry feeling." (Pause about 10 seconds) "Say to yourself, 'I'm angry,' and accept and love yourself for feeling angry. It's okay to have angry feelings." (Pause about 30 seconds)

"When you're ready, come back here to the classroom and open your eyes."

DISCUSSION

Ask the children what happened as they did this. Did they have trouble? Did they have any scary thoughts about what might happen if they let themselves be really angry? If so, ask them to share these and help them to think about whether their fantasy might come true. Finding out that their fantasy is just a fantasy and probably won't come true will make it less frightening. Did they find themselves tensing some part of their body? Were they able to relax and let themselves be angry?

You can do this exercise with other feelings. For instance, you can have them imagine or remember a time when they felt very frightened. Encourage them to let themselves feel that fear: "Feel how scared you are.

Let yourself shake and tremble. If you feel like crying, it's okay to cry. Breathe into your scared feelings and love yourself for feeling scared. It's okay to have those scared feelings."

After you have done this exercise a couple times with different feelings, the children should be able to get in touch with their fantasies much more readily. Fantasies should be checked out against reality so that we don't use them to frighten ourselves into not feeling or acting.

Now that the children have some skills in relaxing and breathing, you can help them integrate their feelings as they occur. They will probably need a lot of permission and encouragement to let themselves feel what they feel and to accept themselves for feeling the way they do.

Regaining Personal Power
Over Feelings

Age Range: Fifth grade to adult

Language and the way we use it can reinforce either a position of powerlessness and passivity, or one of personal power and responsibility. While the learning of language is largely an unconscious process, it is easy to become conscious of how we use words. All we have to do is to listen to ourselves.

By using passive language, we reinforce the misconception that we are stuck in a particular way of responding or acting. For instance, we are taught to think in terms of things "making" us feel certain ways and we reflect this in our language. "She really made me mad," "You hurt my feelings," "Roller coasters scare me," are all examples of how we use language to convince ourselves that we do not have control over our feelings.

The truth is that we have an almost infinite number of ways of responding to people and situations, and we are in control of how we feel. Though it is true that we learn certain response patterns, we can choose to feel and act differently. When we think in terms of "make me feel," we give up our personal power and give others control over how we feel.

We can change the above statements to reflect personal power and personal responsibility by saying instead, "I really felt angry with her" (*I* felt angry; she didn't "make" me); "I feel hurt"; "I'm afraid of roller coasters." These statements reflect that I am in control of how I feel and that I take responsibility for feeling the way I do, rather than pretending it's someone else's fault. When we realize that we are in control of our feelings, we give ourselves the freedom to feel the way we do or choose to feel differently.

Following is an exercise designed to help children own and take responsibility for their feelings.

INSTRUCTIONS

Have the children get into small groups of about four. "Think of a situation in which someone made you angry. Describe what they did and how that made you feel. Everyone in each group take a turn doing that." (Allow all the children to do this)

"Now, describe the same situation again, but this time, after you describe what the other person did or said, own the fact that you *chose* to be angry and say, "I chose to be angry." In your groups, think about and discuss what you could have done or could have chosen to feel instead of anger." (Examples of alternatives: "I could have ignored her," "I could have walked away.")

DISCUSSION

Discuss the exercise with the children and how they felt as they did it. Do they really think someone else can make them feel? Discuss the importance of owning our feelings and taking responsibility for them.

Repeat this exercise with other feelings. You can also use this information to help children own their feelings and take responsibility for how they feel during their daily activities. Remind them to use "I" statements and not to say, "make me feel."

BIBLIOGRAPHY

BERNE, ERIC. *Games People Play*. New York: Grove Press, 1964.

KARPMAN, STEPHEN B. "Script Drama Analysis," *Transactional Analysis Bulletin*, 7 (26), (1968), 39–43.

SCHIFF, JACQUI L. *Cathexis Reader*. New York: Harper & Row, 1975.

STEINER, CLAUDE. *Scripts People Live*. New York: Grove Press, 1974.

8

Parapsychology: Exploring the Mind

Parapsychology gives an opportunity for enhancement of many of your students' self-images. It provides an excellent way to demonstrate how the sciences grow. It helps teach the important intellectual abilities of being open to new information and of recognizing that not all things are clearly true or false; some are in the middle range as far as we know. Parapsychological exercises may help your students develop these abilities. For adolescent reading assignments to accompany this chapter we suggest Larry Kettelkamp's *Sixth Sense*. For your own reading, we recommend pages 107-87 of *The Roots of Consciousness* by Jeffrey Mishlove.

How can parapsychology help your students' self-concepts? For one thing, the more we know about ourselves and each other, the more we find human life fascinating. If we believe we can know things through telepathy or other parapsychological ways, we feel an

157

increased ability to know things and to evaluate ourselves as people. Second (and this is surprisingly frequent), children often seem to have parapsychological experiences, but when they tell their parents or teachers about them, the adults punish, ignore, or ridicule the children. This tells a child that his own experience is worthless and that he is a "freak." Many adults carry along the idea that there is something wrong with them because of ridicule they received for seeing auras, for knowing something is going to happen before it happens, for knowing about people and places they have never seen, and so on. If you start discussing these experiences with adults, it is surprising to find how many remember such incidents from their childhood, but have kept it to themselves for most of their lives. It is usually a relief for them to find out that they aren't crazy.

Children seldom see that the world of knowledge grows and changes. Their experience is just too short for this. One of the ways science grows is by taking in new realms of human experience for systematic examination and understanding. Parapsychological phenomena have been with us at least since Joseph had his dreams in Egypt, and there have been periods of investigation throughout history, but it was only as recently as 1969 that the American Academy for the Advancement of Science accepted parapsychological researchers as affiliate members of AAAS. Here is a clear example of science enlarging its boundaries.

Which professions do you suppose show the greatest interest in experiences beyond our concept of time and space? When asked about this, Dr. Stanislav Grof, whose transpersonal theories are based on seventeen years of research, said it is the physicists and mathematicians. Post-Einsteinian physics and modern math concern changes in time and space and multiple dimensions, as well as domains of parapsychological research.

While the physical scientists are most open to the possibility of ESP (extrasensory perception), psychologists and other social scientists are most skeptical. The *New Scientist,* a British journal, reports from an informal survey that 88 percent of its total readership thinks that ESP is a legitimate scientific undertaking. Twenty-five percent regarded ESP as "an established fact" while an additional 42 percent thought it was a "likely possibility." Physicists and engineers strongly supported the probability of ESP, whereas psychologists rarely did. Perhaps this is because the physical sciences now consider time and space as variable, thus admitting the possibility of different times and spaces. Some suggested renaming ESP "paraphysics."

By no means are parapsychological experiences given full credibility, however, and this is one of the major advantages of teaching about them. Here is a ready-made field to demonstrate to your students that science grows by investigating "new" fields. The truly scientific mind is willing (usually eager, in fact) to consider things that might not be true. It is the fun of investigating these unsure things that makes science enjoyable to scientists. The excitement of exploring the unknown is what keeps many scientists at their work. But even beyond curiosity is the thrill of making the unknown known. Because parapsychology falls in this intriguing gray area, you can help explore this area by experiments in your class.

GETTING SET

When you do ESP exercises, certain attitudes are helpful. The general approach we suggest is open-minded skepticism, a sort of let's-try-it-and-see-what-happens attitude. Trying too hard is likely to interfere with most ESP experiments. This attitude is helpful in another way too. Since the existence of ESP is subject to debate, it will probably be useful to do the exercises below as experiments, and an open-minded approach gives your students practice in this necessary scientific attitude. Besides these advantages, many parents will feel more comfortable if their children are not taught that ESP does definitely exist or does not definitely exist. Current ideas about ESP can be taught similarly to the way the theory of evolution was taught earlier in this century: as an unresolved question about which there are different points of view to be explored.

DEVELOPING THE ESP PERSON

According to a study done with high school students in India (Kanthimana and Rao, 1972), parapsychological ability seems to be related to a series of personality traits. They are listed below:

Positive ESP Scores	Negative ESP Scores
warm, sociable	tense
good-natured, easygoing	excitable
assertive, self-assured	frustrated
tough	demanding
enthusiastic	impatient
talkative	dependent
cheerful	sensitive
quick, alert	timid
adventuresome, impulsive	threat-sensitive
emotional	shy
carefree	withdrawn
realistic, practical	submissive
relaxed	suspicious
composed	depression-prone

This is not to say that only people in the positive list did well in the experiment and that no one in the negative list could do well, but this tendency generally showed up when the researchers considered all the students. You might want to try to encourage the positive traits because they are generally helpful in daily living and learning. Encouraging these traits should help your class's ESP scores, too.

On a day when you notice that your class seems happy and easygoing, stop whatever you're doing and try a quick ESP experiment just for fun. If you can catch them in the right mood, you might find surprising results. Occasionally interrupting the normal class flow for an ESP game can contribute to the positive traits listed above and make your class more exciting. When you do it, do it with an air of fun and excitement.

A fascinating sidelight to psychic development is that a survey of well-known psychics showed that they had only one characteristic childhood experience in common: they all had suffered from severe electric shock before the age of ten. A particularly gifted psychic named Matthew Manning did not remember such an event; however, his mother said she had been so severely shocked three weeks before his birth that she was afraid she would lose him. We do not recommend that your students stick their fingers in live sockets, however! It's interesting to speculate that the increase in electrical gadgets around the home may be developing a generation of psychics. Of course, this can't be the whole story, though, because many people are shocked with no increase in psychic abilities, and many gifted psychics have never been shocked.

Poltergeists

"Poltergeist" means "noisy ghost" and usually shows up in the form of objects falling off shelves or being "thrown" across a room, pictures falling, furniture being overturned, and so forth. Oddly, it usually occurs around an adolescent, one who outwardly is calm and restrained but inwardly is seething with repressed anger. In one such case, involving a nineteen-year-old boy, over 200 objects in a novelty warehouse were moved or broken (Roll and Pratt, 1971). This happened even when no one was present in the room and when the boy was being watched.

The story of Matthew Manning is especially interesting because it illustrates this type of paranormal behavior which is typical of adolescents. Matthew Manning's poltergeist activity started at age eleven in a manner typical of this kind of phenomenon. However, while writing a paper late one night for school, he went into a relaxed state and started writing automatically. He has written in many foreign languages including those he has no conscious knowledge of, and in unusual dialects, such as a rare form of Arabic. Some of his writings were about secret church matters which he received from a dead, former high clergyman in the Greek Orthodox Church, and he even draws pictures that seem to come from artists such as Dürer and Picasso. When Matthew started doing the automatic writing and drawing, the poltergeist activity stopped. Apparently, it was possible to substitute the productive activity for a destructive one. The film *Matthew Manning* is exciting to show adolescents and adults. Matthew describes his experiences in a book called *The Link.*

Extrasensory Perception

Extrasensory perception (ESP) is the name given to four types of parapsychological phenomena: telepathy, clairvoyance, precognition (and retrocognition), and psychokinesis. *Telepathy* is communication from person to person without the use of our usual perceptual systems; in telepathy two people are always involved. In *clairvoyance* there is one person who knows something that his senses apparently can't tell him and that no one else knows. Telepathy and clairvoyance are difficult to understand. However, having radio and television, we are somewhat accustomed to knowing what is going on at a distance, but information from backward and forward in time is more difficult for us to accept.

Precognition is knowing about something before it happens, something that cannot be deduced from available information. For example, if the weatherman predicts rain, this is based on deduction from weather maps and reports from other weather stations. If he could call the throws of fair dice before they were shaken, however, this would be precognition.

The ability to see far into the past and know things that cannot be accounted for by one's lifetime experiences is called *postcognition* or *retrocognition*. Some people claim this is evidence for reincarnation. Others say that thoughts can exist on their own without people thinking them and that the retrocognizer is tuning in to this field of ideas and experiences. Still others say that all things exist throughout time, and the person is traveling across (or backward) through time to the past. A fourth explanation is that a spirit from the past continues to exist and transmits the information to the retrocognizer. Of course, it is possible that more than one of these explanations is true. There is no reason why there has to be only one process. This may be one of those instances when it is best to keep an open mind until we have more information.

For examples of children who unaccountably know about other families they have lived with and other towns where they lived in previous lives, we recommend

Kettelkamp's *Sixth Sense* and Mishlove's *Roots of Consciousness*. These make fascinating stories for children and can add a psychologically based touch of reality to Halloween. For your own information and for examples of the sorts of things that can happen when space, time, and identity change, look at Chapter 5, "Transpersonal Experiences," in Grof's *Realms of the Human Unconscious*.

Psychokinesis (PK) is sometimes included as a type of ESP, and sometimes not. Psychokinesis is the ability to influence things outside the physical body with the mind. The unconscious poltergeist phenomena mentioned above are one example of this. Others are intentional. In the USSR, scientists claim they have several people who have learned to do psychokinesis, but this is exhausting for them to do. In the United States, psychokinetic research is a rapidly changing field that is surrounded with controversy. The Transpersonal Treasure Map at the end of this book will give you some leads to keep track of when following this fast-changing field. Publications of the American Society for Psychical Research, Institute of Noetic Sciences, and *Brain/Mind Bulletin* keep abreast of scientific research in psychokinesis and other parapsychological fields.

No one is really sure whether ESP is a "sixth sense," separate from our sense of touch, sight, smell, sound, and taste. It could be an extremely high degree of one or more of these senses. Our calling it extra*sensory perception* shows we are still thinking of it the same old way. It could be a nonsensory direct intuition, that is, knowledge not arrived at through the senses. It could also be a total combination of feelings throughout the body so that our bodies as a whole act as a perceptual organ. In this view we put ourselves into a body-mind state to do ESP. There is some interesting work along these latter lines.

In a telepathy experiment, one researcher (Dean, 1962) hooked up the subject to a plethysmograph, a machine that measures changes in blood flow. Emotional responses change the amount of blood in the capillaries of the fingers. The agent, or "sender," sent names to the subject, the "receiver," via telepathy. Some names were emotionally important to the subject, others were of no importance. Although the subject was not consciously aware of when the different names were sent, the blood flow showed that his body was aware as the blood flow changed during the emotionally laden names. One of the outcomes of yoga, meditation, or other spiritual disciplines is frequently the development of psychic powers. Since many of these disciplines also teach one to be aware of minor changes in one's body, the research with the plethysmograph supports the idea that telepathy works body to body, rather than mind to mind. According to what they call the Physiological Principle, Drs. Elmer and Alyce Green of the Menninger Foundation say that every change in the mental-emotional state results in a change in the body, and vice versa. Some of these changes may be unconscious, however. Telepathy, then, seems to go from the agent's mind to his body, then to the subject's body. The subject may or may not be sensitive enough to pick up the change in his mind, but his body knows.

Charles Tart of the University of California at Davis did a similar experiment. He connected the subject to a plethysmograph, an electroencephalograph, and a device that records galvanic skin response. The agent was shocked at random intervals, and the subject was supposed to feel when the agent was being shocked. His reports were entirely at random. But his physiological measurements did respond when the agent was shocked. Perhaps we learn not to be aware of all these minor changes in our environment in order not to be at the mercy of every changing event around us. However, if we can learn how to be aware at this fine level, then perhaps we can choose when to "tune in" to these feelings and when to "tune them out." This may be what mediums learn to do.

TELEPATHY

There are many sorts of telepathy exercises you can do with your class. And, you'll have no problem inventing some of your own. In telepathy, the communication goes from one person's mind to another, although, as we pointed out, the message may go via the agent's and subject's bodies. During the exercises it will be helpful if your class is relaxed and in a playful but quiet mood. They should be ready for things to pop into their heads. Either you or a student may be the agent. You might want to ask the class to choose the agent each time; this can help set up a closer relationship between the agent and the subjects. Or you might want to take turns, with each student acting as agent to see who is a good agent.

Turn off the lights and draw the curtains to make the atmosphere more relaxing. Sometimes slow, dreamy music is a help, too. If it isn't too loud, you can keep it playing through the exercises.

Selecting the Targets

This can really be fun and it's a way to develop sensitivity to art at the same time. The exercise tests and helps develop ESP. It can also be used to select target pictures for the ESP experiments that follow. Of course, you may want to choose the pictures yourself, but it is fun to involve the class in this choice and it helps them be aware of how art affects us.

Parapsychologists are finding that emotionally stimulating pictures are better targets than boring cards, numbers, or meaningless symbols. This finding is consistent with the observations that it is usually an emotionally charged event that is involved in spontaneous telepathy—a death or injury, for example.

In selecting your pictures, try to choose those that bring out strong reactions and those that involve the senses. It can be fun to use pictures your class draws or brings in. A good source of ideas for student drawings is to have them illustrate an event from their own dreams. With some classes it will be helpful to use pictures that evoke other sensations as well as sight, such as a chocolate cake or a lemon, a furry rabbit, a lightning storm, or a drum. Other children will react more to the mood of a picture, such as people fighting or wounded, dancers, a religious scene, a calm lake, a still life, a loving mother and child, and so on.

To screen the pictures in order to select the best ones for your "target pool," the student-agent should look at one picture at a time and concentrate on all aspects of it. This will probably take five minutes or so. You can hand him a card with suggestions, such as the sample card below.

Some pictures will suggest activities, for example, you all might decide that a picture of water will be accompanied by a glass of water to drink. A variation on this is to select objects that the agent-sender can actually do things with. These may be used alone or with pictures —for example, a lemon slice to suck, a boxing glove, some soft cotton to feel and play with, money to count,

The activities on this card will help you send your picture to the rest of the class. You may do these in any order, and go back and do them over if you wish. As you do these, keep the class in mind too.

1. Looking at the whole picture, what do you feel? Make that feeling stronger if you can.

2. Pretend you are actually in the picture and can move around in it. In your mind point out things to the class.

3. Imagine you are touching, tasting, or using your other senses on the objects in the picture.

4. If the picture shows something to do, imagine you are doing it with the rest of the class.

5. On a piece of paper, draw some of the things in the picture.

6. Can you think of something else to do?

arithmetic problems, etc. Your class will be able to think of other things.

While the agent-sender is busy becoming involved with the picture, objects, and/or activities (in some place where the rest of the class cannot see her/him), the rest of the class should be relaxed and writing down ideas that occur to them. Often quick sketches will convey the message better than words. When you feel enough time has elapsed, tell the class to write or sketch any last minute ideas, and call the agent in and have him show the picture or object and tell what he did. When you compare the sender's message with a subject-receiver's words and drawings, look for similarities in mood, senses other than sight, and activities that are associated with the target. It is important for learning ESP that the student-subjects know the results of their work immediately. As soon as the agent has finished with one picture, object, or activity, have him return to your classroom to discuss what he did and to show the picture or object. After you have looked for telepathy in one transmission, then try another. Do not have the agent send two or more successive things. This will confuse the feedback.

This exercise is a good one for developing ESP, and by keeping the best pictures or objects you can develop a "target pool" for other ESP exercises.

Learning Telepathy

Equipment: Five pictures that evoke different feelings; the more they differ, the better. They should be the same size and should be put in manila envelopes marked 1 to 5. You might first want to try out many pictures in test runs with your class (see previous exercise). One die is needed for selecting the picture. Each student needs a pencil, and a piece of paper with the numbers 1 through 10 listed in a column.

Procedure: In this exercise the student-subjects should know beforehand what all the pictures are in the "target pool." After the agent has been chosen, and the room and students are set, the die is cast by the agent. The other students must not see which side comes up, which envelope he draws out, and which picture he sends to the others. If you can locate him behind a screen, in an alcove, or otherwise out of sight, this will ensure that there is no leakage of information by his reactions. The agent takes the picture out and looks at it, paying attention to the feelings the picture evokes in himself. The other students write down the picture they think it is. If they feel that it is a guess, they write G after the picture. If they feel somewhat sure of their reception, they put SS after the picture; and if they feel very sure or certain, they put VS after it. With practice they are likely to become more accurate at telepathy and will develop a sense of when it is actually working and when they are merely guessing. An easygoing, leisurely pace is best. You may want to be the timer and after 30 seconds or a minute of telepathy has elapsed, say, "What picture is it?" (Pause for them to answer) "How sure are you?" (Pause) You'll have to use your own sense of timing, as some groups like to go fast and some slowly. When all the students have answered on their papers, say to the agent, "What picture was it?" He responds, and the class marks their answers. This should be done calmly and with as little commotion as possible so as not to break the relaxed atmosphere.

The agent then returns the picture to its envelope and throws the die again. Note: since pictures *are* replaced, it is possible to hit the same picture several times in a row. Your class should be told this.

Apparently, ESP can be learned like other things we do, and it is important for the learner to know whether he was right as soon after he makes his guess as possible. Since there is a likelihood of being right one out of five times, two hits out of a run of ten is most likely. You may want to repeat runs with the same agent or a different one.

Dream Telepathy

This is done just as the previous two exercises are, except that the sender-agent is awake and the receiver-subjects are asleep. Either you or a student agrees to send the target, wheher it is a picture, object, or activity, during the night when the subjects are sleeping. The subjects write down their dreams as soon as they wake up, and you compare target and dreams when they get to school. Here, too, certain aspects of the target may be exaggerated by the dream or may be transformed by it.

Some hints on recording dreams are: Place paper and pen near the bed so they will be handy. Before you go to sleep, tell yourself you will remember your dreams. The more you keep track of dreams and pay serious attention to them, the more you'll learn to remember them. When you wake up after a dream, lie in bed quietly and run the dream through in your mind several times. As you do, notice different dream images. This is likely to bring back some details you otherwise wouldn't remember. Write it down immediately on getting up. It is easy to mistakenly think that we have a dream in our memories, and then find we have forgotten parts of it, or all of it. During the day other details of the dream may come back, so add them to your dream diary. Note: Do not try to analyze or interpret these dreams. That will only make it more difficult to remember them. Sometimes you will find that close friends will have the same dream. You and your class might keep an eye peeled for this.

The book *Dream Telepathy* by Montague Ullman, Stanley Krippner, and Alan Vaughan tells about their dream research at Maimonides Hospital in Brooklyn, which started when one of Dr. Ullman's patients began to dream about the doctor's private life. If students start to dream about your life, don't be too surprised. Children sometimes pick up their parents' dreams too.

Long-Distance Telepathy

The physical distance between agents and subjects doesn't seem to make any difference in a telepathy experiment. You can suggest to your students that they try to link up with a friend or relative in another town or even another country and try long-distance telepathy. Often cousins, aunts and uncles, or grandparents will be willing to help out. Psychic abilities seem to be inherited along the female line of a family, so a grandmother might be just the person. Of course this helps develop a family feeling as it's something people of any age can do together. Pen pals or distant friends are possibilities too. Here again is provided good practice in writing and learning that's in tune with one of the oldest and most basic guiding ideas in Western education: KNOW THY-SELF, as was written at the oracle in ancient Delphi.

When your class does long-distance telepathy, tell them to select a time every day to sit and record what they think the other person has done that day. At the appointed time, they write down what they are receiving and go over what they have done themselves and try to send it to their receiver. The exact time of day for telepathy isn't important, but evening is good because it has the additional benefit of being a "daily review." This review often helps people to assess themselves and their activities and to gain perspective on what they are doing, how they are using their time and energy, and how they will improve the next day.

When your students write down their daily activities, they should also write down where they were and what their feelings were. Since we often think of people at anytime during the day, it also helps if they jot down a word or two whenever they think of their telepathy partner during the day. First, they should make a note of the time, then a word or two about the message they are sending or receiving. Some students will find instantaneous flashes are remarkably accurate.

If the telepathy partner lives in another time zone, you may have to help them figure out the time difference so that the partners are transmitting and receiving at the same time. It is not imperative that the time be kept exactly, but it helps. If daily recording is too much, try some other regular schedule. Daily time in class is possibility.

Also, you'll have to help screen out knowledge of habits. If it's known that grandmother watches soap operas every noon, picking that up doesn't say much about telepathy. If the weather report on TV says it's snowing where the telepathy partner lives, it doesn't require telepathy to guess that he may be shoveling snow or playing in the snow. These cautions are good ways to teach the concepts of prediction, deduction from information, and chance occurrences, too.

An interesting variation on this is for the partners to agree to send each other information on a target, as in the earlier exercises. An object, picture, or activity can be selected and sent along with day-to-day living experiences. They might want to send a word, picture, or thoughts about something they are studying that day in school. In a partner arrangement, each partner should keep a copy of his letter to the other one if possible, or at least notes. They should also keep notes on what they did each day and what they tried to send.

Students in your class may want to be partners for shorter-distance telepathy too. Often it works best between friends.

You may be surprised at how accurate some people are at this process. The book *Thoughts Through Space* by Harold Sherman tells of a long-distance experiment between an airplane pilot in northern Canada and one of his friends thousands of miles away. The pilot went to Canada as part of a search party for a missing Russian flier in the far north. His receiver was able to report specific problems he had with the plane, where he was (even though he deviated from his planned itinerary), his health and moods, and unexpected events such as a toothache, and replacement parts needed for the plane.

CLAIRVOYANCE

Clairvoyance differs from telepathy in that there is a subject (receiver), but there is no agent. In ordinary language, telepathy is "mind reading" or "thought transference," whereas clairvoyance is knowing something that no one else knows and which isn't known through the ordinary senses. In some cases it is uncertain which of the two is working. If a clairvoyant helps police locate a missing ewel, for example, it is possible that the person who lost it knows unconsciouslessly where it is or that the thief knows where he hid it. These instances are usually counted as clairvoyance. If the clairvoyant helps find the body of a missing person who is not the victim of murder, though, this is a clearer case of clairvoyance, since we assume no one else knows the location. The important thing in clairvoyance is that no one knows what has happened until after the guesses, in this case guesses by your class.

Dice, Coins, and Cards

Take a die or coin and put it in a box, paper bag, can, or other opaque container. A file box for 3 by 5 cards works well for this. Shake the container (or have students take turns shaking it). Before you look inside, have each person write down what face he thinks will be up. Then you look. To have the whole class engaged in this, you can divide them into partners and have each pair flip a coin instead of using a box. While this isn't a strictly legitimate ESP experiment, because the students could use a highly developed sense of sight, it serves our purposes in teaching about clairvoyance. It is also considered valid enough to be used at the beginning of football games. With luck, you may develop a student who can be the team clairvoyant by learning to call the toss. Don't laugh. It could be done.

If you want to use cards as a target, it would be preferable to have someone not in your class shuffle them to be sure that subliminal clues don't tip off you or your class. A stack of ten or twenty cards should be put in a safe place, such as a manila envelope. You might want to limit the guessing to just "red" or "black." After you and your students have recorded your guesses, open the envelope and compare the guesses and cards for "hits."

A variation on this is for each student to record his guess for the first card, and for you to lift the first card and reveal what it is. Then they guess for the second card, and you report on it. Since immediate feedback helps in learning, this method is preferred, even though it takes longer.

By changing the targets you can add variety to the game. You might want to use 3 by 5 cards with each student's name, vocabulary words, pictures of things studied, symbols from chemistry or physics, art prints, etc. Younger children can even use numbers and letters. Your students will have ideas for their own card decks, too: popular musicians, sports heros, song titles, cartoons from magazines, and so forth. Souvenir postcards and museum postcard prints can be excellent targets, as well as ways to learn about different places and about art. Of course, these can be used in the telepathy exercises, too. To convert a clairvoyance task to a telepathy task, it takes only one person to know the information and send it to others. Try mixing decks of musicians, sports heros, vocabulary words, and so on. In this case it may be easier to guess the general deck the card is from than to guess which particular card it is. Another variation is to bring in a brand new magazine that your class hasn't seen and try to guess what will be on the next page. For clairvoyance, this has to be a magazine you yourself haven't looked through before, or you'll be doing telepathy. Here again, you'll have to discount pictures that are predictable from the nature of the magazine.

If you have a games section at the back of your room, you might keep ESP materials there for free-time activities. These exercises can turn rainy-day recesses from a horror show into recreational learning.

Relaxed Imagining with Group Judging

Give each student an opaque envelope with a target inside (some of the ones from the exercises above or new ones). If you can't get enough opaque envelopes, put a couple of pieces of paper around each target card. The students then relax, and you tell them they will think of the target in their envelopes. If they want to go to sleep, that's all right. Then they can dream of the target. This works nicely with primary grades that still have a naptime. After the rest period, they compare the picture with the dreams, imaginations, or daydreams.

An alternate way of judging can be used here, and in most other ESP experiments too. Instead of each person opening his own envelope and judging it himself, have everyone write his name on his envelope, and you collect them. You use four or five different targets, and have a spare set to show the class during the judging. The student whose turn it is first describes his dream, daydream, or imaginations to the whole class. Each student matches up the daydream with the picture it fits best. After the whole class has judged which card goes with the daydream, then you look in the envelope to see which is the right match. Then go on to the second student.

In more scientifically controlled ESP experiments, the judges only judge the correspondences and have no other contact with the experiment. Also, false pictures, blank cards, and false daydreams or dreams are added to reduce further the likelihood of good guessing. You might want to slip a false picture into the judging. This method of selecting the correct target oneself or with a panel of judges can be adapted to other ESP experiments. Try it to see if your class likes it. It can give them experience in understanding symbols and feelings too, as different people will change a target to suit their personality. A simple design such as a circle with a square in it will be an oxcart wheel to some, a table to others, a stylized flower to others, a game board, a baseball infield, and so on.

PRECOGNITION

Precognition is knowing about something before it happens. Sometimes it is called "prophecy," "prediction," "premonition," or "seeing the future." For something to classify as precognition, however, it must not be knowable via our usual senses of perception and/or by reason. Reports of precognition are often anecdotal rather than experimental. In the exercises below, the *dream diary* shows an attempt to record one frequent source of these anecdotes, and the experiments are an attempt to study precognition under more carefully controlled conditions.

Throughout history there have been instances of

precognitive dreams. One of the most famous, taken from Kettelkamp's *Dreams,* is a dream of Abraham Lincoln's three weeks before his assassination:

About ten days ago, I retired late. I had been waiting for important dispatches. . . . I soon began to dream. There seemed to be a deathlike stillness about me. Then I heard subdued sobs, as if a number of people were weeping. I thought I left my bed and wandered downstairs. There the silence was broken by the same pitiful sobbing, but the mourners were invisible. I went from room to room. No living person was in sight, but the same mournful sounds of distress met me as I passed along. It was light in all the rooms; every object was familiar to me, but where were all the people who were grieving as if their hearts would break? I was puzzled and alarmed. What could be the meaning of all this? Determined to find the cause of a state of affairs so mysterious and so shocking, I kept on until I arrived in the East Room, which I entered. There I met with a sickening surprise. Before me was a catafalque, on which rested a corpse in funeral vestments. Around it were stationed soldiers who were acting as guards; and there was a throng of people, some gazing mournfully upon the corpse, whose face was covered, others weeping pitifully. "Who is dead in the White House?" I demanded of one of the soldiers. "The President," was his answer. "He was killed by an assassin."

From a more experimental approach we find that successful business executives seem to have a precognitive sense. Researchers at Newark College of Engineering have tested over fifty groups of executives and managers. The subjects punched holes in computer cards to try to guess the results of a computer program that was selected and punched the following day. As would be expected, some of the executives and managers hit on high scores merely by chance, but it also turned out that those with the highest precognition scores increased their company's profits more than those with low precognition scores. Their mental imagery could be a clue to this somehow. When asked to select how they saw time, the high scorers were more likely to see it as a dashing waterfall or galloping horseman than to see it as an old woman spinning, a vast expanse of sky, or a quiet ocean.

An interesting tie-in between precognition, businessmen, and alpha brain wave training provides a possibility of why this happens. Biofeedback researcher Lester Fehmi was training some people to increase alpha brain waves. Without his asking them, some of them said they seemed to be getting along better with their families, friends, and co-workers. Fehmi decided to see if alpha training would help people's social relations and made this the subject of a later study. It did help. Alpha brain waves occur more frequently when a person is quiet and relaxed, but less frequently when he is asleep or wide awake. When doing alpha, a person's area of focus is likely to start to turn inward and his mind begins to drift. When we tie this in with the body-to-body aspect of telepathy that we noted earlier in the telepathy section, it suggests that the increased awareness of what is going on inside themselves may give more successful businessmen a telepathic feeling for what others are doing. This allows them to function better as decision-making executives as well as to be more responsive to people around them. In a study of school counselors, Terry Lesh found that when they practiced Zen meditation (another inward-oriented technique) they became more empathetic, and some of them reported spontaneous telepathy. This too suggests that the body as a whole acts as some sort of receiving device or sense organ to things that are beyond our normal senses. Tuning into the body is one way to be more aware of our environment and others. While the connections among these different observations are only speculations, they do give a certain credibility to intuition, hunches, and "gut feelings." Being able to choose the right kinds of consciousness and being able to put them in the most appropriate order for the task at hand opens a whole new domain for educators.

Basic Precognition Exercises

All the telepathy and clairvoyance exercises can be adapted to precognition. The difference is that in telepathy and clairvoyance the event has already happened, but in precognition it hasn't.

Using the coin-in-the-box and die-in-the-box clairvoyance exercises described earlier, you simply ask the students to guess what face will come up before the box is shaken. You can do three ESP experiments in a row. First, have the class guess which face will come up; this is the precognition experiment. Then shake the box and have them guess which face did come up; this is the clairvoyance experiment. Then look in the box and have them guess which face came up again; this is the telepathy experiment.

Precognitive Dreams

The dream that Abraham Lincoln had is typical of precognitive dreams. We are fortunate that he mentioned it to the U.S. Marshal for the District of Columbia, who wrote it down. The precognitive dreams that people remember are often of crises or disasters, but not always. One problem with these is that usually people don't record them; after the event, a person may claim to have dreamed of it, but there is no record. If you keep a dream diary, it can be used many ways. In addition to experimenting with telepathy, you can search for precognitive events in the dreams. These will often appear when one looks back at dreams of several days to several weeks before. At the time they were dreamed, there may be no indication of any special importance, but when looked back upon, their meaning becomes clearer.

At the Maimonides Hospital in Brooklyn, Montague Ullman, Stanley Krippner, and others conducted a series of dream studies over several years. They found that some subjects could dream of things that were about to happen to them. For example, the experimenters had several sets of possible events planned. During the night when the subject slept, one set of experimenters woke him up and asked him his dreams. These were recorded. After the subject was awake the next morning, a different experimenter selected one of the events at random and put the subject through the experience. Then the transcript of the dreams and the description of the experience were given to outside judges, who tried to match the dreams with the events. The correspondences were remarkably strong, far above chance. These are described in more detail in *Dream Telepathy* by Ullman, Krippner and Vaughan, and *Song of the Siren* by Krippner. One subject dreamed of snow, of everything being white, and of walking in the winter. When he awoke, the second set of experimenters (who knew nothing about his dreams), took him into a room that was painted white and in which everything was covered with white sheets. The room was cold, and the subject had to stay in it for several minutes.

You can do a similar experiment with your class. With or without their help, you can plan some activities. Have them record their dreams. Then after they have recorded them, but not told you about them, you choose one of the activities. If you have six activities, you might choose by rolling a die. The activities should be as different from each other as possible so that it will be easier to spot differences in dreams.

Judging Criteria

The Maimonides group developed a scoring technique that you can use for judging correspondence between dreams and events. They originally used it for comparing art prints with dreams. You can use it with precognitive dreams and with the clairvoyance and telepathy exercises, too. To score a target you look for ten categories and see if the dream, daydream, or imagination matches. The ten items are:

color	human characters
activity	food
mythical characters	body parts
implements	architectural objects
animals	nature scenes

A hit is scored if both the target and the dream show these. If one shows it and the other doesn't, it's a miss. It is not necessary that the hit be exact. Award 10 points for a direct hit, fewer for close misses. For example, a picture of a horse which elicits a dream or day-dream of a horse might be scored as 10 points, while a dream with a donkey in it might be given fewer points.

Central Premonitions Registry

When you and your students have a dream that you think is precognitive, you can officially register the fact that you had it. Then if the event happens, you can confirm the fact that you dreamed it. To register your premonition (dream or otherwise), describe where and when you had it, your address, and what happened in the dream. Include as many details as you can, such as objects around, colors, people, time of day, any words you heard, etc. Keep a copy of the letter for yourself, and send one copy to:

Central Premonitions Registry
Box 482
Times Square Station
New York, N.Y. 10036

PSYCHOKINESIS

Psychokinesis is the ability of the mind to influence objects. "Mind over matter" is the way most people think of it. In PK research some of the effects might be attributed to electrical and magnetic factors, but some are not explainable this way. The unexplainable phenomena have directed people's attention toward the possibility that there is a type of energy that we know very little of. They point out that throughout history we have discovered and developed energies that previously had been unknown. For example, earlier in this century electrical energy was known partially, but we had little idea of some of the things we could do with it. Radiation was almost completely unknown. Since then we have made atomic energy part of our lives. Could there be other types of energy that we still know little of? Are we being egotistical to think that we have discovered all forms of energy? Evidence for this new kind of energy, or new way which energy shows itself, is summarized in Jeffrey Mishlove's *Roots of Consciousness* and Stanley Krippner's *Song of the Siren*. An entire journal is devoted to the study of this energy, *Psychoenergetic Systems*. If this new form of energy does exist, will it offer sweeping changes like those that occurred as we harnessed energy from animals, steam, electricity, and the atom?

From the point of view of what human nature is, psychokinesis not only brings up basic problems, but also sheds light on them. What is the relationship between mind and body? If our minds can affect things without using our bodies, then the mind must exist beyond our bodies. The Field of Mind Theory states that all the body is in the mind, but not all the mind is in the body. The biological approach to the mind-body problem is to suppose that the "mind" is only a name for certain actions of the body, especially actions of the brain and nervous system. Psychokinesis challenges this idea of the mind and brain. When you and your students investigate this area of influencing matter, you are at one of the growing edges of science.

Coins, Cards, and Dice

The telepathy, clairvoyance, and precognition experiments that we have described can be converted to psychokinesis experiments by having the students try to influence the outcome. Before the coin or die is shaken in the box, the class can decide which face they want to come up, and all concentrate on helping that side come up. Or, you can try a heads-team and a tails-team.

You can have the students divide up into pairs and have one partner spin a coin while the other partner tries to make it come up heads or tails. In a card shuffling experiment with playing cards, postcards, 3 by 5 cards, etc., students can try to make a particular card or picture come up on top, or try to influence the shuffle so that more red cards will be in the upper half of the deck. You can think of other variations on this.

Compass

A standard way to test for one kind of PK (there may be different kinds) is to try to influence a compass needle. The compass is put on a table or desk, and the person tries to make it swing away from north. You have to watch carefully to see that no iron is making it deviate from its direction. Jewelry, watches, and keys can influence a sensitive compass. One way to control for this is to have the person who is trying the PK move around near the compass before he tries to influence it. He should get as close to it as he can without touching it or the desk it is on. When it is time to make the needle swing, tell the student that developing intensity and being energetic are likely to help. It helps to imagine that lots of energy is flowing down from one's shoulders into the arms and out the ends of the fingers. Different actions such as flicking off energy from the fingers and pointing the fingers at the compass as if to jab it sometimes do the trick. Since a compass is influenced by magnetic fields, this experiment adds credence to the electromagnetic view of PK.

Suspended Objects

For this experiment you need a large bell jar, aquarium, coffee pot, or other clear glass container, plus a pencil, a key, a knitting needle, or other object that can be suspended. Tie a thin thread around the object and tape the other end of the thread to the inside bottom of the container. When you invert the container, the object will hang from the middle. This position will keep the object from being affected by air movement.

As with the compass, students try to get the target to move without moving the container or the desk it is on. Sometimes putting one hand on one side and the other opposite it works. "Jabbing" and quick actions with the hand may help too. At the Menninger Foundation an Indian Swami made a 14-inch knitting needle swing. The air ducts were sealed to stop movement of the air, and Swami Rama sat four feet from the needle. To make sure he wasn't blowing on the needle, he wore a painter's mask and a plastic shield was attached to the front of it. If you want to tell your class about the details of their experiment, Doug Boyd's book *Swami* describes it (pages 70ff).

Talking to Plants

Do plants respond to human emotions and thoughts? It depends on whom you listen to. Some people say that the original research has been replicated by others. Others say it hasn't. You and your class can find out for yourselves. Give each student some seeds. Bean seeds often are reliable sprouters. Instruct the class to take two identical containers and put the seeds in water, then direct good thoughts to one batch and bad ones to the other. It is important to emphasize that the containers must receive identical treatment except for the love and hate energies. This is more difficult than it seems, so be exact on the directions. Teachers who have tried this find that students mistakenly will use different containers, put the containers in different rooms, water them differently, or give them other unequal treatments. Be sure to explain equal treatment in detail. This is a good way to have students experience the experimental method. One way to keep the water equal is to mark the same water level on each container and to keep the water at that level. This is important because if one batch of seeds grows up faster, they will use up water faster. You can look for two kinds of differences in growth. First, do equal numbers of seeds germinate? Second, do they grow to the same height? To make sure that the containers don't get mixed up, it's useful to tape labels on them: HATE and LOVE.

Thought Photography

This gets fairly expensive, but if you can find the money for film, it's exciting. In *The World of Ted Serios,* a man is described who can sometimes transfer his thoughts to Polaroid film. Do you want to try it? Set up a target the whole class can see. Have them concentrate on the target and try to send it to the camera. This is like telepathy, but with a camera as the subject instead of another person. After the transmitting gets strong, shoot. Point the camera at a blank blackboard. The blackboard should not have any smudges or chalkmarks, but it may be an even gray. Then, when the picture is developed, see what you have.

Metal Bending

Holding keys, nails, spoons, or other metal objects lightly between thumb and forefinger, the students imagine that heat is going into the target and that it's bending. They should not exert much pressure or press the objects on their desks to bend them, but they may massage the object they are holding gently. According to reports from Europe and Japan, when Uri Geller demonstrated this feat on television, many people, especially children by the hundreds, replicated it. Is it trickery, or is there something to it? We leave this up to you and your class to decide.

Psychic Healing

Psychokinesis includes other phenomena such as poltergeists, mentioned earlier, psychic healing, and "things that go bump in the night." *Roots of Consciousness* tells about some of these (pages 161-74). Psychic healing is becoming a recognized field. Some experiments at New York University School of Nursing show that nurses who were trained to heal via a therapeutic touch could affect the hemoglobin values in patients' blood. A newly formed Council of Nurse Healers is trying to gain recognition as a subspecialty within the profession. How about putting your school nurse or biology teachers in touch? One psychic healer has been able to affect the digestive enzyme trypsin.

Summary

Findings and counterfindings abound in parapsychology. We suggest you carefully evaluate both, and keep an open mind. It hardly seems possible that everything that is talked about can be true, but if only one or two things are, our idea of what it means to be a person must change. New ideas of education and learning will follow. The following list from the American Society for Psychical Research provides some fascinating leads, but don't let wishful thinking take you further than the evidence.

9

Transpersonal Values

Transpersonal education places a heavy importance on the development and study of values. There is strong emphasis on values in the upper four stages of Maslow's needs hierarchy: love-belongingness, esteem, self-actualization, and especially transcendence.

The higher values are especially interesting because they seem to form a core of values throughout many cultures and spiritual traditions. The higher that one goes in terms of Maslow's hierarchy, the more similarities there are with other cultures. This may be because these values arise not from the particulars of a culture or of someone's individual background, but from common *peak experiences* or mystical experiences. This is not to say that a specific culture and personal history play no part in values, but that in addition to these influences there are other experiences which contribute to our value systems. This other origin of values seems to rely on direct intuition rather than cultural or individual conditioning.

Peak experiences, mystical experiences, or other transcendent experiences (those in which a person temporarily loses track of an egocentered way of looking at the world) are the sources of this approach to values. One can approach many of these values through ordinary consciousness too; however, in transpersonal experiences the values are immediately apprehended, or intuitively known, rather than developed piecemeal. The peak experience exercise below illustrates one way to experience some of these values.

People who don't realize that transcendence is a normal, healthy human motivation or who are unfamiliar with peak or mystical experiences are baffled by an intuitive approach. Their views are easily understandable. They look at people only as individuals and see society as collections of individuals. To them any moral, ethical, or values decision is made either to benefit the individual directly (when someone acts for his own benefit) or to benefit the individual indirectly by helping the group or society of which he is a part. These two approaches certainly are valid; we do act for those reasons. But we also make value judgments based on non-ego experiences, that is, on our peak experiences or mystical experiences.

To someone ignorant of mankind's natural desire for transcendence and ignorant of its effects, such value judgments might seem to be contrary to concerned social action. The evidence on this shows the opposite to be true. Seeing oneself as part of something larger (and we don't mean just a collection of other people) actually makes one more dedicated to helping others. Self-benefit becomes less important. When Maslow describes transcenders, he says their lives are dedicated to a value or values beyond themselves: justice, truth, mercy, for example. Their peak experiences have put them in touch with these values and have given them the direction and energy to carry them out. In Walter Clark's studies with divinity students, those who had mystical experiences were more dedicated to helping their fellow humans than those who lacked such experiences. In Raymond Moody's study of people who had been clinically dead and resuscitated, *Life After Life,* he found that their temporary egoless state made them less anxious, more caring, and more loving. Psychic healers also say that surpassing the ego is necessary. Counselor-trainees who practiced Zen meditation were more empathetic than those who did not meditate. Charity is the fruit of the tree of transcendence. As pointed out in the parapsychology chapter, telepathy seems to work body-to-body rather than mind-to-mind. Thus, inner awareness and exploration is one door to awareness of others and of things beyond our usual ideas of self. These processes and the reasons they work are some of the puzzles transpersonal psychologists are trying to solve.

It certainly is possible that inner direction can be used as an escape from reality. Anything can be used as an escape by becoming the sole focus of attention. There is no doubt that some people withdraw narcissistically inward to escape social responsibility just as others become addicted to social action as an escape from working on their inner lives. Blindness to the inside is equally blind as blindness to the outside. A whole person grows inwardly and outwardly; if he goes far enough, inner and outer start to complement each other and eventually turn out to be the same. Alternate periods of inward direction and outward direction, of rest and activity, of meditation and action, of verbal and nonverbal, add to each other. Total involvement with one way to the exclusion of the other soon becomes weak and ineffective. As LeShan points out in *How to Meditate,* a primary characteristic of mystics is their efficiency.

The transpersonal values and qualities of peak experiences that follow have been identified as important from a transpersonal point of view. There are probably others that you'll want to add. Since many of them are adult vocabulary, you'll have to translate them into children's language or select those your class can understand.

admiration	benevolence
aliveness	bliss
amusement	brotherhood
appreciation	calmness
awe	caring
beauty	clarity

compassion
completeness
comprehension
courage
creativity
curiosity
desirability
differentiation
ease
ecstasy
effortlessness
ending
energy
enthusiasm
essential
eternity
exuberance
fairness
faith
finality
form
freedom
fulfillment
fun
gaiety
generosity
gentleness
giving
goodness
goodwill

grace
gratitude
harmony
helping
honesty
humor
idiosyncrasy
inclusiveness
independence
individuality
inevitability
infinity
insight
integration
integrity
interconnectedness
intricacy
joy
justice
lawfulness
liberation
light
love
necessity
noncomparability
novelty
oneness
openness
order
orderliness

organization
"oughtness"
patience
peace
perfection
playfulness
positiveness
quiet
reality
receiving
receptivity
relatedness
renewal
richness
rightness
self-determining
self-functioning
self-regulation
self-sufficiency
serenity
service

silence
simplicity
spontaneity
strength
structure
suitability
surprise
synthesis
transcendence
trust
truth
understanding
unity
universality
variety
vitality
wholeness
will
wisdom
wonder

Weekly Word

The above list is an excellent source of vocabulary words, and by studying them students are likely to keep them in mind. Another way to work with these values and qualities is to write one word on the blackboard or post it on the bulletin board for a week. Throughout the week you and your students spot instances of the word and report them in class. The usual sort of vocabulary exercises, such as using them in sentences, or writing stories or plays that demonstrate the quality, are also good ways. Short improvisational plays are fun to do too. It's most important that the students recognize these traits in their own actions and in the behavior of people around them.

Listening to Stories

Myths, poetry, fantasy stories, and classic children's tales often stress these values, although they are seldom called by their abstract names. If your class likes to be read to, a relaxation period leading into a story can make listening a more meaningful experience. Listening also helps the mind to form images of a story and to get in touch with the mythical message and symbolism. Most classical children's stories developed as part of an oral tradition. They were meant to be told and listened to, not read. Listening to a story develops mental abilities that reading it to oneself misses, as anyone who has listened to a story by a campfire can testify. You can't have a campfire in the middle of your classroom, but you can try a candle. It can focus external attention as a campfire does while letting the rest of the mind become absorbed in the story.

In addition to exemplifying qualities and values, myths and folktales give us direct experience with the cultures they come from. Greek, Roman, and other myths express central parts of our culture and psychological truths of human personality. Tales from American Indians or other cultures help us experience some direct contact with them. These stories usually recognize mankind's search for values as an important part of being human. As these stories were refined over generations, many of them became symbolic expressions of common psychological processes. Listening to these stories puts us in contact with these processes and results in better self-knowledge, understanding of others, and an appreciation of literature. Your students might want to write their own myths. This can be fun. Sometimes dreams can be a lead. Joseph Campbell's book, *Myths To Live By*, is a beautiful exposition of the relevance of myths to our daily lives.

Peak Experiences

One of the pathways that leads current educators to a transpersonal view of education is Abraham Maslow's work with peak experiences. While studying self-actualizers, people who were actively realizing their creative potentials, Maslow discovered that they reported experiences in which they temporarily lost sight of their ego boundaries. These "magic moments" seemed especially important to them: they were the highlights of their lives, giving meaning and a feeling of being in touch with a reality beyond their egos. To psychoanalytically trained Maslow, these "oceanic feelings," as the Freudians call them, were signs of unstable personalities. How could it be that Maslow's healthiest people, his examples of the best human development, reported these? This discovery was so much at odds with what he had expected, that it took Maslow seven years to get up enough courage to publish his results.

Since peak experiences seemed to be a lead to the highest human behavior, Maslow decided to explore them further. These explorations led him to the insight that these peaks put people in touch wih a set of values that gave their life guidance and direction. In *Toward a Psychology of Being* Maslow describes these values and his research on peak experiences. Some of your students may have had such experiences. They can happen to all of us, not just self-actualizers or transcenders, although they happen more frequently to these groups. Here is the question Maslow used to study peak experiences:

"I would like you to think of the most wonderful experience or experiences of your life: happiest moments, ecstatic moments, moments of rapture, perhaps from being in love, or from listening to

music, of suddenly 'being struck' by a book or paint-
ing, or from some great creative moment. First list
these."

(Pause several minutes
until students are through listing)

"Now tell me how you feel in such moments,
how you feel different from the way you feel at
other times, how you are at the moment, a different
person in some ways, how the world seems different at that time."

(Pause till the writing slows down; this may
take several minutes, often 10 minutes or longer
with adults)

This can be an interesting in-class writing assignment and can stimulate an exciting discussion. Explain
to your class that you will not grade them on spelling
or grammatical errors. Finally, do not force participa-
tion. All sharing must be true sharing. It will often help
stimulate discussion if you start by mentioning some of
your peak experiences, if you've had them. All sorts of
things can trigger peak experiences.

Since peak experiences are often felt as very personal experiences, some students may want to share how
they felt, but not what the "trigger" was that set off the

peak experience. These may be things such as kissing a special girlfriend or boyfriend, riding a motorcycle through the night, figuring out how to repair a stereo, watching a beautiful sunset, making a football tackle . . . the list goes on endlessly. The important things to notice are the feelings at the time, not what the trigger was.

Do young children have peak experiences? If so, can they write or talk about them? We don't know if there is a limit on the age at which young children can express such experiences. For younger students, you'll have to translate the directions above into their language. Here's one way:

> "I want you to remember times when you were very happy—the happiest times of your life." (Pause)
> "Remember as many happy times as you can." (Pause)
> "Some might be special days like birthdays, Christmas, or going someplace special with your family or friends." (Pause)
> "For some of you it might be a time you did something you're proud of." (Pause)
> "Do you remember when you learned to ride a bicycle and really knew you could ride it? Maybe it was catching a fish, or learning how to swim." (Pause)
> "Maybe it was when your cat had kittens or your dog had puppies." (Pause)

"It could be an ordinary day when you woke up and went outside and everything felt just right." (Pause)

"Maybe it was when you saw someone you missed. Maybe a member of your family or a friend. Maybe after your mother or father was away and came back." (Pause)

"It could be something beautiful, like a rainbow, a sunset, mountains, or anything else that made you feel very, very happy." (Pause)

"Make a list of these very best times in your life." (Pause, repeat the possible triggers above if some students are having a hard time listing these)

"Now how did you feel at these times? Did you feel different?" (Pause)

An alternate here is to have the students draw one of these experiences, or draw a picture of themselves feeling their peak experiences. During the writing or drawing time, you can use the following questions to suggest things. Usually it is best to let the students work on their own first, then use these to suggest other things to write or draw.

"Did time seem to go very fast or very slow?" (Pause)

"Did you notice things that you hadn't seen before?" (Pause)

"Sometimes colors seem brighter than usual." (Pause) "Sometimes sounds sound nicer. Can you remember the colors or sounds of your very special day?" (Pause)

"What about taste or feel? Were these special too?" (Pause)

"How did it feel to be you?" (Pause)

"Have you ever dreamed of one of your special, happy times?" (Pause)

"What was the dream like?" (Pause)

When Maslow had collected hundreds of peak experiences, he compiled them into a typical peak experience. Fourteen qualities were mentioned over and over again. These fourteen are the most common, but many additional words and ideas were used too. Each of these, according to Maslow, blends into the rest, so that they aren't separate and distinct feelings. Maslow compared them to a jewel with fourteen facets, each one reflecting the other thirteen. These are the being-values, felt during peak experiences, those that are felt as good in their own right, *not* because they lead to something else!

wholeness	beauty
perfection	goodness
completion	uniqueness
justice	effortlessness
aliveness	playfulness
richness	truth
simplicity	self-sufficiency

In addition to giving students experience in writing and drawing, these peak experience exercises contribute to their awareness of themselves, to their self-concept. During the discussion period you can point out, "Isn't it nice that we can feel so good sometimes? Don't you like yourself better for feeling this way?"

More than this, however, it helps children learn to be aware of these specific feelings as well as of themselves in general. As we become aware of these feelings, we are likely to pay more attention to the situations that bring them about and to our actions that develop them.

The list of transpersonal values in this chapter can also be used for a smaller-scale class exercise. You can substitute the name of one of the values for the peak experience, compassion or generosity, for example. Your students can remember times when someone helped them and how they felt, or a time when they helped someone else and how they felt then. This adaptation helps put them in touch with transpersonal feelings and values. A person who feels good about his or her past actions is more likely to repeat them in the future.

Shields and Coats of Arms

Many self-concept and human potential exercises can be given a transpersonal flair by simple adaptations. The transpersonal shield is an adaptation of the positive self-image shield described in Canfield and Wells' *100 Ways to Enhance Self-Concept in the Classroom*. Each person draws the outline of a shield or coat of arms. Since there are many different types of shields, your class can choose any shape they want. Or you can hand out a ditto such as the one below.

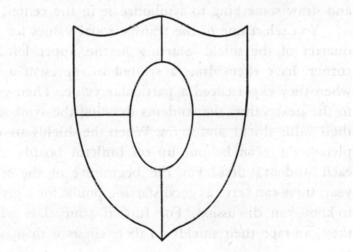

When the shields are drawn, have your class mark off one area in the middle for a drawing, and divide the rest into quarters (see figure). You can use this shield several ways.

Peak Experience and Values Shield

If your class has done the peak experience exercise, you can simply remind them of it and ask them to remember a peak experience and draw a symbol of it in the center space. If they haven't done that exercise, have them remember one of the happiest times in their lives and draw something to symbolize it in the center.

You select one of the transpersonal values for each quarter of the shield. Starting in the upper left-hand corner, have them draw a symbol to represent a time when they experienced a particular value. Then go on to the next value, the students drawing the symbols on their value shield, and so on. When the shields are completed, they can be put up on bulletin boards or on each student's desk. For the beginning of the school year, these can serve as good starting points for a getting-to-know-you discussion. For fun, if your class wishes, they can tape their shields on their chests with masking tape.

If your students aren't familiar with what a symbol is, this exercise can also teach them this. The picture they draw might not actually be a picture of what happened but of something that reminds them of the event. For example, if they had a flat tire on a bicycle and someone helped repair it, they might symbolize helpfulness by a flat tire. If they had a peak experience during a summer hike, they might use a pair of worn out shoes to symbolize the hike.

Integrated-Self Shield

According to the Swiss psychologist Carl Jung, there are four ways that people function in the world. We all have these four abilities to some extent, but one or another will predominate. The Integrated-Self Shield helps people get in touch with the four different ways as they experience them. Using the same five-part shield as above, you start with the outside quarters. Pause after each sentence to give your students time to answer your questions or directions in their own minds, or to make notes.

INSTRUCTIONS

"Think of something you figured out. It might be how to do something, a plan, how to get somewhere, how to build something, or maybe something you had to do in school. Remember a time when you had to reason and think." (Note: If you have been working on some sort of problem solving that requires reasoning, you might want to suggest this—for example, long division, applying mathematical skills, diagramming sentences.) "In the upper left-hand corner, draw a symbol of your *thinking* activity.

"Now remember a time when you had to judge something according to the way you *felt* about it. You probably had your emotions running strong then. Was it good or bad, something you liked or disliked, something agreeable or disagreeable, the right or wrong thing to do? Do you remember how it was to use your values to judge it? It might be something you did or something someone else did. Symbolize your ability to *feel* with a drawing in the lower right-hand corner.

"Can you remember a time when you had to act fast, maybe during an emergency where every second counted? Maybe you or someone you know was about to be hit by a car or hurt some other way, and you yelled or acted quickly to save him. Or, maybe you remember a different activity, one that takes tools to do well. It might be working on a piece of machinery or building something. Maybe it was a hobby that requires you to use tools skillfully. Can you remember how you had to concentrate so that you did everything exactly right? Can you remember the details? Do you remember how you had to pay strict attention to what you were doing? Remember something you did like this, and symbolize it with a drawing in the upper right-hand corner of your shield. This symbolizes your *sensing* ability."

(You can use one of the exercises in the intuition

chapter for the next quarter of the shield. If you have already done an intuition exercise, remind your class of it before beginning these directions.)

"For the questions that I'm going to ask you now, pay attention to hunches and guesses out-of-the-blue. Think of something you like to do. When you think of it, what ideas pop into your mind? Can you remember doing it in the past? How did you start to do it at first? When you think back on it, what other ideas come into your mind? Does this activity say something about you? What kind of person likes to do it? Where do you suppose the activity will take you in the future? What are all the possibilities? What else? Let your mind imagine whatever it wants. What does the activity mean to you? Draw a symbol suggested by these ideas in the lower left-hand corner of your shield. This represents *intuition*." (Give your class time to draw the symbols in each corner of the shield. Tell them you'll come back to the oval in the center later, so they should leave it blank.)

(Later) "The space in the center is still blank, so we'll work on it now. If you're not through with the corners, you can finish them later. Look at your shield. In the upper left-hand corner is your symbol for thinking. This is the thinking part of you. In the upper right-hand corner is your symbol for sensation. This is what you see, hear, taste, touch, and smell. Below that is your way of showing feeling. It is how you feel about things. Next to that, in the lower left-hand corner, is a way you visualize intuition. Intuition shows you that you can know things that you can't account for by reason or sensation.

"Somehow we all manage to do these different things and to combine them in our lives. Some people are better at one of these four than they are at the others, but we all possess them all to some degree. How do you go about using these four? Who is it that mixes together or coordinates these different functions or activities? Imagine that these four symbols are all combined into one brand-new symbol. As you look at the four symbols on your shield, does another symbol come to mind? In the center of your shield draw this new symbol. It is a symbol for you and your ability to control and use all four different activities. It is you the manager, coordinator, director, or boss of the other four."

The Beauty Meditation

This is one of the most enjoyable things to do that we know of. The example given here is for beauty, but it could just as well be a Harmony Meditation, Wholeness Meditation, or meditation based on any of the other transpersonal values. This type of meditation works any time, but is especially useful at the beginning of a class to bring the minds together, or at the end of a day to give a feeling of closure. It is an especially good way to end meetings and send people out with a good feeling.

Depending on the age and maturity of your class, you will have to judge the length of the pauses. Generally, long pauses are best. Before beginning, the class should be relaxed and calm. One of the centering or relaxation exercises is a good way to begin. Teachers of outdoor education like to use these meditations outside, particularly on a starry night. Adults love this experience, too. Once the class is calm and settled, eyes closed, you begin:

"I would like you to think of several things that have brought out strong feelings of beauty in you, things that you have experienced and which make you feel aware of beauty. They might be man-made, such as music or a work of art. They may be scenes from nature, a relationship with someone else, an idea, anything that makes you respond with a feeling that you are experiencing beauty. For a few minutes now, think of these things and refeel the feelings of aesthetic joy." (Long pause)

"Now select the thing or event that brings out the strongest feeling in you." (Pause)

"Pay attention to that experience and run it through in your mind. When you come to the end, go through it again, only slower. Each time you go through it, try to be aware of more details so that you can reexperience it as fully as possible." (Long pause)

"Keep that experience running through your mind, and this time pay attention to how it is affecting you, to how you respond to it. Be aware of what your body and emotions feel." (Pause)

"Now make those feelings stronger and stronger." (Long pause)

"Let the memory of the beautiful thing fade back into your unconscious, and keep those feelings going." (Pause) "Keep the feelings of beauty going and pay attention to how you feel." (Long pause)" Now watch that feeling and keep it going. At the same time, pay attention to what I'm saying. The feeling you are experiencing is something you were able to bring up and recreate through your mind. The actual object of beauty wasn't there, but you could imagine it. Your responses to the beautiful object and your feelings about it are real. They result from the way you used your mind. You created this beautiful feeling in yourself with your mind, and you can carry it with you out of this room and reexperience it whenever you want.

"Get in touch with that feeling again now." (Short pause) "As you leave the room, carry the feeling with you (to your next class, on your way home, etc.) and remember that you can recreate it whenever and wherever you want, just by thinking about it."

Authors' Postscript

By now you've probably tried some of these exercises with your children, classes, or clients. How did they go? We'd like to know. Have you invented some transpersonal techniques of your own, maybe a fantasy journey or an intuition exercise that you thought up? How about sharing it with others? We'd like to pass the word along to other teachers and counselors.

If enough good ideas can be put together, soon there will be another book of transpersonal ways to teach and counsel written by teachers and counselors for other teachers and counselors. If you are willing to share your ideas, please write them up and send them to us. Include the age and level of the students, a description with enough detail so that others can easily follow what you did and said, an evaluation and description of what the students are to do, and your evaluation of the activity and how the class liked it. We will collect these, and with your permission, perhaps pass them along in another centering book. Be sure to include your name and address, and keep a copy for yourself since we will not be able to send them back.

Gay Hendricks   *or*

School of Education

University of Colorado

Colorado Springs,

    Col. 80907

Thomas B. Roberts

Department of Human

    Learning and

    Development

162 Gabel Hall

Northern Illinois

    University

DeKalb, Ill. 60115

Even if you don't have an activity to pass along, let us hear from you. One of the joys of transpersonal education is making connections with others who are expanding their sense of centeredness and exploring the heights of the human potential. Since we are all expressions of the universe, every step we take toward personal harmony facilitates the larger harmony of the universe. We dedicate this book to all those who are harmonizing themselves and the world. Thank you for reading it.

Bibliography

A Transpersonal Education
Treasure Map

A word about these items: In selecting the items
to include in this bibliography and resource guide, our
main criterion was usefulness to the reader. Thus, some
entries only tangentially related to transpersonal education are included, because they lead to associated fields
or they provide a foundation for understanding transpersonal approaches to teaching, counseling, and working
with children. Not everything on this list can be considered transpersonal.

We are skeptical about some of these items, too, and
urge you to keep your critical abilities sharp when reading them. To be quite honest, a few of them look outright

nutty to us, but we remember that some of the ideas we now take seriously once looked strange to us too. Some of these items would be considered anti-transpersonal; they should remind us that a full understanding of any field requires critical examination and that areas of study advance by constantly questioning and reexamining themselves.

The scope and depth of transpersonal techniques and research are much greater than we had expected when we started to compile this list. The field is growing at an accelerating rate, as can be seen by the large number of recent entries. A few years ago biofeedback, meditation, yoga, relaxation, guided imagery, and brain hemisphere specialization were on the fringes of education. They were unheard of by most professionals. Now, thanks to the people whose writings (and other media) appear here, a new door has opened to help us reach traditional goals and even go beyond them to new kinds of learning, to new ways of teaching, and to higher objectives. To those of you whose work appears on this list, thank you for your contribution to the improvement of education. Your efforts are helping a new generation develop their full capacities. We can well imagine you didn't have an easy time pioneering a new field.

One area missing from here is a bibliography of children's literature which develops transpersonal values. If you are looking for a long, difficult, and valuable activity, such a list would be a great help to others. Finally, our thanks to those many people who suggested items to us so that we could pass along these suggestions. Your gracious help has made this bibliography and resource guide possible. If anyone has items to suggest for a future expanded edition, we'd like to hear from you.

Good luck as you explore these sources. We hope you will feel as we do: this bibliography is a treaure map to better teaching, counseling, parenting, and being.

ART, MUSIC, AND LITERATURE

ANGELOTTI, MICHAEL, *et al.* "Heart Rates: A Measure of Reading Involvement," *Research in the Teaching of English*, 9, no. 2 (February 1975), 192–99.

ASSAGIOLI, ROBERTO. "A Psychological Method for Learning Languages." Issue no. 3, Psychosynthesis Research Foundation, New York.

BECKER, JOHN E. "The Law, the Prophets, and Wisdom: On the Functions of Literature," *College English*, 37, no. 3 (November 1975), 254–64.

BONNY, HELEN. *Creative Listening, Vol. 1: Music and Imagination Experiences For Children.* Stereo record. Institute for Consciousness and Music, Baltimore, Md., 1973.

———. *Creative Listening, Vol. 2: Dancing Around the World and Surprise Journey.* Institute for Consciousness and Music, Baltimore, Md., 1975.

———, and LOUIS SAVARY. *Music and Your Mind: Listening With a New Consciousness.* New York: Harper & Row, 1973.

CLARK, WILMA. "Literature, Language, and Human Consciousness," *College English*, 37, no. 6 (February 1976), 605–12.

Excellent. English teachers and foreign language teachers should read this.

DE LUBICZ, ISHA SCHWALLER. *HER-BAK, Vol. 1, The Living Face of Ancient Egypt.* Baltimore: Penguin Metaphysical Library, 1972. A speculative account of the early life and training of an Egyptian boy during ancient times.

DURR, R. A. *Poetic Vision and Psychedelic Experience.* New York: Dell Publishing Co., 1976.

EATON, MANFORD L. "Induce and Control: Bio-Music Is Here Today," *Music Educators' Journal,* 59 (January 1973), 54–57.

EDMONDSON, NELSON. "Logical Empiricism and Religious Myth: Considerations Relevant to the Teaching of General Humanities," *Journal of General Education,* 27, no. 3 (February 1975), 205–18.

English in Australia, "Resources: The Supernatural," 25 (November 1973), 32–33.

FLETCHER, DAVID. "Birth Trauma Writing," *Teachers and Writers Collaborative Newsletter,* 6, no. 1 (February 1974), 46–48.

———. "Trusting the Imagination," *Teachers and Writers Collaborative Newsletter,* 7, no. 1 (February 1975), 19–20.

GARDNER, HOWARD, *et al.* "Artistic Symbols in Early Childhood," *New York University Education Quarterly,* 6, no. 4 (Summer 1975), 13–21.

GOUFFE, MARIE. *Treasures Beyond the Snows.* Wheaton, Ill.: Children's Quest Book, Theosophical Publishing House. For children 8 to 12.

GRAHL, URSULA. *The Wisdom in Fairytales.* Spring Valley, N.Y.: Anthroposophic Press (Rudolf Steiner—Waldorf Education).

HEAD, J. G. "From Spring to Winter: The How, When and Why of Mythology." Paper presented at the Annual Meeting of the Secondary School English Conference, Boston, April 1976, ERIC, ED-123-651, 1976.

HIGGINS, JAMES E. *Mystical Fancy in Children's Literature.* New York: Teacher's College Press, Columbia University, 1970.

IZARD, JANET WRIGHT. *Mandala Coloring Pad.* Garden City, N.Y.: Doubleday, 1973.

KEYES, MARGARET FRINGS. *The Inward Journal (Arts as Psychotherapy for You).* Milbrae, Calif.: Celestial Arts, 1974.

KOCH, KENNETH. *Rose, Where Did You Get That Red?* New York: Random House, 1973.

―――. *Wishes, Lies, and Dreams: Teaching Children to Write Poetry.* New York: Chelsea House, 1970.

LABIANCA, D. A., and W. J. REEVES. "Interdisciplinary Approach to Science and Literature," *Journal of Chemical Education,* 52 (January 1975), 66–67.

MASLOW, ABRAHAM H. "Peak Experiences in Education and Art," *The Humanist,* September/October 1970, pp. 29–31.

McKIM, ROBERT H. *Experiences in Visual Thinking,* ERIC, ED-073-690, 1972. Monterey, Calif.: Brooks/Cole, 1972.

―――. "Relaxed Attention," *Journal of Creative Behavior,* 8, no. 4 (Fourth Quarter, 1974), 265–76. (Excerpt from *Visual Thinking.*)

MILES, H. C. "Art and the Superconscious." Psychosynthesis Research Foundation, Report No. 5, New York.

PESKANZER, S. C. "Thoughts on C. S. Lewis and the Chronicles of Narnia," *Language Arts,* 53 (May 1976), 523–26.

ROSENBAUER, W. "Art Education and the Development of the Whole Man." Psychosynthesis Research Foundation, Report No. 3, New York.

SASOWSKY, NORMAN. "Awakening Higher Consciousness Through Art." Paper presented at National Association for Art Education, Saint Louis, 1976. Department of Art, University of Delaware, Newark, 1971.

SCHÄFER, GEORG, and NAN CUZ. *In the Kingdom of Mescal: A Fairy Tale for Adults.* Berkeley, Calif.: Shambala Publications, 1970.

SHAH, IDRIES. "The Teaching Story: Observations on the Folklore of our 'Modern' Thought." In Robert E. Ornstein, ed., *The Nature of Human Consciousness.* New York: Viking, 1974.

―――. *Caravan of Dreams.* Baltimore, Md.: Penguin, 1972.

―――. *The Exploits of the Incomparable Mulla Nastrudin.* New York: E. P. Dutton, 1972.

―――. *Pleasantries of Mulla Nastrudin.* New York: E. P. Dutton.

―――. *Tales of the Dervishes.* New York: E. P. Dutton, 1970.

SHEDLOCK, MARIE. *The Art of the Story-Teller.* New York: Dover, 1952.

SIFF, D. "Working with Unconscious Thinking in Freshman Composition: Dream Papers," *English Journal,* 64 (December 1975), 31–36.

SONG, SUNMIN. "Anthropology and Myth," *Indiana Social Studies Quarterly,* 28, no. 3 (Winter 1975-76), 8–23.

STOTT, J. C. "Anatomy of a Masterpiece: The Borrowers," *Language Arts,* 53 (May 1976), 538–44.

STRZEPEK, JOSEPH. "Fiction and the Human Potential," in *Four Psychologies Applied to Education: Freudian, Behavioral, Humanistic, Transpersonal,* ed. T. Roberts, pp. 366–72. New York: John Wiley & Sons, 1975.

WAGNER, M. J. "Effect of Music and Biofeedback on Alpha Brainwave Rhythms and Attentiveness," *Journal of Research in Music Education,* 23 (Spring 1975), 3–13.

WEBB, DONALD A. "Archetypes to Ashes: From Superstar to Superfly—And Back Again? *Indiana Social Studies Quarterly,* 28, no. 3 (Winter 1975-76), 50–56.

Weewish Tree. Kachina Dolls, 3, no. 5 (February 1975), 8–9.

WILSON, BARBARA KER. "A Visit to Dreamtime," *Wilson Library Bulletin*, 49, no. 10 (June 1975), 720–27. Aboriginal Folklore of Australia and New Zealand.

Yoga Coloring Book. Homestead, Fla.: Svarga Ashrama Press (P.O. Box 309).

BIOFEEDBACK

ASTOR, MARTIN. "Biofeedback: The Westernization of Eastern Wisdom." Mimeo. Queens College, CUNY, Flushing, N.Y., forthcoming.

————. "Biofeedback in Counseling and Education: A Critical Evaluation." Mimeo. Queens College, CUNY, Flushing, N.Y., forthcoming.

Biofeedback Research Society. *Biofeedback and Self-Regulation*. University of Colorado Medical College, Denver, 1973. A bibliography of 800 references representing 850 authors.

BITTING, ANDY. *Biofeedback and Meditation in High School*, Ph.D. dissertation, California School of Professional Psychology, San Francisco, 1976.

BRAUD, L. W., M. N. LUPIN, and W. G. BRAUD. "The Use of EMG (electromyographic) Biofeedback in the Control of Hyperactivity," *Journal of Learning Disabilities*, 8, no. 7 (August-September 1975), 420–25.

BROWN, BARBARA B. *The Biofeedback Syllabus*. Springfield, Ill.: Charles C Thomas, 1975. Useful descriptors are: applications, children, child development, cognitive, cognition, ESP, hyperkinesis, operant conditioning.

BUDZYNSKI, THOMAS H., and JOHANN STOYVA. "Biofeedback Techniques in Behavior Therapy," in *Biofeedback and Self-Control, 1972.* Chicago: Aldine Publishing Co., 1973.

DANSKIN, D. G., and E. D. WALTERS. "Biofeedback and Voluntary Self-Regulation: Counseling and Education," *Personnel and Guidance Journal,* 51, no. 9 (1973), 633–38.

ENGELHARDT, LORETTA. "Application of Biofeedback Techniques Within a Public School Setting." Paper presented at the Seventh Annual Meeting of the Biofeedback Research Society, Colorado Springs, February 27-March 2, 1976. Reprint available from Biofeedback Research Society.

GREEN, ELMER E., ALYCE M. GREEN, and E. DALE WALTERS. "Voluntary Control of Internal States: Psychological and Physiological," *Journal of Transpersonal Psychology,* 2, no. 1 (1970), 1–26.

HAIGHT, MARYELLEN J., and G. JAMPOLSKI. "An Experience with Biofeedback in a Public High School," *Journal of Bio-feedback,* Winter 1974.

HARDYCK, CURTIS D., DELBERT W. ELLSWORTH, and LEWIS F. PETRINOVICH. "Feedback of Speech Muscle Activity during Silent Reading: Rapid Extinction." In *Biofeedback and Self-Control.* Chicago: Aldine Publishing Co., 1971.

———. L. PETRINOVICH, and D. W. ELLSWORTH. "Feedback of Speech Muscle Activity During Silent Reading: Rapid Extinction," *Science,* 154 (1966), 1467–68.

Involuntary Control (movie), 21 minutes, color. New York: John Wiley & Sons, 1972. Biofeedback.

JACOBSON, LAURIE. "Feedback on Biofeedback," *Human Behavior,* July 1974, pp. 47–51.

JAMPOLSKY, GERALD G., and MARYELLEN J. HAIGHT. "A Special Technique for Children with Reading Problems," *Academic Therapy,* 10, no. 3 (Spring 1975), 333–38.

KAMIYA, JOANNE GARDNER, MARYELLEN J. HAIGHT, and GERALD G. JAMPOLSKY. "A Biofeedback Study in a High School."

Paper presented at the Sixth Annual Meeting, Biofeedback Research Society, February 1, 1975, Monterey, Calif.

KETTELKAMP, LARRY. *A Partnership of Mind & Body: Biofeedback.* New York: William C. Morrow & Co., 1976. Juvenile.

KING, MARJORIE. "Biofeedback in the High School Curriculum," *Journal of Humanistic and Transpersonal Education,* 1, no. 1, forthcoming 1977.

KNIRK, F. G., and W. A. SPINDELL. "Indirect (Biofeedback) Measurement in Instructional Technology," *Education Technology,* 15 (June 1975), 33–35.

LAZARUS, RICHARD S. "A Cognitively Oriented Psychologist Looks at Bio-Feedback," *American Psychologist,* 30, no. 5 (May 1975), 553–61.

Learning Magazine. Biofeedback. Poster 13. May 1973.

McDONALD, S. L. "Feedback-Based EEG Alpha Training in Pre-Adolescent Children," Special Education Cooperative of South Cook County, 1125 Division St., Chicago Heights, Ill.

MONTER, KAREL. "The Attention Level Analyzer," *The Journal of Bio-Feedback,* 2, no. 1 (Spring-Summer 1974), 22–23.

MOORE, W. H., JAMES R. DUNSTER, and MARY K. LANG. "The Effects of Alpha Bio-Feedback Conditioning On Stuttered Verbal Behavior: Case Report and Some Clinical Applications," *The Journal of Bio-Feedback,* 2, no. 2, Winter-Spring 1974.

MULHOLLAND, THOMAS B. "It's Time to Try Hardware in the Classroom," *Psychology Today,* 7, no. 7 (December 1973), 103–4.

―――. "Training Visual Attention," *Academic Therapy,* 10, no. 1 (Fall 1974), 5–17.

MULHOLLAND, T. B., and G. GASCON. "A Quantitative EEG Index of the Orienting Response in Children," *Electroencephalography and Clinical Neurophysiology,* 33, no. 3 (September 1972), 295–301.

NEWTON, FREDERICK A., et al. "Biofeedback Training of 40-Hz EEG Activity in Humans: Hardware, Procedures, and Data." Paper presented at the Seventh Annual Meeting of the Biofeedback Research Society, Colorado Springs, February 27-March 2, 1976. Reprint available from Biofeedback Research Society.

NIDEFFER, ROBERT M. "Alpha and the Development of Human Potential," in Biofeedback and Self-Control 1972. Chicago: Aldine Publishing Co., 1973.

PARSKY, LARRY M. Biofeedback-Induced Suppression of Subvocalization in Sixth Grade Reading Disabled Children: Effects on Reading Comprehension and Vocabulary. Ph.D. dissertation, University of Michigan, 1975. University Microfilm 76-9484.

RØRVIK, D. M. "The Theta Experience," Saturday Review, May 1973, pp. 46–51.

RUGH, JOHN D., and ROBERT L. SCHWITZGEBEL. "Biofeedback Apparatus: List of Suppliers," Behavior Therapy, 6, no. 2 (March 1975), 238–40.

SCHAEFER, SIGRID, and ROLF R. ENGEL. "Operant Control of Autonomic Functions: Biofeedback Bibliography," Perceptual and Motor Skills, 36 (1973), 863–75.

SCHMEIDLER, G., and L. LEWIS. "Mood Changes After Alpha Feedback Training." Perceptual and Motor Skills, 32 (1971), 709.

SCHWITZGEBEL, RALPH K. "Development and Legal Regulation of Coercive Behavior Modification Techniques with Offenders." Washington, D.C.: U.S. Government Printing Office, February 1971.

SCHWITZGEBEL, R. L., and J. D. RUGH. "Of Bread, Circuses, and Alpha Machines" (Special issue: Instrumentation in Psychology), American Psychologist, 30, no. 3 (1975), 371–78.

WAITE, MITCHELL. "Alpha Brain Waves and Biofeedback Training," Popular Electronics, December 1972, pp. 33–38.

————. "Build an Alpha Brain Wave Feedback Monitor," *Popular Electronics,* January 1973, pp. 40–45.

BRAIN HEMISPHERES AND PHYSIOLOGY

BOGEN, JOSEPH E. Educational Aspects of Hemispheric Specialization, *U.C.L.A. Educator,* 17, no. 2 (Spring 1975), 24–32.

Brain Information Service. *Cerebral Dominance, Laterality and Handedness.* Bibliography #79A, UCLA, Los Angeles.

Brain/Mind Bulletin, "Brain Research Gives Impetus to Education Reform," 1, no. 9 (March 15, 1976), 1–2.

Brain/Mind Bulletin, "Integrated Frameworks for Learning Explored at Twin California Symposia," 1, no. 16 (July 5, 1976), 3.

Brain/Mind Bulletin, "Massachusetts Conferees Consider Genetic Basis for Human Potential," 1, no. 24 (November 1976), 2.

Brain/Mind Bulletin, " 'Vitamins Can Change Brain Function': Pauling," 1, no. 24 (November 1, 1976), 3.

Brain/Mind Bulletin, "University Conference: Split-brain Research and Education," 1, no. 2 (December 15, 1975), 1–2.

BUZAN, TONY. *Use Both Sides of Your Brain.* New York: E. P. Dutton, 1976.

"Chemical Theory of Memory Gains Support," *Chemical and Engineering News,* 51, no. 48 (November 1973), 20.

COHEN, GILLIAN. "Hemispheric Differences in the Effects of Cuing in Visual Recognition Tasks," *Journal of Experimental Psychology: Human Perception and Performance,* 1, no. 4 (November 1975), 366–73.

CRINELLA, FRANCIS M., et al. "Unilateral Dominance Is Not Related to Neuropsychological Integrity," *Child Development*, 42, no. 6 (December 1971), 2033–54.

DON, NORMAN. "Electroencephalographic Correlates of Focusing and the Alterations of Conscious Experience," in *Research in Experimental Focusing*, ed. L. Olsen, forthcoming 1977.

ECCLES, JOHN C. "Brain and Consciousness," *Naturwissenschaften*, 60, no. 4 (April 1973), 167–76.

GALIN, DAVID. "Implications for Psychiatry of Hemispheric Specialization," *Archives of General Psychiatry*, 71 (1974), 572–83.

GAZZANIGA, MICHAEL S. "Review of the Split Brain," *U.C.L.A. Educator*, 17, no. 2 (Spring 1975), 9–12.

GRADY, MICHAEL P. "Students Need Media for a Balanced Brain," *Audiovisual Instructor*, 21, no. 9 (November 1976), 46–48.

HARRIS, LAUREN JAY. "Interaction of Experiential and Neurological Factors in the Patterning of Human Abilities: The Question of Sex Differences in 'Right Hemisphere' Skills." ERIC, ED-119-854, 1975.

HELLIGE, JOSEPH. "Hemispheric Processing Differences Revealed by Differential Conditioning and Reaction Time Performance," *Journal of Experimental Psychology: General*, 104, no. 4 (December 1975), 309–26.

HUNTER, MADELINE. "Right-Brained Kids in Left-Brained Schools," *Today's Education*, 65, no. 4 (November-December 1976), 45–48.

IANNAZZI, MARIE. "Brain Asymmetry," *Science Teacher*, 42, no. 1 (January 1975), 47–48.

JERISON, HARRY J. "Evolution of the Brain," *U.C.L.A. Educator*, 17, no. 2 (Spring 1975), 1–8.

KONICEK, RICHARD D. "Seeking Synergism for Man's Two-Hemisphere Brain: The UMass Mess continued," *Phi Delta Kappan*, 57, no. 1 (September 1975), 37–39.

KRASHEN, STEPHEN D. "The Major Hemisphere," *U.C.L.A. Educator*, 17, no. 2 (Spring 1975), 17–23.

LILLY, JOHN C. "Learning Motivated by Subcortical Stimulation: The 'Start' and 'Stop' Patterns of Behavior." In H. H. Jasper, *et al.*, eds., *Reticular Formation of the Brain*. Boston: Little Brown Publishing Co., 1958.

McGLANNAN, FRANCES, ed. "Research of Interest," *Journal of Learning Disabilities*, 9, no. 2 (February 1976), 81–84. Roles of pupil size, hemisphere specialization, and maternal stress.

MACKWORTH, JANE F. "Information Processing Models of Reading: A Developmental Approach." Paper presented at the Annual Meeting of the International Reading Association, Anaheim, Calif., May 1976. ERIC, ED-123-580.

MINTZBERG, HENRY. "Planning on the Left Side and Managing on the Right," *Harvard Business Review*, July/August 1967, pp. 49–58.

MOLFESE, DENNIS L., *et al.* "Cerebral Assymetry: Changes in Factors Affecting Its Development." Paper presented at the New York Academy of Sciences Conference on Origins and Evolution of Language and Speech, September 1975. ERIC, ED-121-420.

MURPHY, PHILIP, *et al.* "Effects of Simultaneous Divergent EEG Feedback from Both Cerebral Hemispheres on Changes in Verbal and Spatial Tasks." Paper presented at the Seventh Annual Meeting of the Biofeedback Research Society, Colorado Springs, February 27-March 2, 1976. Reprint available from Biofeedback Research Society.

NEBES, ROBERT D. "Man's So-Called 'Minor' Hemisphere," *U.C.L.A. Educator*, 17, no. 2 (Spring 1975), 13–16.

PAPCUN, GEORGE, *et al.* "Is the Left Hemisphere Specialized for Speech, Language and/or Something Else?" ERIC, ED-113-971. American Institute of Physics, New York, February 1974.

PELLETIER, KENNETH, and ERIK PEPER. "The Chutzpah Factor in

the Psychophysiology of Altered States of Consciousness," in *Transpersonal Education: A Curriculum for Feeling and Being*, eds. Gay Hendricks and James Fadiman. Englewood Cliffs, N.J.: Prentice-Hall, Inc., 1976.

POLIDORA, JAMES. *Biology of the Mind/Body: A Course of Study*. P.O. Box 709, Davis, Calif. $2.00, 1975.

RENNELS, MAX R. "Cerebral Symmetry: An Urgent Concern for Education," *Phi Delta Kappan*, March 1976, 471–72.

SAMPLES, ROBERT E. "Educating for Both Sides of the Human Mind," *Science Teacher*, 42, no. 1 (January 1975), 21–23.

———. "Learning with the Whole Brain," *Human Behavior*, 4 (February 1975), 16–23, 79.

———. "Are You Teaching Only One Side of the Brain?" *Learning*, February 1975, 25–28.

SELTZ, JUDITH. "The Brain: Magic Window on Behavior," *Grade Teacher*, 88, no. 9 (May-June 1971), 26–30.

SPERRY, ROGER W. "Left-Brain, Right-Brain," *Saturday Review*, 2, no. 23 (August 9, 1975), 30–33.

SULLIVAN, E. A. "Medical, Biological, and Chemical Methods of Shaping the Mind," *Phi Delta Kappan*, April 1972.

SURWILLO, WALTER W. "Word-Association Latency in Normal Children During Development and the Relation of Brain Electrical Activity," *Psychophysiology*, 10 (1973), 254.

———. "Human Reaction Time and Period of the EEG in Relation to Development," *Psychophysiology*, 8 (1971), 468.

UCLA Educator, 17, no. 2 (Spring 1975). Entire issue is on brain-learning research.

CHILD DEVELOPMENT

ALEXANDER, F. MATTHIAS. *The Alexander Technique: Writing of F. Matthias Alexander*, "Child Training and Education." New York: University Books, 1970.

ANASTASIOW, NICHOLAS. "Updating Intellectual Growth in Children and Bioplasmic Forces," *Phi Delta Kappan*, LV, no. 8 (April 1974), 561–62.

ARASTEH, A. REZA. "A Critique of the Literature on Developmental Psychology," Section I of *Toward Final Personality Integration*, pp. 3–49. New York: John Wiley and Sons, 1975.

BOULDING, ELSIE. *Children and Solitude*. Pendle Hill Pamphlet No. 125. Wallingford, Penn.: Pendle Hill, 1962.

————. *Born Remembering*. Wallingford, Penn.: Pendle Hill, 1975.

Brain/Mind Bulletin, "Infant's Relationship With Mother Can Establish Lifelong Patterns of Stress," 1, no. 24 (November 1, 1976), 1–2.

CONKLIN, JOHN. *Rejoice, Rejoice, the Child is Born!* (working title). Manuscript in preparation. Board of Health, Edmonton, Canada.

DANCING, DICK. *My Mind Is an Ocean*. Spiritual Community Publications, Box 1080, San Rafael, Calif. 94902. Poems, koans, and prophecies, written by children.

EHRENWALD, JAN. "Mother-Child Symbiosis: Cradle of ESP," *Psychoanalytic Review*, 58, no. 3 (Fall 1971), 455–66.

FROMMER, EVA A. *Voyage Through Childhood into the Adult World*. Elmsford, N.Y.: Pergamon. (Rudolf Steiner—Waldorf Education), 1969.

GLAS, NORBERT. *Early Childhood*. Spring Valley, N.Y.: Anthroposophic Press (Rudolf Steiner—Waldorf Education).

————. *Conception, Birth and Early Childhood*. Spring Valley, N.Y.: Anthroposophic Press.

GOUFFE, MARIE. *The Way of a Child*. London: Rudolf Steiner Press, 1940.

GRAHL, URSULA. *The Exceptional Child*. Spring Valley, N.Y.: Anthroposophic Press (Rudolf Steiner—Waldorf Education).

GRUNELIUS, ELIZABETH. *Early Childhood Education and the Wal-*

dorf Plan. Spring Valley, N.Y.: Anthroposophic Press (Rudolf Steiner—Waldorf Education).

HARWOOD, A. C. *The Way of a Child.* Spring Valley, N. Y.: Anthroposophic Press (Rudolf Steiner—Waldorf Education).

HODGSON, A. M. "Birth to Adulthood—A Systematic Study," *Systematics, Journal of the Institute for Comparative Study of History, Philosophy and the Sciences* (5-7 Kingston Hall, Kingston Upon Thames, Surrey). Gurjieff influence.

KOENIG, KARL. *Brothers and Sisters.* Spring Valley, N.Y.: Anthroposophic Press (Rudolf Steiner—Waldorf Education).

———. *The First Three Years of Childhood.* Spring Valley, N.Y.: Anthroposophic Press (Rudolf Steiner—Waldorf Education).

NEUMANN, ERICH. *The Child.* New York: G. P. Putnam's Sons, 1974.

OGLETREE, EARL J. "Intellectual Growth in Children and the Theory of 'Bioplasmic Forces,'" *Phi Delta Kappan,* 1974, 407–12. Also in T. Roberts, ed., *Four Psychologies Applied to Education: Freudian, Behavioral, Humanistic, Transpersonal,* pp. 426–37. New York: John Wiley & Sons, 1975.

PEARCE, JOSEPH CHILTON. *The Magical Child,* forthcoming.

VON HEYDEBRAND, CAROLINE. *Childhood: A Study of the Growing Soul.* Spring Valley, N.Y.: Anthroposophic Press (Rudolf Steiner—Waldorf Education).

WICKS, FRANCES G. *The Inner World of Childhood.* New York: Appleton-Century, 1966. The effects of adults' unconscious on children's dreams and fantasies. Jungian.

COUNSELING, GUIDANCE, THERAPY

ASTOR, MARTIN. "Transpersonal Approaches to Counseling," *Personnel and Guidance Journal,* 50, no. 2 (1972), 801–8.

————. "Transpersonal Counseling as a Form of Transcendental Education," *Counseling and Values,* 19, no. 2 (February 1975), 75–82.

BECK, CARLTON E. "Synergy and Counseling," *Counseling and Values,* 18, no. 1 (February 1973), 7–13.

BECK, MICHAEL. "Externalization of the Toxic Introject," *Journal of Family Counseling,* 3, no. 2 (February 1975), 12–15.

BERGER, E. "Zen Buddhism, General Psychology, and Counseling Psychology," *Journal of Counseling Psychology,* 9, no. 2 (1962), 122–27.

BINDRIM, PAUL. "Facilitating Peak Experiences," in *Ways of Growth: Approaches to Expanding Awareness,* chapter 11, ed. Herbert A. Otto and John Mann. New York: Pocket Books, 1971.

BRADLEY, JANE. *Self-Direction: Finding One's Own Path.* Montreal: Canadian Institute of Psychosynthesis, 1975.

Brain/Mind Bulletin, " 'Altered States' Effective in Variety of Therapies and Growth Techniques," 1, no. 22 (October 4, 1976), 2.

BROWN, H. ALAN. "Role of Expectancy Manipulation in Systematic Desensitization," *Journal of Consulting and Clinical Psychology,* 41, no. 3 (December 1973), 404–11.

CLARK, WALTER HOUSTON. "The Place of Drugs in the Religion of the Counter Culture," *Research in Education.* ERIC, ED-065-429, 1972.

Counseling and Values. February 1975 issue is on transpersonal counseling.

COX, DANIEL J. "Differential Effectiveness of Electromyograph Feedback, Verbal Relaxation Instructions, and Medication Placebo with Tension Headaches," *Journal of Consulting and Clinical Psychology,* 43, no. 6 (December 1975), 892–97.

CRAMPTON, MARTHA. "Answers from the Unconscious," *Synthesis,* 1, no. 2 (1975), 140–51.

DANSKIN, D. G. "Biofeedback in Counseling and Education." Paper presented at the First Annual Symposium on Biofeedback for Counseling, Education, and Psychotherapy, Veterans Administration Hospital, Topeka, Kansas, October 1973.

DANSKIN, D. G., and E. D. WALTERS. "Biofeedback Training as Counseling," *Counseling and Values*, 19, no. 2 (February 1975), 116–22.

DAVISON, GERALD C. "A Procedural Critique of 'Desensitization' and the Experimental Reduction of Threat," *Journal of Abnormal Psychology*, 74, no. 1 (February 1969), 88–89.

DEAN, STANLEY, ed., *Psychiatry and Mysticism*. Chicago: Nelson-Hall, 1975.

DEIKMAN, ARTHUR. *Personal Freedom*. New York: Grossman Publishers, The Viking Press, 1976.

DETTERMAN, DOUGLAS K. "The Von Restorff Effect and Induced Amnesia: Production by Manipulation of Sound Intensity," *Journal of Experimental Psychology (Human Learning and Memory)*, 1, no. 5 (September 1975), 614–28.

FRY, P. S. "Effects of Desensitization Treatment on Core-Condition Training," *Journal of Counseling Psychology*, 20, no. 3 (May 1974), 214–19.

FUJITA, K., and S. TAKIDO. "Sermon and Counseling from the Buddhist Point of View," *Psychologia*, 5, no. 4 (December 1962), 181–84.

GENDLIN, EUGENE T. "Focusing," *Psychotherapy: Theory, Research and Practice*, 6, no. 1 (Winter 1969), 4–15.

GLASSER, W. "Positive Addiction Theory," *Journal of School Health*, 45 (December 1975), 564.

GRIM, PAUL F. "Psychotherapy by Somatic Alteration," *Mental Hygiene*, 53, no. 3 (July 1969), 451–58.

GUMAER, JIM, and RICHARD VOORNEVELD. "Affective Education with Gifted Children," *Elementary School Guidance and Counseling*, 10, no. 2 (December 1975), 86–94.

HANKOFF, L. D. "Adolescence and the Crisis of Dying," *Adolescence*, 10, no. 39 (February 1975), 373–89.

HAWKINSON, JUDITH R. "Teaching About Death," *Today's Education*, 65, no. 3 (1976), 41–42.

HEAPS, RICHARD A., and TERRY R. SEAMONS. "Group Desensitization: Techniques and Problems of Application." Paper presented at the American Personnel and Guidance Association Convention, Chicago, March 25-30, 1972. ERIC, ED-065-815, March 1972.

HENDRICKS, GAY. *Transpersonal Therapy: Principles and Techniques*, manuscript in preparation.

HENSCHEN, THOMAS. "Biofeedback–Induced Reverie: A Counseling Tool," *Personnel and Guidance Journal*, 54, no. 6 (1976), 327–28.

HENSLER, DONNA L. "Awareness Techniques: A Model for Personal Growth," *Counseling and Values*, 19, no. 3 (April 1975), 197–204.

JOHN, JOSEPH. "J. Krishnamurti: A Noneudaemonistic Approach to Guidance," *Counseling and Values*, 19, no. 4 (July 1975), 254–58.

JOHNSON, A., and S. SZUREK. "The Genesis of Antisocial Acting Out in Children and Adults," *Psychoanalytic Quarterly*, Vol. 21, 1952.

JONES, FRANCES W., and DAVID S. HOLMES. "Alcoholism, Alpha Production, and Biofeedback," *Journal of Consulting and Clinical Psychology*, 44, no. 2 (April 1976), 224–28.

KATER, DONNA, and JEANETTE SPIRES. "Biofeedback: The Beat Goes On," *The School Counselor*, 23, no. 1 (September 1975), 16–21.

LESH, TERRY V. "Zen Meditation and the Development of Empathy in Counselors," *Journal of Humanistic Psychology*, 10, no. 1 (Spring 1970), 39–74. Abridged in Roberts, T., ed., *Four Psychologies Applied to Education: Freudian, Behav-*

ioral, Humanistic, Transpersonal, pp. 537–50. New York: John Wiley & Sons, 1975.

LEVENTHAL, ALLAN M., and DONALD K. PUMROY. "Training in Behavioral Therapy: A Case Study," *Journal of College Student Personnel,* 10, no. 5 (September 1969), 296–301.

LIVINGSTON, DIANE D. *Transcendental States of Consciousness and the Healthy Personality: A Theoretical Overview,* unpublished doctoral dissertation, Department of Psychology, University of Arizona, Tucson, 1976.

MAUPIN, EDWARD M. "Zen Buddhism: A Psychological Review," *Journal of Consulting Psychology,* 26, no. 4 (1962), 362–78.

McGAREY, ROBERT. *Increases in Self-Actualization Resulting from Peak Experiences.* New College, Sarasota, Fla., May 31, 1974. A.R.E. Clinic, Phoenix, Ariz.

MELONE, ROBERT A. "The Way Is in Your Will With Recovery, Inc.," *Counseling and Values,* 19, no. 2 (February 1975), 131–34.

NISHIJIMA, Y. "On the Problems of Theories of Psychotherapy and Counseling," *Psychologia,* 7 (1964), 55–59.

NORDBERG, R. B. "Mysticism—Its Implications for Helping Relationships," *Counseling and Values,* 19, no. 2 (February 1975), 99–109.

O'CONNELL, VINCENT, and APRIL O'CONNELL. *Choice and Change: An Introduction to the Psychology of Growth.* Englewood Cliffs, N.J.: Prentice-Hall, Inc., 1974. The second half includes dream interpretation, the mythical self, relaxation, and centering.

O'HANLON, WILLIAM, and ROBERT McGAREY. "Transpersonal Counseling,' A.R.E. Clinic, Phoenix, undated, 5 pp. typed.

PARKER, CAROL L. "A Desensitization Group for Adult Community Leaders," *Personnel and Guidance Journal,* 54, no. 1 (September 1975), 48–49.

PAYNE, BURYL. *Getting There Without Drugs.* New York: Viking, 1973.

PULVINO, CHARLES J., and JAMES L. LEE. "Counseling According to Don Juan," *Counseling and Values,* 19, no. 2 (February 1975), 125–30.

PULVINO, CHARLES J. "Psychic Energy: The Counselor's Undervalued Resource," *Personnel and Guidance Journal* (September 1975), 29–32.

RICKLES, WILLIAM H. "Some Theoretical Aspects of the Psychodynamics of Successful Biofeedback Treatment." Paper presented at the Seventh Annual Meeting of the Biofeedback Research Society, Colorado Springs, February 27-March 2, 1976. Reprint available from Biofeedback Research Society.

ROHM, C. E. TAPIE. "Anxiety, Systematic Desensitization, and Pain." Paper presented at the Seventh Annual Meeting of the Biofeedback Research Society, Colorado Springs, February 27-March 2, 1976. Reprint available from Biofeedback Research Society.

ROSENFELD, EDWARD. *The Book of Highs: 250 Ways to Alter Consciousness Without Drugs.* New York: Quadrangle Books, The New York Times Book Company, 1973. A good followup on Andrew Weil's idea that the desire to explore consciousness is a natural human trait.

ROSENZVEIG, FRED. "Psychosynthesis with Adolescents." Paper presented to Workshop on Adolescents, Canadian Institute of Psychosynthesis, Montreal, 1975.

SCHEIDLER, THOMAS. "Application of Psychosynthesis Techniques to Child Psychotherapy." Psychosynthesis Research Foundation, New York.

SCISSONS, EDWARD H., and LLOYD J. WJAA. "Systematic Desensitization of Test Anxiety: A Comparison of Group and Individual Treatment," *Journal of Consulting and Clinical Psychology,* 41, no. 3 (December 1973), 470.

SKOVHOLT, T. M., and R. W. HOENNINGER. "Guided Fantasy in Career Counseling," *Personnel Guidance Journal,* 52, no. 10 (1974), 693–96.

STEWART, ROBERT A. "Self-Actualization as the Basis of Psychotherapy: A Look at Two Eastern-Based Practices, Transcendental Meditation and Alpha Brain Wave Biofeedback," *Social Behavior & Personality*, 2, no. 2 (1974), 191–200.

STONE, WINIFRED O. "Transcendent Counseling for Blacks: A Modular-Conceptual Theory." Paper presented at the 1973 Second Annual Region V, TRIO Conference, Fontana, Wisconsin. Bowling Green State University, Bowling Green, Ohio.

SUTHERLAND, ANN, *et al.* "Comparison of Three Behavioral Techniques in the Modification of Smoking Behavior," *Journal of Consulting and Clinical Psychology*, 43, no. 4 (August 1975), 443–46.

VAHIA, N. S. "Psychophysiologic Therapy Based on the Concepts of Patanjali," *American Journal of Psychotherapy*, 27, no. 4, October 1973.

ZYCHOWICZ, MARLENE JANE. *American Indian Teachings as a Philosophical Base for Counseling and Psychotherapy.* Unpublished Doctoral Dissertation, Northern Illinois University, DeKalb, 1975.

CREATIVITY AND INTUITION

BROWN, GEORGE I. "The Creative Sub-Self," in *Ways of Growth: Approaches to Expanding Awareness,* chapter 13, ed. Herbert A. Otto and John Mann. New York: Pocket Books, 1971.

CLINCHY, BLYTHE. "The Role of Intuition in Learning," *Today's Education*, 64, no. 2 (March/April 1975), 48–51.

COHN, RUTH C. "Training Intuition," in *Ways of Growth: Approaches to Expanding Awareness,* chapter 15, ed. Herbert A. Otto and John Mann. New York: Pocket Books, 1971.

DEBONO, EDWARD. *Lateral Thinking: Creativity Step by Step.* New York: Harper and Row, 1970.

Durio, H. F. "Mental Imagery and Creativity," *Journal of Creative Behavior*, 9, no. 4 (1975), 233–44.

Farrell, M. A. "Intuitive Leap of Unscholarly Lapse?" *Mathematics Teacher*, 68 (February 1975), 149–52.

Gowan, John Curtis. *The Development of the Creative Individual*. San Diego, Calif.: Knapp (Box 7234), 1972.

———. *The Development of the Psychedelic Individual*. Creative Education Foundation, 1300 Elmwood Ave., Buffalo, N.Y. 14222, 1974.

———. "Trance, Art, and Creativity," *Journal of Creative Behavior*, 9, no. 1 (1975), 1–11.

———. *Trance, Art and Creativity*. Buffalo, N.Y.: Creative Education Foundation, State University College, 1975.

Green, Elmer, Alyce Green, and E. Dale Walters. "Psychophysiological Training for Creativity." Paper presented at the 1971 meeting of the American Psychological Association, Washington, D.C., 1971. Research Department, The Menninger Foundation, Topeka.

Joesting, Joan, and Robert Joesting. "Torrance's Creative Motivation Inventory and Its Relationship to Several Personality Variables (including ESP)," *Psychological Reports*, 24, no. 1 (1969), 30.

Khatena, Joe. "Creative Imagination, Imagery, and Analogy," *Gifted Child Quarterly*, 19, no. 2 (Summer 1975), 149–60.

———. "Creative Imagination and What We Can Do to Stimulate It." ERIC, ED-116-430.

Krippner, Stanley. "Creativity and Psychic Phenomena," *Gifted Child Quarterly*, 7, no. 6 (Summer 1963), 51–62.

MacKinnon, Donald M. "Creativity and Transliminal Experience," *Journal of Creative Behavior*, 5, no. 4 (Fourth Quarter 1971), 227–41.

Maslow, Abraham H. "The Creative Attitude." Psychosynthesis Research Foundation, Report No. 10, New York.

SAMPLES, ROBERT E. "Kari's Handicap: The Impediment of Creativity," *Saturday Review*, July 15, 1967, 56–57.

SAVARY, LOUIS. *Creativity in Children*. Institute for Consciousness and Music, Baltimore, Md., 1974.

SCHAEFER, CHARLES E. "The Importance of Measuring Metaphorical Thinking in Children," *Gifted Child Quarterly*, 19, no. 2 (Summer 1975), 140–48.

SCHOEN, STEPHEN M. "LSD and Creative Attention," in *Ways of Growth: Approaches to Expanding Awareness*, chapter 14, ed. Herbert A. Otto and John Mann. New York: Pocket Books, 1971.

SIMONTON, DEAN K. "Creativity, Task Complexity, and Intuitive versus Analytical Problem Solving," *Psychological Reports*, 37 (1975), 351–54.

TORRANCE, E. PAUL, *et al. Needed Research on Creativity*. ERIC, ED-113-640, September 1973.

WECKOWICZ, THADDEUS E., *et al.* "Effect of Marijuana on Divergent and Convergent Production Cognitive Tests," *Journal of Abnormal Psychology*, 84, no. 4 (August 1975), 386–98.

DREAMS AND SLEEP

COHEN, DAVID B. "To Sleep, Perchance to Recall a Dream: Repression Is Not the Demon who Conceals and Hoards Our Forgotten Dreams," *Psychology Today*, May 1974, 50–54.

COHEN, DAVID B., and GARY WOLFE. "Dream Recall and Repression: Evidence for an Alternative Hypothesis," *Journal of Consulting and Clinical Psychology*, 41, no. 3 (December 1973), 349–55.

FOWLER, M. J., *et al.* "Sleep and Memory," *Science*, 179 (January 19, 1973), 302–4.

HART, JOSEPH T. "Dreams in the Classroom," *Experiment and Innovation: New Directions in Education at the University of California,* 4 (1971), 51–66. Also available from Institute for Integrative Psychology, University of California, Irvine, Calif. 92664.

HAYES, ROSEMARY. "Do You Have Your Dream for English?" in *Four Psychologies Applied to Education: Freudian, Behavioral, Humanistic, Transpersonal,* ed. T. Roberts. New York: John Wiley & Sons, 1975.

JONES, RICHARD M. *Dreams and Poetry* (working title). Unpublished manuscript. Olympia. Wash.: The Evergreen State College.

KETTLEKAMP, LARRY. *Dreams.* New York: William Morrow and Co., 1968.

KUPRIANOVICH, L. "The Process of Instruction During Sleep Can Be Regulated," *TechnikaMolodezhi* (Moscow), 11 (1965), 26.

McLEESTER, DICK. *Welcome to the Magic Theatre: A Handbook for Exploring Dreams.* Amherst Mass.: Food for Thought Publications, P.O. Box 331.

NATIONAL INSTITUTE OF MENTAL HEALTH (DHEW), Bethesda, Md. "Current Research on Sleep and Dreams," ERIC, ED-049-506, 1965.

NELL, RENEE, "Guidance Through Dreams," in *Ways of Growth: Approaches to Expanding Awareness,* chapter 16, ed. Herbert A. Otto and John Mann. New York: Pocket Books, 1971.

PIRMANTGEN, PATRICIA. "What Would Happen to the American Psyche If, Along with Homerooms, Flag Saluting, and I.Q. Testing, Schools Had Daily Dream Sharing?" in *Transpersonal Education: A Curriculum for Feeling and Being,* ed. Gay Hendricks and James Fadiman. Englewood Cliffs, N.J.: Prentice-Hall, Inc., 1976.

ROSSI, ERNEST L. "Growth, Change and Transformation in

Dreams," *Journal of Humanistic Psychology,* II, no. 2 (1971), 147–69.

RUBIN, F. "Learning and Sleep: The Theory and Practice of Hypnopaedia." John Wright, 1971.

SAMPLES, ROBERT, and CHERYL CHARLES. "Dream Dragons," *Essentia,* Tiburon, Calif.

TRUPIN, E. W. "Correlates of Ego-level and Agency Communion in Stage REM Dreams of 11-13 Year Old Children," *Journal of Child Psychology and Psychiatry,* 17 (July 1976), 169–80.

WERLIN, ELENA. "Movies in the Head," *K-Eight,* November-December 1971, 36–52.

WOODS, RALPH L., and HERBERT B. GREENHOUSE. *The New World of Dreams.* New York: Macmillan, 1974.

YAROUSH, RITA, *et al.* "Effects of Sleep on Memory, II: Differential Effect of the First and Second Half of the Night," *Journal of Experimental Psychology,* 88, no. 3 (June 1971), 361–66.

FANTASY AND IMAGINATION

BEGG, I., and M. C. ANDERSON. "Imagery and Associative Memory in Children," 21 (June 1976), 480–89.

BENDER, BRUCE G., and JOEL R. LEVIN, "Imagery Generation and Motor Activity in Young Children: Trick or Feat?" Technical Report No. 358. ERIC, ED-121-447, 1975.

BODEM, MARGUERITE M. "The Role of Fantasy in Children's Reading," *Elementary English,* 52, no. 4 (April 1975), 470–71, 538.

BROWN, CHARLES T. "The Pleasures of Self-Talk," ERIC (microfiche), ED-077-042, April 1973.

CAMPBELL, JOSEPH, *Myths to Live By.* New York: Bantam, 1973.

CANFIELD, JACK, and PAULA KLIMEK. *Fantasy in the Classroom,* manuscript in preparation.

————. "Guided Imagery in the Classroom," *Journal of Humanistic and Transpersonal Education,* 1, no. 1, forthcoming 1977.

CASKEY, OWEN L., and MURIAL H. FLAKE. *Suggestive-Accelerative Learning: Adaptations of the Lozonov Method.* Iowa City: SALT, 1976.

CLARK, FRANCES VAUGHAN. "Learning through Fantasy," in *Transpersonal Education: A Curriculum for Feeling and Being,* ed. Gay Hendricks and James Fadiman. Englewood Cliffs, N.J.: Prentice-Hall, Inc., 1976.

————. "Approaching Transpersonal Consciousness Through Affective Imagery in Higher Education." Ph.D. dissertation. California School of Professional Psychology. Ann Arbor: Xerox University Microfilms, 1973, #73-19,777.

————. "Fantasy and Imagination," in *Four Psychologies Applied to Education: Freudian, Behavioral, Humanistic Transpersonal,* ed. T. Roberts. New York: John Wiley & Sons, 1975.

CRAMER, EUGENE H. "A Study of the Relationships Among Mental Imagery, Reading Comprehension, and Reading Attitude of Eleventh and Twelfth Grade Students." Ph.D. dissertation, University of Wisconsin, Madison. University Microfilms, Ann Arbor, Mich. 75-27,999, 1975.

————. "Pictures in Your Head: A Discussion of Relationships Among Mental Imagery, Reading Comprehension, and Reading Attitude." Paper presented at the Annual Meeting of the International Reading Association, Anaheim, Calif., 1976. ERIC, ED-122-263.

CRAMPTON, MARTHA. "The Use of Mental Imagery in Psychosynthesis," *Journal of Humanistic Psychology,* 9, no. 2 (Fall 1969), 139–53.

CREW, LOVIE. "Tapping the Imagination," *Exercise Exchange*, 18, no. 2 (Spring 1974), 2–5.

CROSSLEY, R. "Education and Fantasy," *College English*, 37, no. 3 (1975), 281–93.

DEMCHIK, MICHAEL JOSEPH. "An Analysis of the Effects of Short-Term Image-Provoking Training on the Teaching and Learning Patterns of Junior High School Science and Nonscience Teachers and their Students as Measured by Selected Classroom Observational Instruments." Ed.D. Dissertation, West Virginia University. University Microfilms, 74-199, Ann Arbor, Mich., 1973.

DESOILE, R. Trans. F. Harorian. *The Directed Daydream*. Psychosynthesis Research Foundation, Issue No. 18, New York.

DILLEY, JOSIAH S. "Mental Imagery," *Counseling and Values*, 19, no. 2 (February 1975), 110–15.

EBERLE, ROBERT F. *Scamper: Games for Imagination Development*. Buffalo, N.Y.: DOK Publishers (771 East Delavan Ave.).

Elementary English, Fantasy and Science Fiction, 52, no. 5 (May 1975), 620–30.

FLANNERY, MERLE. "Images and Aesthetic Consciousness," *Art Education*, 27, no. 3 (March 1974), 4–7.

FREYBERG, JOAN T. "Increasing Children's Fantasies: Hold High the Cardboard Sword," *Psychology Today*, 8, no. 9 (February 1975), 63–64.

GUMENIK, WILLIAM E. "Imagery and Association in Incidental Learning," ERIC, ED-118-616, 1974.

HAIGHT, MARYELLEN J. "Holistic Education Through Imagery and Biofeedback." Paper presented at the annual meeting of the Association of Humanistic Psychology, Estes Park, Col., August 1975.

HOLLIDAY, W. G. "Conceptualizing and Evaluating Learner Aptitudes Related to Instructional Stimuli in Science Education," *Journal of Research and Science Teaching,* 13 (March 1976), 101–9.

HOPKINS, L. B. "Fantasy Flights Circa 1976," *Teacher,* 93 (April 1976), 34ff.

JONES, RICHARD M. "Involving Fantasies and Feelings." In *Facts and Feelings in the Classroom,* Louis J. Rubin, ed. New York: Viking-Compass, 1973.

KHATENA, JOE. "Creative Imagination Imagery: Where Is It Going?" Paper presented at the Annual Meeting of the American Educational Research Association, San Francisco, April 1976. ERIC, ED-123-648, 1976.

————. "Imagination Imagery of Children and the Production of Analogy," *Gifted Child Quarterly,* 19 (Winter 1975), 310–15.

————. "Original Verbal Imagery and Its Sense Modality," *Gifted Child Quarterly,* 20 (Summer 1976), 180–86.

KING, CORWIN P. "Imagery and Information Processing: Some Implications for Therapeutic Communication." ERIC, ED-075-883, 1973.

KLINGER, ERIC. *Structure and Functions of Fantasy.* New York: John Wiley & Sons, 1971.

KULHARY, R. W., and I. SWENSON. "Imagery Instructions and the Comprehension of Text," *British Journal of Educational Psychology,* 45, Part 1 (February 1975), 47–51.

LESGOLD, ALAN M., *et al.* "Imagery Training and Children's Prose Learning," *Journal of Education Psychology,* 67, no. 5 (October 1975), 663–67.

MACINNES, C. "Easy to Visualize," *Times Educational Supplement,* No. 3159, December 19, 1975, p. 11.

MASSEY, SARA. "The Importance of Fantasy," *Today's Education,* 64, no. 1 (January/February 1975), 42–43.

McNARY, SUSAN, *et al.* "Interrelationships Among Psychological Measures of Cognitive Style and Fantasy Predisposition in a

Sample of 100 Children in the Fifth and Sixth Grades, *Educational and Psychological Measurement*, 35, no. 2 (Summer 1975), 477–85.

MEESON, P. "Imagination in Art and Art Education," *Journal of Aesthetic Education*, 9 (October 1975), 55–68.

MEZNARICH, RICHARD, ROBERT HABES, and CLAUDIA BINTER, "How Three Teachers Use Fantasy Journeys," in *Transpersonal Education: A Curriculum for Feeling and Being*, ed. Gay Hendricks and James Fadiman. Englewood Cliffs, N.J.: Prentice-Hall, Inc., 1976.

MWANALUSHI, MUYUNDA. "Imagery in Children's Memory for Patterns," *Developmental Psychology*, 12, no. 1 (January 1976), 78.

PASKANZER, SUSAN CORNELL. "A Case For Fantasy," *Elementary English*, 52, no. 4 (April 1975), 472–75.

PRESSLEY, G. MICHAEL. "Mental Imagery Helps Eight-Year-Olds Remember What They Read." Paper presented at the Annual Meeting of the American Educational Research Association, San Francisco, 1976. ERIC, ED-123-595.

———. "Mental Imagery Helps Eight-Year-Olds Remember What They Read," *Journal of Educational Psychology*, 68 (June 1976), 355–59.

PULASKI, MARY ANN. "The Rich Rewards of Make Believe," *Psychology Today*, 7, no. 8 (January 1974), 68–74.

RAPKIN, MAURICE. *The Power of Pretend*. Available from the author: 10480 Santa Monica Boulevard, Los Angeles, Calif. 90025.

RICHARDSON, C. C. "Reality of Fantasy," *Language Arts*, 53 (May 1976), 549–51ff.

ROBERTS, THOMAS B., BENJAMIN S. WESTHEIMER, and FRANK ZUMMALLEN. *Learning Through Fantasy*, manuscript in preparation.

ROSENZVEIG, FRED. "Four Gifts—a Fantasy Journey." Mimeographed, 3 pp. Canadian Institute of Psychosynthesis, Montreal.

SAMPLES, ROBERT E. *The Metaphoric Mind: Womb of Human Consciousness.* Palo Alto, Calif.: Addison-Wesley, Publishing Co., 1976.

————. "Intuitive Mode: Completing the Educational Process," *Media and Methods,* 11 (May 1975), 24–25ff.

STARK, STANLEY. "An Essay in Rorschach Revisionism, with Special Reference to the Maslowian Self-Actualizer: I. Innovation Versus Imagination, Idealism, Mysticism, Romanticism," *Perceptual and Motor Skills,* 33, no. 2 (1971), 343–57.

STROM, ROBERT D. "The Merits of Solitary Play," *Childhood Education,* 52, no. 3 (January 1976), 149–52.

SUMMERFIELD, G. "Making Room for Fantasy: Interview," *Times* (London) *Literary Supplement,* no. 3179 (May 7, 1976), pp. 26–27.

ZUCK, J. E. "Religion and Fantasy," *Religious Education,* 70 (November 1975), 586–604.

FOUNDATIONS AND THEORETICAL BACKGROUND

ARNHEIM, RUDOLF. *Visual Thinking.* Los Angeles: University of California Press, 1969.

ASRANI, U. "The Psychology of Mysticism," *Main Currents in Modern Thought,* 25 (1969), 68–73.

ASSAGIOLI, ROBERTO. The Conflict between the Generations and the Psychosynthesis of the Human Ages. Issue no. 31, Psychosynthesis Research Foundation, New York.

BARAVALLE, HERMAN. *Rudolf Steiner as Educator.* Spring Valley,

N.Y.: Anthroposophic Press (Rudolf Steiner—Waldorf Education).

————. *The International Waldorf School Movement.* Spring Valley, N.Y.: Anthroposophic Press (Rudolf Steiner—Waldorf Education).

Brain/Mind Bulletin, "Education: Overcoming Old Psychologies," 1, no. 1 (December 15, 1975), 3.

Brain/Mind Bulletin, "Transpersonal Education Panelists Urge Soft Sell, Integrated Philosophy," 1, no. 21 (September 6, 1976), 1, 3.

BRUNER, JEROME. *On Knowing: Essays for the Left Hand.* New York: Atheneum, 1965.

BURKE, O. M. "A Few Well-Chosen Words," in *Transpersonal Education: A Curriculum for Feeling and Being,* ed. Gay Hendricks and James Fadiman. Englewood Cliffs, N.J.: Prentice-Hall, Inc., 1976.

CANFIELD, JACK. "Internal Wisdom." P.O. Box 575, Amherst, Mass.

CHRISTENSEN, J. A. "Cosmic Consciousness," *Media and Methods,* 11, no. 6 (February 1975), 18–21.

CONKLIN, JOHN. "Transpersonal Education: Step Two for John Conklin," *Journal of Humanistic and Transpersonal Education,* 1, no. 1, forthcoming 1977.

ELKIND, DAVID. "Freud, Jung, and the Collective Unconscious," *The New York Times Magazine,* October 4, 1970.

ELLWOOD, ROBERT S. *Religious and Spiritual Groups in Modern America.* Englewood Cliffs, N.J.: Prentice-Hall, Inc., 1973.

FADIMAN, JAMES. *Hemiconceptual Realities In Nonordinal Spaces: An Autobiography.* Chakra, Calif.: Potananda Press, undated.

————, and ROBERT FRAGER. *Personality and Personal Growth.* New York: Harper & Row, 1976.

FRAGER, ROBERT. "Transpersonal Education," in *Transpersonal Education: A Curriculum for Feeling and Being,* ed. Gay Hendricks and James Fadiman. Englewood Cliffs, N.J.: Prentice-Hall, Inc., 1976.

————. "A Proposed Model for a Graduate Program in Transpersonal Psychology," *Journal of Transpersonal Psychology,* 6, no. 2 (Fall 1974), 163–66.

————. *A Transpersonal Psychology Graduate Program.* Transpersonal Psychology Institute, P.O. Box 2364, Stanford, Calif. 94305, Winter, 1975.

GARDNER, JOHN FENTRESS. *The Experience of Knowledge: Essays on American Education.* Garden City, N.Y.: Waldorf Press, Adelphi University (Cambridge Ave.), 1975.

GLAS, WERNER. *The Waldorf School Approach to History.* Spring Valley, N.Y.: Anthroposophic Press (Rudolf Steiner—Waldorf Education).

GORDON, WILLIAM. *The Metaphorical Way of Learning and Knowing.* Cambridge, Mass.: Porpoise Books, 1966.

GREELEY, ANDREW M. "Sociology of the Paranormal: A Reconnaissance," *Sage Papers in The Social Sciences—Studies in Religion and Ethnicity.* Series 90-023, Vol. 2. Beverly Hills: Sage Publications.

————, and WILLIAM McCREADY. "Are We a Nation of Mystics?" *New York Times Magazine,* January 26, 1975, pp. 12–25.

GREEN, ELMER, and ALYCE GREEN. *Beyond Biofeedback.* New York: Delacorte, 1977.

GROF, STANISLAV. *Realms of the Human Unconscious: Observations from LSD Research.* New York: Viking, 1975. Paperback, New York: E. P. Dutton, 1976. See especially chapter on transpersonal experiences. One of the major works in psychology this century.

HALL, MANLY P. *Basic Principle of Domestic Psyche and Bringing Philosophy to Children.* Philosophical Research Society

Inc. (3910 Los Felez Boulevard, Los Angeles, Calif. 90027), 1964.

HARDING, D. E. "From *On Having No Head*," in *Transpersonal Education: A Curriculum for Feeling and Being,* ed. Gay Hendricks and James Fadiman. Englewood Cliffs, N.J.: Prentice-Hall, Inc., 1976.

HARGROVE, ROBERT. "The School of the Ignoramus." Editorial. *East-West Journal,* 4, no. 8 (1974), 2.

HARMAN, WILLIS W. "The New Copernican Revolution," *Journal of Transpersonal Psychology,* 1, no. 2 (Fall 1969), 21–30. Social-cultural background.

HARONIAN, FRANK. "The Repression of the Sublime." In *The Proper Study of Man,* pp. 239–46. James Fadiman, ed. New York: Macmillan, 1971. Reprinted in *Synthesis,* 1, no. 1 (Spring 1974), 51–62, 92.

HAYASHI, TETSUMARO. "Zen and the Samurai Tradition," *Indiana Social Studies Quarterly,* 28, no. 3 (Winter 1975-76), 73–83.

HEARD, GERALD. *The Five Ages of Man: The Psychology of Human History.* New York: Julian Press, 1963.

HENDRICK, NANCY. "A Program in the Psychology of Human Consciousness," *Journal of Transpersonal Psychology,* 3, no. 2 (1971), 145–49.

HENDRICKS, GAY. "Educators' Checklist: Questions to Ask Ourselves about Schooling," in *Transpersonal Education: A Curriculum for Feeling and Being,* ed. Gay Hendricks and James Fadiman. Englewood Cliffs, N.J.: Prentice-Hall, Inc., 1976.

Humanistic and Transpersonal Education, Journal of, "Transpersonal Education: An Initial Resource Guide," 1, no. 1, forthcoming 1977.

HUXLEY, ALDOUS. "From *Island*," in *Transpersonal Education: A Curriculum for Feeling and Being,* ed. Gay Hendricks and James Fadiman. Englewood Cliffs, N.J.: Prentice-Hall, Inc., 1976.

————. "Education of the Amphibian," *Tomorrow and Tomorrow and Tomorrow, and other essays.* New York: Harper & Row, 1964.

————. "Education on the Nonverbal Level," *Daedelus,* 41, no. 2 (Spring 1962), 279–93. Also in Richard M. Jones, ed. *Contemporary Educational Psychology.* New York: Harper 1967.

————. Introduction to *The Perennial Philosophy,* pp. iv–vii. Cleveland: Meridian Books, The World Publishing Co., 1968.

JOEL, DAVID. "Naropa: The University of Wholeness," *East/West Journal,* 4, no. 8 (September 1974), 14–15.

JUNG, CARL GUSTAV. *Psychology and Education.* Princeton, N.J.: Princeton University Press, Bollinger Series, 1971.

KANTOR, ROBERT. "The Affective Domain and Beyond," *Journal for the Study of Consciousness,* vol 3, no. 1 (January-June 1970), 20–42. Abridged in *Four Psychologies Applied to Education: Freudian, Behavioral, Humanistic, Transpersonal,* ed. T. Roberts. New York: John Wiley & Sons, 1975.

KATZ, RICHARD. "Education for Transcendence." In *Preludes for Growth.* New York: Free Press, 1973.

————. "Education for Transcendence: Lessons for the !Kung Zhu/twasi," *Journal of Transpersonal Psychology,* 5, no. 2 (Fall 1973), 136–55.

KOBAYASHI, V. N. "Quest for Experience: Zen, Dewey and Education," *Comparative Education Review,* 5, no. 3 (February 1962), 217–22.

KOJI, SATO. "Editorial: With the Cosmic Perspective," *Psychologia: An International Journal of Psychology in the Orient,* 14, no. 1 (March 1971), 1–2.

KRISHNAMURTI, JIDDU. *Education and the Significance of Life.* New York: Harper and Row, 1953.

Krishnamurti On Education. New Delhi: Orient Longman Ltd., 1974.

KRISHNAMURTI, J. "From *Education and the Significance of Life,*" in *Transpersonal Education: A Curriculum for Feeling and Being,* ed. Gay Hendricks and James Fadiman. Englewood Cliffs, N.J.: Prentice-Hall, Inc., 1976.

LEONARD, GEORGE. "The Human Potential," *Education and Ecstasy,* Chapter 2. New York: Delacorte Press, 1968.

LESHAN, LAWRENCE. *The Medium, The Mystic, and The Physicist.* New York: Ballentine Books, Random House, 1975. Psychic Healing.

LEVEY, R. M. "Happenings in Education: Courses in the Occult," *PTA Magazine,* 68, no. 3 (February 1974), 2–3.

LOFGREN, R. "The School as a Living Organism." Psychosynthesis Research Foundation. Report No. 1, New York.

MARIN, PETER. "The New Narcissism." *Harper's,* no. 251, December 1975, pp. 45–50.

MASLOW, ABRAHAM H. "Lessons From the Peak-Experiences," *Journal of Humanistic Psychology,* 2, no. 2 (1962), 9–18.

———. *The Farther Reaches of Human Nature.* New York: Viking, 1971.

McBRIDE, A. "From Zen to the Cloud of Unknowing," *Momentum,* 7 (May 1976), 31–33.

McLAUGHLIN, FRANK. "In the Form of Krisna," *Media and Methods,* 9, no. 1 (September 1972), 23–27.

McWATERS, BARRY. "An Outline of Transpersonal Psychology: Its Meaning and Relevance for Education," in *Four Psychologies Applied to Education: Freudian, Behavioral, Humanistic, Transpersonal,* ed. T. Roberts. New York: John Wiley & Sons, 1975.

———. "A Comparative Analysis of Diverse Schemata of Transpersonal Psychology," unpublished doctoral dissertation, United States International University, San Diego, Calif., 1972.

MILES, H. C. "Design for Tomorrow." Psychosynthesis Research Foundation. Report No. 4, New York.

MILLER, JOHN P. "Consciousness Expansion," in *Humanizing the Classroom: Models of Teaching in Affective Education.* New York: Praeger Publishers, 1976.

MISHLOVE, JEFFREY. *The Roots of Consciousness: Psychic Liberation through History, Science, and Experience.* New York: Random House, 1975. Survey of historical and current research on consciousness, excellent source book and bibliography.

MORRIS, JOSEPH. *Psychology and Teaching: A Humanistic View.* New York: Random House, forthcoming 1977.

MURPHY, MICHAEL. "Education for Transcendence," *Journal of Transpersonal Psychology,* 1, no. 1 (Spring 1969), 21–32. Also in T. Roberts, ed., *Four Psychologies Applied to Education: Freudian, Behavioral, Humanistic, Transpersonal,* pp. 438–47. New York: John Wiley & Sons, 1975.

MUSES, C. "The Present Dilemma in Psychotherapy, Religion, and Education," *Journal for the Study of Consciousness,* Vol. 2, no. 2, July-December 1969.

———. "Taint Necessarily So: A New Look at Education," *Journal for the Study of Consciousness,* 4, no. 2 (1971), 101–4.

NARANJO, CLAUDIO. "The Oneness of Experience in the Ways of Growth," in *The One Quest.* New York: Viking Press, 1973, pp. 123–28.

NORDBERG, R. B. *The Teenager and the New Mysticism.* New York: Richards Rosen Press, 1973.

———. "Paths to Mysticism in the 1970's." *Counseling and Values,* 17, no. 3 (1973), 167–75.

NORTHRUP, F. S. C. *Meeting of East and West.* New York: Macmillan, 1960.

ORNSTEIN, ROBERT E. "The Education of the Intuitive Mode." In *The Psychology of Consciousness,* Chapter 7. San Francisco: W. H. Freeman, 1972; New York: Pelican-Penguin, 1975.

PARSONS, JAMES B. "New Paradigms to Re-present the Past: The Psychedelic Approach." Paper presented at American Historical Association, New York, December 1971. University of California at Riverside.

PEARCE, JOSEPH CHILTON. *Crack in the Cosmic Egg*. New York: Pocket Books, 1973.

———. *Exploring the Crack in the Cosmic Egg*. New York: Julian, 1974.

RAM DASS, BABA. "Toward a Higher Education," *East/West Journal*, 4, no. 8 (September 1974), 16–17.

REDMOND, HUGH. "A Pioneer Program in Transpersonal Education," *Journal of Transpersonal Psychology*, 6, no. 1 (1974), 8–10.

REISER, O. L. "Synthesis as the Function of Philosophy." Psychosynthesis Research Foundation, Report No. 8, New York.

RING, KENNETH. "An Essay on Transpersonal Living," *Journal of Humanistic and Transpersonal Education*, 1, no. 1, forthcoming 1977.

ROSENBAUER, W. "Some Thoughts on a New Approach to Education." Psychosynthesis Research Foundation, New York.

SAMPLES, ROBERT E. "Toward a Synergy of Mind: Psychological Premises for Education Before 1984," *Essentia*, The Evergreen State College, Olympia, Wash. Mimeographed, 23 pp., 1974.

———. *Where All Things Belong* (movie). Essentia, Tiburon, Calif., 1975.

SAMUELS, MIKE, and NANCY SAMUELS. *Seeing with the Mind's Eye*. New York: Random House, Bookworks, 1975.

SHAH, IDRIES. "How Knowledge Was Earned," in *Transpersonal Education: A Curriculum for Feeling and Being*, ed. Gay Hendricks and James Fadiman. Englewood Cliffs, N.J.: Prentice-Hall, Inc., 1976.

———. *Wisdom of the Idiots*. New York: E. P. Dutton, 1971.

SMITH, CAM. *Buckminster Fuller to Children of Earth.* Garden City, N.Y.: Doubleday and Co., Inc., 1972.

STAUDE, JOHN R., and MALCOLM R. WALLEY, eds. *Consciousness, Energy, and Change.* Forthcoming.

STORY, M. L. "Education and the New Puritanism," *Clearing House,* 47, no. 9 (May 1973), 515–18.

SULLIVAN, E. A. *The Future: Human Ecology and Education.* Homewood, Ill.: ETC Publications (18512 Pierce Terrace), 1975.

SWAIN, JOHN W. *Eastern Philosophical Assumptions and Practices in Relation to Transpersonal Process Curricula,* University of Northern Colorado, Greeley, Colo. Winter 1974. Ed.D. Dissertation.

TAFT, RONALD. "Peak Experiences and Ego Permissiveness, *Acta Psychologica,* 29, no. 1 (February 1969), 35–64.

TART, CHARLES T. "Altered States of Consciousness." In Lyle E. Bourne, Jr., and Bruce R. Ekstrand, *Psychology: Its Principles and Meanings,* Chapter 8. New York: Holt, Rinehart, and Winston, 1976. Good introduction to the study of altered states of consciousness.

————. "Some Assumptions of Orthodox, Western Psychology," in *Transpersonal Psychologies,* ed. Charles T. Tart. New York: Harper & Row, 1975. Stunningly insightful.

TOMPKINS, P. K. "On Paradoxes in the Rhetoric of the New England Transcendentalists," *Quarterly Journal of Speech,* 62 (February 1976), 40–48.

TZU, CHUANG. "The Joy of Fishes," in *Transpersonal Education: A Curriculum for Feeling and Being,* ed. Gay Hendricks and James Fadiman. Englewood Cliffs, N.J.: Prentice-Hall, Inc., 1976.

VAN KAAM, A. "The Third Force in European Psychology." Psychosynthesis Research Foundation, Issue No. 9, New York.

VARGIU, JAMES. "Global Education and Psychosynthesis." Psychosynthesis Research Foundation, Issue No. 27, New York.

WEIL, ANDREW. Excerpts from *The Natural Mind*, pp. 19–25. Boston: Houghton Mifflin Co., 1972. In T. Roberts, ed., *Four Psychologies Applied to Education: Freudian, Behavioral, Humanistic, Transpersonal*, pp. 421–25. New York: John Wiley & Sons, 1975. On natural human desire to explore consciousness.

WILBER, KEN. "Psychologica Perennis: The Spectrum of Consciousness," *Journal of Transpersonal Psychology*, 7, no. 2 (1975), 105–32.

YEOMANS, THOMAS. "Search for a Working Model: Gestalt, Psychosynthesis, and Confluent Education," in George I. Brown, Thomas Yeomans, and Liles Grizzard, *The Live Classroom: Innovation Through Confluent Education and Gestalt*, Chapter 14. New York: Viking, 1974.

ZIMBARDO, PHILIP. "Transpersonal Psychology and Maslow's Hierarchy," *Psychology and Life Newsletter*, 3, no. 2 (Fall 1975), 2.

——, and FLOYD RUCH. "Altered States of Consciousness." In Zimbardo and Ruch, *Psychology and Life*, Chapter 7, Glenview, Ill.: Scott, Foresman & Co., 1975. Good background chapter on states of consciousness.

HYPNOSIS

ARNETTE, J. L., and T. H. CARTER. "Use of Hypnosis and Self-Hypnosis for Assisting Students with Academic Problems," *Journal of College Student Personnel*, 16 (November 1975), 522.

ARONS, HARRY. *Hypnosis for Speeding Up the Learning Process*. Irvington, N.J.: Power Publishers, Inc., 1974.

ASTOR, MARTIN. "Learning Through Hypnosis," *Educational Forum*, May 1971, 447–55.

CHAPPIE, DAVID ALEXANDER. "Can Waking Suggestion Be As Effective as Hypnosis In Increasing Reading Efficiency? A Consideration for Educational Application." ERIC ED-067-615, 1971.

DALE, RALPH ALAN. "Hypnosis and Education," ERIC, ED-087-710, 1972.

DESAU, GEORGE. "Hallahan High Pre and Post Testing." Silva Mind Control International, Laredo, Texas.

DIAMOND, MICHAEL JAY, *et al.* "The Use of Direct Instructions to Modify Hypnotic Performance: The Effects of Programmed Learning Procedures," *Journal of Abnormal Psychology*, 84, no. 2 (April 1975), 109–13.

EDMONSTON, WILLIAM E., JR., and HERBERT E. MARKS, III. "The Effects of Hypnosis and Motivational Instructions on Kinesthetic Learning," *The American Journal of Clinical Hypnosis*, 9, no. 4 (April 1967), 252–55.

———, and MICHAEL PE-SIN. "Hypnosis as Related to Learning and Electrodermal Measures," *The American Journal of Hypnosis: Clinical, Experimental, Theoretical*, 9, no. 1 (July 1966), 31–51.

EGAN, RICHARD M., and WILLIAM EGAN. "The Effect of Hypnosis on Academic Performance," *The American Journal of Clinical Hypnosis*, 11, no. 1 (July 1968), 31–34.

EVANS, FREDERICK J., and JOHN F. KIHLSTROM. "Contextual and Temporal Disorganization During Posthypnotic Amnesia," ERIC, ED-123-534, 1975.

FRANZINI, LOUIS R., and ROY D. McDONALD. "Marijuana Usage and Hypnotic Susceptibility," *Journal of Consulting and Clinical Psychology*, 40, no. 2 (April 1973), 176–80.

GILBERT, JAMES E., and THEODORE X. BARBER. "Effects of Hypnotic Induction, Motivational Suggestions, and Level of Suggestibility on Cognitive Performance," *The International Journal of Clinical and Experimental Hypnosis,* 20, no. 3 (1972), 156–68.

HARLEY, WILLARD F., JR., and WILLARD F. HARLEY, SR. "The Effect of Hypnosis on Paired-Associate Learning," *Journal of Personality,* 36, no. 3 (September 1968), 331–40.

JAMPOLSKY, GERALD G. "Use of Hypnosis and Sensory Motor Stimulation to Aid Children with Learning Problems," *Journal of Learning Disabilities,* 3 (November 1970), 29–34.

―――, and MARYELLEN J. HAIGHT. "A Special Technique for Children with Reading Problems," *Academic Therapy,* 10, no. 3 (Spring 1975), 333–37.

KETTLEKAMP, LARRY. *Hypnosis, the Wakeful Sleep.* New York: William Morrow and Co., 1975. Grades 4-6.

KRAUSS, BEATRICE J. "Effect of Hypnotic Time Distortion Upon Free-Recall Learning," *Journal of Abnormal Psychology,* 83, no. 2 (April 1974), 140–44.

KRIPPNER, STANLEY. "The Use of Hypnosis with Elementary and Secondary School Children in a Summer Reading Clinic," *American Journal of Clinical Hypnosis,* 4, no. 4 (April 1965), 261–66.

―――. "The Use of Hypnosis and the Improvement of Academic Achievement," *Journal of Special Education* (Fall 1970), 451–60.

―――, and PAUL R. BINDLER. "Hypnosis and Attention: A Review," *American Journal of Clinical Hypnosis,* 16, no. 3 (January 1974), 166–67.

LIEBERT, ROBERT M., NORMA RUBIN, and ERNEST R. HILGARD. "The Effects of Suggestions of Alertness in Hypnosis on Paired-Associate Learning," *Journal of Personality,* 33, no. 4 (December 1965), 605–12.

LONDON, PERRY, and LESLIE M. COPPER. "Reactivation of Memory by Hypnosis and Suggestion." ERIC, ED-037-796, 1968.

LONDON, PERRY, *et al.* "More Hypnosis in the Unhypnotizable:

Effects of Hypnosis and Exhortation on Rote Learning," *Journal of Personality,* 34, no. 1 (March 1966), 71–79.

McCORD, HALLACK. "Hypnosis as an Aid to Increasing Adult Reading Efficiency," *Journal of Developmental Reading,* 6 (Autumn 1962), 64–65.

———. "Improving Reading Ability Through Combined Tutoring and Hypnotherapy," *Journal of Developmental Reading,* 7, no. 2 (Winter 1964), 141–42.

MELNICK, J., and R. W. RUSSELL. "Hypnosis versus Systematic Desensitization in the Treatment of Test Anxiety," *Journal of Counseling Psychology,* 23 (July 1976), 291–95.

MORDEY, THEOBOLD, and DOUGLAS DENIKE. "Enhancement of Achievement Motivation by Post-Hypnotic and Waking Suggestion," *American Journal of Clinical Hypnosis,* 13, no. 3 (January 1971), 198–205.

MORGAN, WILLIAM P. "Postdoctoral Fellowship Program in Educational Research," Final Technical Report (Hypnosis), ERIC, ED-045-596, 1970.

MORRIS, FREIDA. *Self-Hypnosis in Two Days.* New York: E. P. Dutton, 1975.

MUTKE, PETER H. C. "Increased Reading Comprehension Through Hypnosis," *American Journal of Clinical Hypnosis,* 9 (4) (1967), 262–66.

ORNE, MARTIN T. "Hypnosis, Motivation, and the Ecological Validity of the Psychological Experiment." In W. J. Arnold and M. M. Page, eds., *Nebraska Symposium on Motivation: 1970,* University of Nebraska Press, Lincoln, 1971.

OSTRANDER, SHEILA, and LYNN SCHROEDER. "Artificial Reincarnation," *Psychic Discoveries Behind the Iron Curtain,* Chapter 12. New York: Bantam Books, 1971. Also in T. Roberts, ed., *Four Psychologies Applied to Education: Freudian, Behavioral, Humanistic, Transpersonal,* pp. 487–97. New York: John Wiley & Sons, 1975.

SIMMONS, ROY D., JR. "The Relative Effectiveness of Systematic

Desensitization and Hypnosis in Alleviating Test Anxiety in Community College Students," doctoral dissertation. Walden University, February 1976. ERIC, ED–124–265.

SLOTNICK, ROBERT S., ROBERT M. LIEBERT, and ERNEST R. HILGARD. "The Enhancement of Muscular Performance in Hypnosis Through Exhortation and Involving Instruction," *Journal of Personality*, March 1965, pp. 37–45.

SPRINKLE, R. LEO. "Anxiety Management Training Through Self-Hypnosis," ERIC, ED–067–590, 1972.

STINSON, ROBERT C. "Hypnosis and Learning," *Pennsylvania School Journal*, May 1964, pp. 418–19.

SWIERCINSKY, DENNIS, and WILLIAM C. COE. "Hypnosis, Hypnotic Responsiveness, and Learning Meaningful Material," *The International Journal of Clinical and Experimental Hypnosis*, XVIII, no. 3 (July 1970), 217–22.

———. "The Effect of Alert Hypnosis and Hypnotic Responsiveness on Reading Comprehension," *The International Journal of Clinical and Experimental Hypnosis*, XIX, no. 3 (July 1971), 146–53.

WEITZENHOFFER, ANDRE M. *Hypnotism: An Objective Study in Suggestibility*. New York: John Wiley & Sons, Inc., 1963. See Chapter 13, "Influence of Hypnotic Suggestion on Memory and Learning."

WOODY, ROBERT H. "Self-Help Experiences," *NASPA Journal*, 10, no. 4 (April 1973), 339–43. Hypnosis.

ZIEGENFUSS, BEATRICE W. "Hypnosis: A Tool for Education," *Education* (April 1962), 505–7.

MEDITATION

BARTELS, WAYNE JOHN. "The Effects of a Western Meditation on a Measure of Self-Actualization." Unpublished doctoral dissertation. Stillwater, Oklahoma: Oklahoma State University. 1976.

BOLEN, JEAN S. "Meditation and Psychotherapy in the Treatment of Cancer," *Psychic*, 4, no. 6 (July 1973), 19–23.

Brain/Mind Bulletin, "First Folsom TM Study: Inmates' Self-Image Is Improved," 1, no. 24 (November 1, 1976), 1–2.

COLLIER, R. W. "The Effect of Transcendental Meditation Upon University Academic Attainment," Proceedings of the Pacific Northwest Conference on Foreign Languages. In Press, 1973.

DENNISTON, DENISE, and PETER MCWILLIAMS. *The TM Book: How to Enjoy the Rest of Your Life*. Allen Park, Mich.: Versemonger Press, 1975.

DRISCOLL, FRANCIS. "TM as a Secondary School Subject," *Phi Delta Kappan*, 54, no. 4 (December 1972), 236–37. Also in T. Roberts, ed., *Four Psychologies Applied to Education: Freudian, Behavioral, Humanistic, Transpersonal*, pp. 525–27. New York: John Wiley & Sons, 1975.

FRUMKIN, LYNN R., and ROBERT R. PAGANO. "Meditation and Right Hemispheric Functioning." Paper presented at the Seventh Annual Meeting of the Biofeedback Research Society, Colorado Springs, February 27–March 2, 1976. Reprint available from Biofeedback Research Society.

HENDRICKS, GAY, and RUSSELL WILLS, "A Basic Meditation," in *Transpersonal Education: A Curriculum for Feeling and Being*, ed. Gay Hendricks and James Fadiman. Englewood Cliffs, N.J.: Prentice-Hall, Inc., 1976.

HJELLE, LARRY A. "Transcendental Meditation and Psychological Health," *Perceptual and Motor Skills*, 39 (1974), 623–28.

HODGSON, JOAN. *Hullo Sun*. Novato, Calif.: Inner Light Foundation (P.O. Box 761).

"Is TM Religious or Secular? U.S. District Court to Decide," *Phi Delta Kappan*, June 1976, p. 660.

KANELLAKOS, DEMETRI P. *The Psychobiology of Transcendental Meditation: An Annotated Bibliography*, Maharishi International University, Fairfield, Iowa, Spring 1973.

KEEFE, T. "Meditation and the Psychotherapist," *American Journal of Orthopsychiatry,* 45 (April 1975), 484–89.

KUNA, D. J. "Meditation and Work," *Vocational Guidance Quarterly,* 23 (June 1975), 342–46.

LANGFORD, CRICKET. *Meditation for Little People.* Novato, Calif.: Inner Light Foundation, 1974.

LESHAN, LAWRENCE. *How to Meditate: A Guide To Self-Discovery.* Boston: Little, Brown Publishing Co., 1974.

LEVINE, PAUL H. "Transcendental Meditation and the Science of Creative Intelligence," *Phi Delta Kappan,* 54, no. 4 (December 1972), 231–35.

LINDEN, WILLIAM. "The Relation Between the Practice of Meditation by School Children and Their Levels of Field Dependence-Independence, Test Anxiety and Reading Achievement," *Journal of Consulting and Clinical Psychology,* 41, no. 1 (August 1973), 139–43.

Maharishi International University. *Research Index: A Listing of Researchers Engaged in TM/SCI-Related Research.* Fairfield, Iowa, Spring 1973.

———. *Fundamentals of Progress: Scientific Research on Transcendental Meditation.* Fairfield, Iowa, 1974. Revised periodically.

MAUPIN, EDWARD W. "Meditation," in *Ways of Growth: Approaches to Expanding Awareness,* Chapter 17, ed. Herbert A. Otto and John Mann. New York: Pocket Books, 1971.

MORRIS, JOSEPH. "Meditation in the Classroom," *Learning,* 5, no. 4 (December 1976), 22–27.

NARANJO, CLAUDIO, and ROBERT ORNSTEIN. *On the Psychology of Meditation.* New York: Viking, 1971.

NIDICH, SANFORD, WILLIAM SEEMAN, and T. DRESKIN. "Influence of Transcendental Meditation: A Replication," *Journal of Counseling Psychology,* 20, No. 6 (1973), 565–66.

NORDBERG, R. B. "Meditation: Future Vehicle for Career Exploration," *Vocational Guidance Quarterly,* 22 (June 1974), 267–71.

OTTENS, J. "Effects of Transcendental Meditation Upon Modifying the Cigarette Smoking Habit," *Journal of School Health,* 45 (December 1975), 577–83.

PEERBOLTE, M. "Meditation for School Children," *Main Currents in Modern Thought,* 24 (1967), 19–21.

PELLITIER, KENNETH R. "Influence of Transcendental Meditation Upon Autokinetic Perception," *Perceptual and Motor Skills,* 39 (1974), 1031–34.

POSNER, M. J. "TM—What Is It?" *The Massachusetts Teacher,* May-June 1972.

ROZMAN, DEBORAH. *Meditating with Children.* Boulder Creek, Calif.: University of the Trees Press (P.O. Box 644), 1975.

RUBOTTOM, AL E. "Transcendental Meditation and Its Potential Uses for Schools," *Social Education,* December 1972, 851–57. Also in T. Roberts, ed., *Four Psychologies Applied to Education: Freudian, Behavioral, Humanistic, Transpersonal,* pp. 514–24. New York: John Wiley & Sons, 1975.

SEEMAN, WILLIAM, SANFORD NIDICH, and THOMAS BANTA. "Influence of Transcendental Meditation on a Measure of Self-Actualization," *Journal of Counseling Psychology,* 19, no. 3 (1972), 184–87.

SHAFII, MOHAMMAD. "Silence in the Service of Ego: Psychoanalytic Study of Meditation," *International Journal of Psycho-Analysis,* 54 (1973), 431–43.

———, RICHARD LAVELY, and ROBERT JAFFE. "Meditation and Marijuana," *American Journal of Psychiatry,* 131, no. 1 (January 1974), 60–63.

STEK, R. J., and B. A. BASS. "Personal Adjustment and Perceived Locus of Control Among Students Interested in Meditation," *Psychological Reports,* 32 (1973), 1019–22.

TIME, "Tempest over TM," March 1, 1976.

TIMMONS, BEVERLY, and JOE KAMIYA. "The Psychology and

————. "The Relationship Between Level of ESP Scoring and Physiology of Meditation and Related Phenomena: A Bibliography," *Journal of Transpersonal Psychology,* 2, no. 1 (1970), 41–59.

————, and DEMETRI P. KANELLAKOS. "The Psychology and Physiology of Meditation and Related Phenomena: Bibliography II," *Journal of Transpersonal Psychology,* 6, no. 1 (1974), 32–38.

TRAYNHAM, RICHARD N. *The Effects of Experimental Meditation, Relaxation Training, and Electromyographic Feedback on Physiological and Self-Report Measures of Relaxation and Altered States of Consciousness,* unpublished doctoral dissertation, University of Arkansas, Fayetteville, 1976.

TRUCH, STEPHEN. "TM: A Boon for Teachers?" *The Alberta Teachers Association Magazine,* May-June 1972.

VAN DUSEN, WILSON. "On Meditation," in *Transpersonal Education: A Curriculum for Feeling and Being,* ed. Gay Hendricks and James Fadiman. Englewood Cliffs, N.J.: Prentice-Hall, Inc., 1976.

WHITE, JOHN, ed. *What Is Meditation?* Garden City, N.Y.: Anchor, 1974.

WILLIAMS, GURNEY III. "Transcendental Meditation: Can It Fight Drug Abuse?" *Science Digest,* February 1972.

PARAPSYCHOLOGY AND UNUSUAL PHENOMENA

ANDERSON, MARGARET. "Clairvoyance and Teacher-Pupil Attitudes in Fifth and Sixth Grades," *Journal of Parapsychology,* 21 (March 1957), 1–12.

Student Class Grade," *Journal of Parapsychology*, 23 (March 1959), 1–18.

————, and ELSIE GREGORY. "A Two-year Program of Tests for Clairvoyance and Precognition with a Class of Public School Pupils," *Journal of Parapsychology*, 23 (September 1959), 149–77.

————, and R. A. MCCONNELL. "Fantasy Testing for ESP in a Fourth and Fifth Grade Class." *Journal of Psychology*, 52 (1961), 491–503.

————, and RHEA WHITE. "Teacher-Pupil Attitudes and Clairvoyance Test Results," *Journal of Parapsychology*, 20 (September 1956), 141–57.

————. "A Further Investigation of Teacher-Pupil Attitudes and Clairvoyance Test Results," *Journal of Parapsychology*, 21 (June 1957), 81–97.

————. "ESP Score Level in Relation to Student's Attitude Toward Teacher-Agents Acting Simultaneously," *Journal of Parapsychology*, 22 (1958), 20–28.

————. "The Relationship Between Changes in Student Attitude and ESP Scoring," *Journal of Parapsychology*, 22 (September 1958), 167–74.

————. "A Survey of Work on ESP and Teacher-Pupil Attitudes," *Journal of Parapsychology*, 22 (December 1958), 246–68.

BELOFF, JOHN. "The Study of the Paranormal as an Educative Experience," in *Education in Parapsychology*, ed. Betty Shapin and Lisette Coly. New York: Parapsychology Foundation, 1976.

BRIER, ROBERT M. "A Mass School Precognition Test," *Journal of Parapsychology*, 33, no. 2 (June 1969), 125–35.

BURT, C. "Experiments on Telepathy in Children," *British Journal of Statistical Psychology*, Part I, 12 (May 1959), 55–99.

CHILD, IRVIN L. "Parapsychology in the Liberal-Arts Curriculum," in *Education in Parapsychology,* ed. Betty Shapin and Lisette Coly. New York: Parapsychology Foundation, 1976.

COHEN, DANIEL. *ESP, The Search Beyond the Senses.* New York: Harcourt, Brace, Jovanovich, 1973. High school and adult.

COOKE, AILEEN H. *Out of the Mouth of Babes: Extra Sensory Perception in Children.* Cambridge and London: James Clarke & Co. Ltd., 1968.

DAVIS, GARY, JAMES M. PETERSON, and FRANK H. FARLEY. "Attitudes, Motivation, Sensation Seeking, and Belief in ESP as Predictors of Real Creative Behavior," *The Journal of Creative Behavior,* 8, no. 1 (First Quarter 1974), 31–39.

DEAN, E. DOUGLAS. "The Plethysmograph As an Indicator of ESP," *Journal of the Society for Psychical Research,* 41 (1962), 351–53.

DEGUISNE, ARNON. "Two Repetitions of the Anderson-White Investigation of Teacher-Pupil Attitudes and Clairvoyance Test Results, Part I: High School Tests," *Journal of Parapsychology,* 23 (September 1959), 196–207.

DELANEY, OLIVER J. "The Occult: Diabolica to Alchemists, *R.Q.,*" 11 (February 1971), 7–14.

DOMMEYER, FREDERICK C. "Parapsychology and the Teaching of Philosophy," in *Education in Parapsychology,* ed. Betty Shapin and Lisette Coly. New York: Parapsychology Foundation, 1976.

EHRENWALD, JAN. "The Occult," *Today's Education,* 60, no. 6 (September 1971), 28–30.

———. "Telepathy and the Child-Parent Relationship," *Journal of the American Society for Psychical Research,* 48 (1954), 43–55.

EISENBUD, JULE. *The World of Ted Serios.* New York: Paperback Books, 1976.

EVANS, CHRISTOPHER. "Parapsychology—What the Questionnaire Revealed," *New Scientist,* January 25, 1973, p. 209.

FEILD, RESHAD. "The Hows and Whys of Power Points," in *Transpersonal Education: A Curriculum for Feeling and Being,* ed. Gay Hendricks and James Fadiman. Englewood Cliffs, N.J.: Prentice-Hall, Inc., 1976.

FEWKES, REV. RICHARD. "Parapsychology and Religion" (Curriculum Kit). Unitarian Universalist Psi Symposium at Old Ship Church, Hingham, Mass. Junior high through adult. Slides, games, tests, discussion tools. Rev. Fewkes, 644 Main Street, Norwell, Mass.

FISHER, GARY. "Self-Actualization of Paranormals," *Journal of Personality Assessment,* 35, no. 5, October 1971.

FITZHERBERT, J. "The Role of Extra-sensory Perception in Early Childhood," *Journal of Mental Science,* 106 (1960), 1560–67.

FOSTER, A. "ESP Tests with American Indian Children," *Journal of Parapsychology,* 7, no. 2 (June 1943), 94–103.

FREEMAN, JOHN, "A Precognition Test with a High School Science Club," *Journal of Parapsychology,* 28, no. 3 (September 1964), 214–21.

———. "Sex Differences and Target Arrangement: High School Tests of Precognition," *Journal of Parapsychology,* 30, no. 4 (December 1966), 227–35.

GARDNER, EDWARD L. *Fairies—A Book of Real Fairies.* London: Theosophical Publishing House Ltd. (68 Great Russell St.), 1945. "Authenticated" photographs of children with real fairies!

GOUFFE, MARIE. *Fairies at Work and at Play.* London: Theosophical Publishing House, Ltd., 1929.

GREEN, C. E., M. E. EASTMAN, and S. T. ADAMS. "Birth Order and Family Size and Extrasensory Perception," *British Journal of Social and Clinical Psychology,* 5, no. 2 (June 1966), 150–52.

GREENWALD, ANTHONY G. "Significance, Nonsignificance, and Interpretation of an ESP Experiment," *Journal of Experimental Social Psychology*, 11, no. 2 (March 1975), 180–99.

HANSEL, C. E. M. "Experiments on Telepathy in Children," *British Journal of Statistical Psychology*, 13, Part 2 (November 1960), 175–78.

HEINLEIN, J. H., and C. P. HEINLEIN. "What Is the Role of ESP in Objective Testing at the College Level?" *Journal of Psychology*, 46, Part II (October 1958), 319–28.

HODSON, GEOFFRY. *The Miracle of Birth. A Clairvoyant Study of Prenatal Birth.* Wheaton, Ill.: Theosophical Publishing House Ltd., 1929.

HUMPHREY, B. M. "ESP and Intelligence," *Joournal of Parapsychology*, 9 (1945), 7–16.

JOHNSON, MARTIN. "Parapsychology and Education," in *Education in Parapsychology*, ed. Betty Shapin and Lisette Coly. New York: Parapsychology Foundation, 1976.

Journal of Communication, "Paranormal Communication: A Symposium," 25 (Winter 1975), 96–194.

KANTHIMANA, B. K., and K. R. RAO. "Personality Characteristics of ESP Subjects," *Journal of Parapsychology*, 36 (1972), 56–70. Research done with Indian high school students.

KETTLEKAMP, LARRY. *Haunted Houses.* New York: William Morrow and Co., 1968. Grades 5–9.

———. *Sixth Sense.* New York: William Morrow and Co., 1970. Grades 5-9.

———. *Investigating UFO's.* New York: William Morrow and Co., 1971. Grades 5-9.

KRIPPNER, STANLEY. "Parapsychology and Humanistic Psychology: The Educational Interface," in *Education in Parapsychology*, ed. Betty Shapin and Lisette Coly. New York: Parapsychology Foundation, 1976.

———. "Coding and Clairvoyance in a Dual-Aspect Test With Children," *Perceptual and Motor Skills*, 20 (1965), 745–48.

————. *Song of the Siren: A Parapsychological Odyssey.* New York: Harper & Row, 1975. Interesting summary and sourcebook. Much good information well-told. Useful bibliography.

————, and GARDNER MURPHY. "Parapsychology and Education," *Journal of Humanistic Psychology,* 13, no. 4 (Fall 1973), 17–20. Also in T. Roberts, ed., *Four Psychologies Applied to Education: Freudian, Behavioral, Humanistic, Transpersonal.* New York: John Wiley & Sons, 1975.

————, and R. DAVIDSON. "Paranormal Events Occurring During Chemically Induced Psychedelic Experience and Their Implications for Religion," *Journal of Altered States of Consciousness,"* 1 (1974), 175–84.

LAB-AIDS, INC., *ESP Kit No. 44,* Farmingdale, N.Y., 1967.

LANG, J. JOHN. "Scientism and Parapsychology," *Counseling and Values,* 19, no. 2 (February 1975), 91–97.

LAYTON, BRUCE D., and BILL TURNBULL. "Belief, Evaluation, and Performance on an ESP Task," *Journal of Experimental Social Psychology,* 11, no. 12 (March 1975), 166–79.

LOUWERENS, N. G. "ESP Experiments with Nursery School Children in the Netherlands," *Journal of Parapsychology,* 24 1960), 75–93.

MANNING, MATTHEW. *The Link.* New York: Ballantine, 1976.

MARCUSE, F. L., and M. E. BITTERMAN. "Classroom Demonstration of 'Psychical Phenomena,'" *Journal of Abnormal Psychology,* 39 (April 1944), 238–43.

Matthew Manning: Study of a Psychic (movie), George Ritter Films, Ltd., 2264 Lakeshore Blvd. West, Toronto, Ontario, M8V 1A9, Canada.

McBURNEY, DONALD H. "ESP in the Psychology Curriculum," *Teaching of Psychology,* 3, no. 2 (April 1976), 66–69.

McCONNELL, R. A. *ESP: A Curriculum Guide.* New York: Simon & Schuster, 1971.

MOODY, RAYMOND. *Life After Life.* New York: Bantam, 1976.

Morriss, James E. "Parapsychology in the Secondary School Curriculum," in *Education in Parapsychology,* ed. Betty Shapin and Lisette Coly. New York: Parapsychology Foundation, 1976.

Onetto, Brenio. "Education in Parapsychology: Systematic Courses or Free Experimental Research Training," in *Education in Parapsychology,* ed. Betty Shapin and Lisette Coly. New York: Parapsychology Foundation, 1976.

Overmire, T. G. "Sixth Sense: Nonsense?" *American Biology Teacher,* 23 (March 1961), 139–40.

Parapsychology Foundation, *Education in Parapsychology.* Proceedings of the 1975 International Conference of the Parapsychology Foundation, August 14-16, San Francisco. Parapsychology Foundation, New York, 1976.

Pauli, Enrique Novillo. "Parapsychological Education in Argentina," in *Education in Parapsychology,* ed. Betty Shapin and Lisette Coly. New York: Parapsychology Foundation, 1976.

Peters, R. A., et al. "Some Trials in a Case of Alleged Telepathy," *Journal of the American Society for Psychical Research,* 44, no. 738, 1968.

Peterson, James W. *Some Profiles of Non-Ordinary Perception.* M.A. Thesis, University of California, Berkeley, 1974.

————. "Extrasensory Abilities of Children: An Ignored Reality?" *Learning,* December 1975, 10–14.

Porter, Jean. *Psychic Development.* New York: Random House, 1974.

————. "From *Psychic Development,*" in *Transpersonal Education: A Curriculum for Feeling and Being,* ed. Gay Hendricks and James Fadiman. Englewood Cliffs, N.J.: Prentice-Hall, Inc., 1976.

Radford, Ruby L. *The Enchanted Hill.* Wheaton, Ill.: Theosophical Publishing House, 1968. A children's book on ESP (fictional narrative).

RANDALL, JOHN L. "Card-Guessing Experiments with Schoolboys," *Journal of the American Society for Psychical Research*, 47, no. 761 (1974), 421–32.

RAO, K. RAMAKRISHNA. "Teaching of Parapsychology in India and the Andhra Experiment," in *Education in Parapsychology*, ed. Betty Shapin and Lisette Coly. New York: Parapsychology Foundation, 1976.

RHINE, J. B. "ESP—Can It Influence Teaching?" *Education Summary*, September 12, 1959, pp. 4–5.

———. "A Review of Current Needs and Expectations," in *Education in Parapsychology*, ed. Betty Shapin and Lisette Coly. New York: Parapsychology Foundation, 1976.

RILLING, MARK E., CLARE PETTIJOHN, and JOHN Q. ADAMS. "A Two-Experimenter Investigation of Teacher-Pupil Attitudes and Clairvoyance Test Results in the High School Classroom," *Journal of Parapsychology*, 25 (December 1961), 247–59.

RIVERS, OLIVIA B. "An Exploratory Study of the Mental Health and Intelligence of ESP Subjects," *Journal of Parapsychology*, 14 (December 1950), 267–77.

ROGO, D. SCOTT. *Methods and Models for Education in Parapsychology*, Parapsychological Monograph No. 14, Parapsychology Foundation, New York, 1973.

———. "Some Criticisms of Education in Parapsychology," in *Education in Parapsychology*, ed. Betty Shapin and Lisette Coly. New York: Parapsychology Foundation, 1976.

ROLL, W. G., and J. G. PRATT. "The Miami Disturbances," *Journal of the American Society for Psychical Research*, 65, no. 4 (October 1971), 409–54. Poltergeist activity with a nineteen-year old male.

RYZL, MILAN. *How to Develop ESP in Yourself and Others*. Available from the author, Box 9459, Westgate Station, San Jose, Calif. 95157.

SANDERSON, G. D. "Educational Psychology: The Challenging Frontier," *Science Education*, 49 (December 1965), 433–46. A review of parapsychology, especially in the classroom.

———. "Report on an Experiment on the Relationship Between Teacher-Pupil Extrasensory Transfer and Letter Grades," *Science Education*, 49 (December 1965), 446–52.

SCHMEIDLER, GERTRUDE. "Recruiting for Research," in *Education in Parapsychology*, ed. Betty Shapin and Lisette Coly. New York: Parapsychology Foundation, 1976.

———. "Using ESP: Science Fiction or Applied Science," *Counseling and Values*, 19, no. 2 (February 1975), 135–40.

SCHNEIDER, JOHN E. "Mind to Mind Communication: Nonverbal Influence?" *Theory Into Practice*, October 1971, pp. 259–63.

SCHWARZ, B. E. "Telepathic Events in a Child One and Three and a Half Years of Age," *International Journal of Parapsychology*, Vol. 3/4, pp. 5–52, 1961.

———. *Parent-Child Telepathy*. New York: Garrett-Helix, 1971.

SHAPIN, BETTY and LISETTE COLY. "Education in Parapsychology." Proceedings of an International Conference Held in San Francisco, August 14–16, 1975. Parapsychology Foundation, Inc., New York, 1976.

SHERMAN, HAROLD. *Thoughts Through Space*. London: Frederick Muller, Publisher, 1971.

SHIELDS, ELOISE. "Comparison of Children's Guessing Ability (ESP) with Personality Characteristics," *Journal of Parapsychology*, 26 (1962), 200–10.

SPERLING, M. "Children's Interpretation and Reaction to the Unconscious of Their Mothers," *International Journal of Psychoanalysis*, 31 (1950), 36–41.

STANFORD, REX G. "Preparing for a Carer in Parapsychology," in *Education in Parapsychology*, ed. Betty Shapin and Lisette Coly. New York: Parapsychology Foundation, 1976.

TARG, RUSSELL, and HAROLD PUTHOFF. "Information Transmission Under Conditions of Sensory Shielding," *Nature,* October 19, 1974, pp. 602–7.

————, and DAVID B. HURT. "Use of an Automatic Stimulus Generator to Teach Extra Sensory Perception." Paper presented at the IEEE International Symposium on Information Theory, January 1972. Stanford Research Institute, Menlo Park, Calif. In T. Roberts, ed., *Four Psychologies Applied to Education: Freudian, Behavioral, Humanistic, Transpersonal.* New York: John Wiley & Co., 1975.

TART, CHARLES T., *Learning to Use Extrasensory Perception.* Chicago: University of Chicago Press, 1976.

————. *The Application of Learning Theory to ESP Performance.* Psychological Monographs, No. 15, 1975, Parapsychology Foundation, Inc., 29 West 57th St., New York, N.Y.

VAN BUSSCHBACH, J. G. "An Investigation of Extrasensory Perception in School Children," *Journal of Parapsychology,* 17 (September 1953), 210–14.

————. "A Further Report on an Investigation of ESP in School Children," *Journal of Parapsychology,* 19 (June 1955), 73–81.

————. "An Investigation of ESP Between Teacher and Pupils in American Schools," *Journal of Parapsychology,* 20 (June 1956), 71–80.

————. "An Investigation of ESP in the First and Second Grades of Dutch Schools," *Journal of Parapsychology,* 23 (December 1959), 227–37.

VAN DE CASTLE, R. L. "A Review of ESP Tests Carried Out in the Classroom," *International Journal of Parapsychology,* 1 (Autumn 1959), 84–99.

————. "The Cuna Indians of Panama," *Journal of Communication,* 25, no. 1 (Winter 1975), 183–90.

VASSE, C., and P. VASSE. "ESP Tests with French First Grade School Children," *Psychological Abstracts,* 33, item 9768 (1959), 947.

WHITE, RHEA A., "The Role of the Library in Education for Parapsychology," in *Education in Parapsychology,* ed. Betty Shapin and Lisette Coly. New York: Parapsychology Foundation, 1976.

————. *Surveys in Parapsychology: Reviews of the Literature with Updated Bibliographies.* Metuchen, N.J.: Scarecrow Press. Due late 1975 or early 1976.

————, and JEAN ANGSTADT. "A Resume of Research at the A.S.P.R. into Teacher-Pupil Attitudes and Clairvoyance Test Results, 1959–1960," *Journal of the American Society for Psychical Research,* 55 (October 1961), 142–48.

————, and JEAN ANGSTADT. "A Review of Results and New Experiments Bearing on Teacher-Selection Methods in the Anderson-White High School Experiments," *Journal of the American Society for Psychical Research,* Vol. LIX, no. 1, January 1965.

————, and L. DALE. *Parapsychology: Sources of Information,* Metuchen, N.J.: Scarecrow Press, 1973. Annotated bibliography of 282 books on parapsychology.

WILLIAMS, CHESTER S. "Psi and the School." East Texas State University, Texarkana.

Readings Recommended by the Education Department, American Society for Psychical Research

* BELOFF, JOHN. "The Study of the Paranormal as an Educative Experience," *Parapsychology Review,* November/December 1975.

* CHILD, IRVIN L. "Parapsychology in the Liberal Arts Curriculum," *Parapsychology Review,* March/April 1976.

FEWKES, REV. RICHARD. "Parapsychology and Religion" (Curriculum Kit). Unitarian Universalist Psi Symposium at Old Ship Church, Hingham, Mass. Junior high through adult. Slides, games, tests, discussion tools. Rev. Fewkes, 644 Main Street, Norwell, Mass. 02061. $15.

HONORTON, CHARLES. "Parapsychology and Education—circa 1972: An Appreciation of McConnell's *ESP Curriculum Guide,*" *Journal of the American Society for Psychical Research,* October 1972.

RHINE, LOUISA. *Manual for Introductory Experiments in Parapsychology,* Institute for Parapsychology, College Station, Box 6847, Durham, N.C. 27708. $1.

ROBINSON, DIANA. "Planning a Course in Parapsychology," *Parapsychology Review,* November/December 1973.

ROGO, D. SCOTT. "A Guide to Juvenile Literature on Parapsychology," *Parapsychological Review,* May/June 1976.

———. *Methods and Models for Education in Parapsychology.* Parapsychological Monographs No. 14. Parapsychology Foundation, 1973.

———. "Three Approaches to the Teaching of Parapsychology," *Parapsychology Review,* January/February 1972.

SCHINDLER, HELEN. "My Introduction to Parapsychology (As a Student)," *Parapsychology Review,* March/April 1974.

* SCHMEIDLER, GERTRUDE R. "Recruiting for Research," *Parapsychology Review,* January/February 1976.

SHIELDS, ELOISE. "12 Tapes of Introductory Talks on Parapsychology for Junior and Senior High School Students and Teachers." Speed Cassette Duplication, P.O. Box 337, Manhattan Beach, Calif. 90266.

* VAUGHAN, ALAN. "(Overview) Education in Parapsychology," *Parapsychology Review,* November/December 1975.

YARD, ILA Z. "Birth of a New Psi Research Association," *Parapsychology Review,* November/December 1971.

* Items marked with asterisk will be combined and available in:

Education in Parapsychology. Proceedings of 1975 International Conference by the Parapsychology Foundation, August 14–16, San Francisco. Parapsychology Foundation, Fall 1976.

For additional information and the latest news in parapsychology and education, write:

Education Department
American Society for Psychical Research
5 West 73rd Street
New York, N.Y. 10023

PHYSICAL EDUCATION, BODY TECHNIQUES, YOGA, SPORTS, AND HEALTH

Academy of Parapsychology and Medicine. *The Dimensions of Healing.* Los Altos, Calif., 1974.

Academy of Parapsychology and Medicine. *The Varieties of Healing Experience: A Symposium.* Los Altos, Calif., 1974.

ADLER, CHARLES S., and SHEILA MORRISSEY ADLER. "The Pragmatic Application of Biofeedback to Headaches—A Five-Year Clinical Follow-Up." Paper presented at the Seventh Annual Meeting of the Biofeedback Research Society, Colorado Springs, February 27–March 2, 1976. Reprint available from Biofeedback Research Society.

Ananda Marga Publications, *Teaching Asanas: An Ananda Marga Manual for Teachers.* Los Altos Hills, Calif.: Ananda Marga (27160 Moody Road).

AUROBINDO, SRI, and the MOTHER. *On Physical Education.* Mt. Tremper, N.Y.: Matagiri.

CARR, RACHEL. *Be a Frog, a Bird or a Tree: Creative Yoga Exercises for Children.* Garden City: N.Y.: Doubleday and Co., 1973.

CERUTTY, PERCY WELLS. *Essays on Sport and Life.* San Francisco: Lodestar Press, 1973.

CHAMPION, BABA RICK. *Yoga Tennis: Awareness Through Sports.* A.S.I.A., Inc., Suite 11, 2803 North 7th Ave., Phoenix, Ariz., 85007, 1973.

CLEMENTS, WARREN. "Yoga May Offer Hope for Disturbed Children," *The Montreal Star,* July 19, 1972, p. G–1.

COLLETTO, JERRY, with JACK L. SLOAN. *Yoga Conditioning and Football.* Celestial Arts, 231 Adrian Road, California, 94030, 1975.

CRISWELL, ELEANOR. "Experimental Yoga Course for College Students: A Progress Report," *Journal of Transpersonal Psychology,* 2, no. 1 (1970), 71–78.

————, and MARYELLEN HAIGHT. "Biofeedback and Education," *Somatics,* 1, no. 1, Fall 1976.

DEVRIES, HERBERT A., "Physical Education, Adult Fitness Programs: Does Physical Activity Promote Relaxation? *Journal of Physical Education and Recreation,* 46, no. 7 (September 1975), 53–54.

DONATH, A. M. DUBACK. *The Basic Principles of Eurythmy.* Spring Valley, N.Y.: Anthroposophic Press (Rudolf Steiner—Waldorf Education).

DOUST, DUDLEY. "Tony Jacklin—Mystical Perception in Sport," *The (London) Sunday Times,* April 1970, pp. 32–33.

FELDENKRAIS, MOSHE. *Awareness Through Movement.* New York: Harper & Row, 1972.

————. *Body and Mature Behavior: A Study of Anxiety, Sex,*

Gravitation, and Learning. New York: International University Press, 1949.

FRUHLING, M., J. V. BASMAJIAN, and T. G. SIMARD. "A Note on the Conscious Control of Motor Units by Children Under Six," *Journal of Motor Behavior,* 1 (1969), 65.

GALLWEY, W. TIMOTHY. *The Inner Game of Tennis.* New York: Random House, 1974.

GREEN, ELMER E., ALYCE GREEN, and E. DALE WALTERS. "Biofeedback for Mind-Body Self-Regulation, Healing and Creativity." Paper given at symposium *The Varieties of Healing Experience,* DeAnza College, Cupertino, Calif., sponsored by the Academy of Parapsychology and Medicine and by Lockheed Missile and Space Corp. Research Department, The Menninger Foundation, Topeka.

HARI DAS, BABA and L. CONTE. *Yoga Is Love Coloring Book.* Lakemont, Ga.: CSA Press.

HENDERSON, JOSEPH. *Thoughts On The Run,* P.O. Box 366, Mountain View, Calif., 1970. Cross-country running.

HOUTS, JO ANN. "Feeling and Perception in the Sport Experience," *Journal of Health, Physical Education, and Recreation,* 41, no. 8 (October 1970), 71–72.

HUDDLESTON, O. "Flexibility Exercises for Physical Fitness," *Archives of Physical Medicine and Rehabilitation,* 45 (1964), 581–84.

JACKSON, IAN. *Yoga and the Athlete.* Mountain View, Calif.: World Publications, 1975.

JACOBSON, GARY. "Coach Endorses TM for that Better Dive, 'It's a Means of Resting,' " (University of) *Minnesota Daily,* Tuesday, January 9, 1973.

KASER-CANNON, LINDA. "P.E. Inside Out: What to Do Until the Biofeedback Machine Arrives." Mimeographed. Faculty of Education, Simon Fraser University, Burnaby, B.C. Canada, V5A 1S6. Undated.

KHANNA, YOGIRAJ SHRI. *Yoga for Children (and Parents)*. Newton, Mass.: Maha Yoga Publications, 1974.

KISS, MICHAELINE. *Yoga for Young People*. New York: Pocket Books, 1973.

KOTSES, HARRY, *et al.* "The Effect of Operant Conditioning of the Frontalis Muscle on Peak Expiratory Flow in Asthmatic Children." Paper presented at the Seventh Annual Meeting of the Biofeedback Research Society, Colorado Springs, February 27–March 2, 1976. Reprint available from Biofeedback Research Society.

LEONARD, GEORGE. "Why Johnny Can't Run," *The Atlantic Monthly*, August 1975a, pp. 55–60.

——. "Physical Education for Life," *Today's Education*, September–October 1975b, pp. 75–76.

——. *The Ultimate Athlete*. New York: Viking, 1975c.

——. "Why Johnny Can't Run: And Other Gym Class Scandals," in *Transpersonal Education: A Curriculum for Feeling and Being*, ed. Gay Hendricks and James Fadiman. Englewood Cliffs, N.J.: Prentice-Hall, Inc., 1976.

LUND, MORTEN. "Inner Skier: A New Way of Learning," Part 1, *SKI*, November 1975, pp. 74–76, 135, 137; Part 2, December 1975, pp. 90–92.

MASTERS, ROBERT. "The Psychophysical Experience," *Saturday Review*, February 22, 1975, pp. 30–31.

McKINNEY, WAYNE C., and PHYLLIS FORD, "What Is the Professional Doing About Education for Leisure?" *Journal of Health, Physical Education, and Recreation*, 43, no. 5 (May 1972), 49–53.

MURPHY, MICHAEL. *Golf In The Kingdom*. New York: Viking, 1972.

——. "Sport as Yoga: Altered States of Consciousness and Extraordinary Powers," *The Esalen Catalog*, October–December 1974, pp. 4–7.

————, and JOHN BRODIE. "I Experience a Kind of Clarity," *Intellectual Digest*, 3, no. 5 (January 1973), 19–22.

National Council on Wholistic Therapeutics in Medicine. *Healing Source Contact Directory.* New York: Doubleday and Co., due 1977.

New Games Foundation. *New Games Book.* San Francisco (P.O. Box 7901).

RAPPAPORT, BERNARD S. "Carnal Knowledge: What the Wisdom of the Body Has to Offer Psychotherapy," *Journal of Humanistic Psychology,* 15, no. 1 (Winter 1975), 49–70.

REICH, LEONARD. "Try Not to Think About It," *Runner's World Magazine,* February 1974, p. 17.

RICHARD, MICHAEL. "Attention Training: A Pilot Program in the Development of Autonomic Control," *Contemporary Education,* 43, no. 3 (January 1972), 57–60. Also in T. Roberts, ed., *Four Psychologies Applied to Education: Freudian, Behavioral, Humanistic, Transpersonal.* New York: John Wiley & Sons, 1975.

ROHE, FRED. *The Zen of Running.* New York: Random House; Bookworks, Berkeley, 1974.

SCHOFIELD, LEON J., JR., and STEPHANIE ABBHUL. "The Stimulation of Insight and Self-Awareness through Body-Movement Exercise," *Journal of Clinical Psychology,* 31, no. 4 (October 1975), 745–46.

SEREDA, LYNN. "Inner Voyage." Vancouver, B.C.: Light-House Publications, 1975.

————. "Inner Voyage," 2 phonograph records. Radha Record Pressings Ltd., P.O. Box 2199, Burnaby, B.C., Canada, V6B–3V7.

SHEALY, C. NORMAN. "Biogenic Technique in Management of Pain." Paper presented at the Seventh Annual Meeting of the Biofeedback Research Society, Colorado Springs, February 27–March 2, 1976. Reprint available from Biofeedback Research Society.

SHUTZ, WILLIAM C. "Education and the Body," in *Transpersonal Education: A Curriculum for Feeling and Being,* ed. Gay Hendricks and James Fadiman. Englewood Cliffs, N.J.: Prentice-Hall, Inc., 1976.

SMITH, ADAM. "Sport Is a Western Yoga," *Psychology Today,* October 1975, pp. 48–51, 74, 76.

SPINO, MIKE. *Beyond Jogging: The Innerspaces of Running.* Millbrae, Calif.: Celestial Arts, 1976.

VAN BATHNER, F. *Gymnastic Education.* Spring Valley, N.Y.: Anthroposophic Press (Rudolf Steiner–Waldorf Education).

WALLACE, J. MACDONALD. "Health Education in the Field of Adult Education," *Adult Education* (London), 47, no. 1 (May 1974), 10–16.

ZEBROFF, KAREEN, and PETER ZEBROFF. *Yoga for Happier Children.* Vancouver, B.C.: Fforbez Enterprises, Ltd.

ZWAIG, MARILYN S. *Yoga for Children of All Ages.* Phonograph record. Marilyn Zwaig Rossner, 3949 St. Antoine St., Montreal, Quebec, Canada.

RELAXATION

BECHTEL, JAMES E., and REGIS MCNAMARA. "Relaxation as a Factor in Semantic Desensitization," *Journal of Consulting and Clinical Psychology,* 43, no. 6 (December 1975), 925.

BENSON, HERBERT, JOHN F. BEARY, and MARK P. CAROL. "The Relaxation Response," *Psychiatry,* 37, no. 1 (February 1974), 37–46.

BERNSTEIN, D. A., and T. D. BORKOVER. *Progressive Relaxation*

Training: A Manual for the Helping Professions. Champaign, Ill.: Research Press, 1975.

CHANG-LIANG, R., and D. R. DENNEY. "Applied Relaxation as Training in Self-Control," *Journal of Counseling Psychology,* 23 (May 1976), 163–89.

COURSEY, ROBERT D. "Electromyograph Feedback as a Relaxation Technique," *Journal of Consulting and Clinical Psychology,* 43, no. 6 (December 1975), 825–33.

EDWARDS, MARIGOLD A. "The Role of Tension Control in Education." Paper presented at the First Meeting of the American Association for the Advancement of Tension Control, October 12-13, 1974, Chicago, Ill. University of Pittsburgh, Pittsburgh, Penn. 15213.

ELLIOT, JAMES. "ESP and Relaxation," *Personal Growth,* no. 21 (1974), 13–17.

FORBES, D. S., and S. T. LIFRAK. "Psycho-aquanetics: Water Relaxation Approach," *Journal of Physical Education and Recreation,* 47 (June 1976), 52–53.

FREDERICK, A. B. "Biofeedback and Tension Control," *Journal of Physical Education and Recreation,* 46 (October 1975), 25–28.

————, ed. "A Brief Report of Solicited and Contributed Papers." Proceedings of the First Meeting of the American Association for the Advancement of Tension Control, October 12-13, 1974, Chicago, Ill. In McGuigan, F. J., ed., *Tension Control.* Blacksburg, Va.: University Publications, 1975.

————. "The Literature of Tension—A Selected List," Mimeographed. Department of Physical Education, University of Wisconsin, Superior, Wisc. 54880.

————. "Relaxation: A Fourth 'R' for Education," ERIC, ED-106-261, 1975.

GOLFRIED, MARVIN R., and CHRISTINE S. TRIER. "Effectiveness of Relaxation as an Active Coping Skill," *Journal of Abnormal Psychology,* 83, no. 4 (August 1974), 348–55.

LINDUFF, FLORENCE S. "Scientific Relaxation." Mimeographed. University of Colorado Medical Center, Department of Physical Medicine, Denver, undated.

LUPIN, MIMI, LENDELL W. BRAUD, WILLIAM BRAUD, and WILLIAM F. DUER. "Effects of Relaxation Tapes Upon Children and Their Parents," *Academic Therapy*. Forthcoming.

MARSHALL, MICHAEL, and CHARLES BEACH. "Method for Incorporating Tension Control into the Elementary School Curriculum," in *Proceedings of the Second Meeting of the American Association for the Advancement of Tension Control*, 1976.

————. "Tension Control at Michigan State University." Paper presented to the American Association for the Advancement of Tension Control, October 12, 1974.

MEYER, ROBERT G., and ROSEANNE REED. "Reduction of Test Anxiety Via Autogenic Therapy," *Psychological Reports*, 35, no. 1, Part 2 (August 1974), 649–50.

NDLOVU, SIKHANYISO D. "Role of Educational Behavioral Objectives in Tension Control: The Affective and Psychomotor Domains." Paper presented at the First Meeting of the American Association for the Advancement of Tension Control, October 12-13, 1974, Chicago. Upstate Medical Center, Syracuse University, Syracuse, New York.

O'NEIL, HAROLD F., JR., *et al.* "The Effects of Anxiety Reduction Techniques on Anxiety and Computer-Assisted Learning and Evaluation of College Students: Final Report," ERIC, ED-076-060, December 1972.

O'ROURKE, ROBERT. "Yes, We *Can* Help Kids Relax," *Learning*, 5, no. 4 (December 1976), 24–25.

PAUL, GORDON L. "Physiological Effects of Relaxation Training and Hypnotic Suggestion," *Journal of Abnormal Psychology*, 74, no. 4 (August 1969), 425–37.

SHOWERS, MARIAN, and C. TIMOTHY DICKEL. "Recognition and Treatment of Tension in the Elementary School Child." In

Proceedings of the Second Meeting of the American Association for the Advancement of Tension Control, University Publications, Blacksburg, Va., 1976.

STEINHOUS, ARTHUR H., and JEANNE E. NORRIS. "Teaching Neuromuscular Relaxation." ERIC, ED-003-278, 1964.

STOUDENMIRE, JOHN. "A Comparison of Muscle Relaxation Training and Music in the Reduction of State and Trait Anxiety," *Journal of Clinical Psychology,* 31, no. 3 (July 1975), 490–92.

STROUGHAN, JAMES H., and W. HENRY DUFORT. "Task Difficulty, Relaxation, and Anxiety Level During Verbal Learning and Recall," *Journal of Abnormal Psychology,* 74, no. 5 (October 1969), 621–24.

VOLPE, RICHARD. "Feedback Facilitated Relaxation Training in School Counseling," *Canadian Counsellor,* 9, no. 3/4 (June 1975), 202–12.

RELIGIOUS SCHOOLS AND SPIRITUAL DEVELOPMENT

A Course in Miracles. Huntington Station, N.Y.: Coleman Graphics (One Huntington Quadrangle).

ABDULLAH, RAMJOO. *Sobs and Throbs: Sufism Reoriented.* (1300 Boulevard Way, Walnut Creek, Calif.) Out of print. An account of the Prem Ashram, a school for children set up by Meher Baba in the 1920's.

ALLEN, PAUL, ed. *Rudolf Steiner's Curative Education.* Spring Valley, N.Y.: Anthroposophic Press (Rudolf Steiner–Waldorf Education).

AUROBINDO, SRI. "A National System of Education—Some Preliminary Ideas." Pamphlet. Pondicherry, India: Sri Aurobindo Ashram, 1970.

————. *The Human Cycle.* Mt. Tremper, N.Y.: Matagiri, 1971.

————, and the MOTHER. *On Education.* Mt. Tremper, Matagiri.

————. *Centenary Booklets on Education.* Mt. Tremper, N.Y.: Matagiri.

AUROBINDO, SRI SOCIETY. *Sri Aurobindo and the Mother on Education.* Three pamphlets. Pondicherry, India, 1972.

BAILEY, ALICE A. *Education in the New Age.* Pamphlet adapted from book of the same title. New York: World Goodwill, 1954.

————. *Education in the New Age.* New York: Lucis Publishing Co., 1971.

BARAVALLE, HERMAN. *The Waldorf Plan.* Spring Valley, N.Y.: Anthroposophic Press (Rudolf Steiner–Waldorf Education).

BARBANELL, SYLVIA. *When A Child Dies.* London: Spiritualist Press, 1942.

BERENDS, POLLY BERRIEN. *Whole Child—Whole Parent—A Spiritual and Practical Guide to the First Four Years of Parenthood.* New York: Harper's Magazine Press, 1975. A resource guide for children's literature and toys.

BHATTACHARYA, P. K. *A Scheme of Education.* Mt. Tremper, N.Y.: Matagiri.

CAPRIO, BETSY. "Experiments in Spiritual Growth," *a.d. correspondence: Personal Reflections On Catholic Life,* pp. 2–6, July 19, 1975.

————. *Experiments in Growth.* Notre Dame, Ind.: Ave Maria Press, 1976.

CHINMOY, SRI. *Siddhartha Becomes the Buddha: A Book of Spiritual Plays* (for children). New York: Sky Publishers, 1973.

CLARK, WALTER HOUSTON, et al. *Religious Experience: Its Nature and Function in the Human Psyche.* Springfield, Ill.: Charles C Thomas, 1973.

Dowsett, Norman C., and Dr. Sita Ram Jayaswal. *Education of the Child.* Pondicherry, India: Sri Aurobindo Society, 1974.

Edmunds, Francis. *Rudolf Steiner Education.* Spring Valley, N.Y.: Anthroposophic Press (Rudolf Steiner–Waldorf Education).

Hartman, David T. "Expanding Our Teaching," *Church Teachers,* November 1976, pp. 14–15.

Harwood, A. C. *The Recovery of Man in Childhood. A Study in the Educational Work of Rudolf Steiner.* London: Hodder and Stoughton, 1958. Also Spring Valley, N.Y.: Anthroposophic Press.

Jordan, Daniel C., and Donald T. Streets. "Guiding the Process of Becoming: The ANISA Theories of Curriculum and Teaching," *World Order,* 7, no. 4 (Summer 1973), 29–41.

————. "The ANISA Model," *World Order,* Spring 1972. Bahai work in forming a holistic educational model.

Joshi, Kireet, and Yvonne Artaud. *Exploration in Education.* Mt. Tremper, N.Y.: Matagiri, 1974.

————. *Exploration in Education: Two Essays.* Pondicherry, India: Sri Aurobindo, Ashram, 1974.

Kahn, Sufi Inayat. *Education from Before Birth to Maturity.* London: Sufi Publishing Co., 1974.

Kalinowski, Michael F., and Daniel C. Jordan. "Being and Becoming: The ANISA Theory of Development," *World Order,* 7, no. 4 (Summer 1973), 17–28. (World Order, a Baha'i magazine: 415 Linden Ave., Wilmette, Ill. 60091.) ANISA Model work is centered at the University of Massachusetts in Amherst. Write Daniel C. Jordan, School of Education, University of Massachusetts, Amherst.

Keller-Von Asten, H. *Encounter with the Infinite: Projective Geometry.* Spring Valley, N.Y.: Anthroposophic Press (Rudolf Steiner–Waldorf Education).

KENNET, JIYU ROSHI. "The Education of the Buddhist Child," in *Transpersonal Education: A Curriculum for Feeling and Being,* ed. Gay Hendricks and James Fadiman. Englewood Cliffs, N.J.: Prentice-Hall, Inc., 1976.

KETTLEKAMP, LARRY. *Religions East and West.* New York: William Morrow and Co., 1972. Grades 4-6.

KYBER, MANFRED. *The Three Candles of Little Veronica—The Story of a Child's Soul in This World and the Other.* Garden City, N.Y.: The Waldorf Institute for Liberal Education, 1972.

THE MOTHER (Mira Richard). *Ideal Child.* Mt. Tremper, N.Y.: Matagiri.

MUKHERJEE, H. B. *Education for Fullness: A Study of the Educational Thought and Experiment of Rabindranath Tagore.* London: Asia Publishing House. An account of Santineketan, a children's school set up near Calcutta by Tagore during the early part of this century.

OGLETREE, EARL J. "Rudolf Steiner: Unknown Educator," *Elementary School Journal,* 74, no. 6 (March 1974), 344–52.

————, JOHN A. RACKAUKAS, and THEO BUERGEN. "Waldorf Education for the Disadvantaged Child," In E. Ogletree, ed., *The Socially Disadvantaged,* Vol. II, pp. 233–45. MSS Information Corp., New York, 1974.

————. "The Socially Disadvantaged: A Rationale and New Concept of Human Development." In E. Ogletree, ed., *The Socially Disadvantaged,* Vol. II, pp. 141–75. MSS Information Corporation, New York, 1974.

PERCEVAL, H. W. "The Child, Mother, Where Did I Come From? and How to Help the Child Remember." Part II of *Man and Woman and Child.* New York: The World Publishing Co., 1951.

PETERS, FRITZ. *Boyhood with Gurdjieff.* Baltimore: Penguin, 1972.

PIETZNER, CARLO, ed. *Aspects of Curative Education.* Spring Valley, N.Y.: Anthroposophic Press (Rudolf Steiner–Waldorf Education).

PROGOFF, IRA. *The Well and the Cathedral, The White Robed Monk, The Star/Cross* (3 books). New York: Dialogue House, 1971.

RAIZIZUN, MAY M. *Your Own Little Elf*. Quest Book for Children. Wheaton, Ill.: Theosophical Publishing House, 1969.

RICHARD, MIRA (see Mother)

ROSICRUCIAN FELLOWSHIP. *Rosicrucian Principles of Child Training*. Oceanside, Calif. (222 Mission Ave., P.O. Box 713, 92054).

———. *Horoscopes of Children*. Vol. I and Vol. II. Oceanside, Calif.

———. *Aquarian Age Stories for Children*. Vols. 1-6. Oceanside, Calif.

SANFORD, J. A. "Jesus, Paul, and Death Psychology," *Religious Education*, 68 (November 1973), 673–89.

SOCIETY OF BROTHERS, ed. *Children in Community*. Rifton, N.Y.: Plough Publishing House, 1975.

Spiritual Community Guide. The Clarity of Children, pp. 108–9. San Rafael, Calif.: Spiritual Community Press, 1972.

SPIRITUAL COMMUNITY PUBLICATIONS. *A Pilgrim's Guide to the Planet Earth*. Box 1080, San Rafael, Calif. 94902.

———. *The Spiritual Community Guide for North America, 1975-1976*, Box 1080, San Rafael, Calif. 94902.

"Spiritual Education–Two Public School Teachers Take a Look at Gurukula," *Back to Godhead*, Vol. 10, no. 11.

STEINER, RUDOLF. *Art of Education*. Spring Valley, N.Y.: Anthroposophic Press (Rudolf Steiner–Waldorf Education).

————. *Education and Modern Spiritual Life.* Spring Valley, N.Y.: Anthroposophic Press (Rudolf Steiner—Waldorf Education).

————. *Curative Education.* Spring Valley, N.Y.: Anthroposophic Press.

————. *Education and Modern Spiritual Life.* Spring Valley, N.Y.: Anthroposophic Press (Rudolf Steiner—Waldorf Education).

————. *Eurythmy as Visible Speech.* Spring Valley, N.Y.: Anthroposophic Press (Rudolf Steiner—Waldorf Education).

————. *Lectures to Teachers.* Spring Valley, N.Y.: Anthroposophic Press (Rudolf Steiner—Waldorf Education).

————. *Practical Course for Teachers.* Spring Valley, N.Y.: Anthroposophic Press (Rudolf Steiner—Waldorf Education).

————. *Roots of Education.* Spring Valley, N.Y.: Anthroposophic Press (Rudolf Steiner—Waldorf Education).

————. *Spiritual Ground of Education.* Spring Valley, N.Y.: Anthroposophic Press (Rudolf Steiner—Waldorf Education).

————. *Study of Man.* Spring Valley, N.Y.: Anthroposophic Press (Rudolf Steiner—Waldorf Education).

————. *The Essentials of Education.* Spring Valley, N.Y.: Anthroposophic Press (Rudolf Steiner—Waldorf Education).

————, *et al. Education as an Art.* Blauvelt, N.Y.: Rudolf Steiner Pub. Co., 1970.

————, WALLACE, and HARWOOD. *Eurythmy.* Spring Valley, N.Y.: Anthroposophic Press (Rudolf Steiner—Waldorf Education).

————. *Discussions with Teachers.* London: Rudolf Steiner Press, 1967.

————. *Education as a Social Problem.* Spring Valley, N.Y.: Anthroposophic Press, 1969.

————. *The Education of the Child in the Light of Anthroposophy.* London: Rudolf Steiner Press, 1965.

————. *Human Values in Education.* London: Rudolf Steiner Press, 1971.

————. *The Kingdom of Childhood.* London: Rudolf Steiner Press, 1974. Also Spring Valley, N.Y.: Anthroposophic Press, 1974.

————. *A Modern Art of Education.* London: Rudolf Steiner Press, 1972.

————. *The Younger Generation. Educational and Spiritual Impulses for Life in the Twentieth Century.* Spring Valley, N.Y.: Anthroposophic Press, 1967.

STEINER, RUDOLF PRESS. (35 Park Rd., London NW1 6XT). "The Spiritual Ground of Education" (9 lectures); "The Kingdom of Childhood" (7 lectures); and "The Essentials of Education" (5 lectures). 1974.

VON ARNIM, GEORG. "Imitation and the Body-Scheme," *The Cresset,* 13, no. 4 (1967), 15–31. Reprinted in Earl J. Ogletree ed., *The Socially Disadvantaged,* Vol. II. MSS Information Corp., New York, 1974.

WILCOX, MARY, and JAMES S. WHITT. "Is the Church Teaching Both Sides of the Brain?" *Church Teachers,* 3, no. 5 (April 1976).

WILKINSON, RAY. *Questions and Answers on Waldorf Education.* Spring Valley, N.Y.: Anthroposophic Press (Rudolf Steiner —Waldorf Education).

WOLKISER, DONICA. "My Life in the Steiner Schools," *East/West Journal,* 4, no. 8 (September 1974), 10–12.

YOGANANDA, PARAMAHANSA. *Autobiography of a Yogi.* "Founding a Yoga School at Ranchi" and "Rabindranath Tagore and I Compare Schools," pp. 237–308. Los Angeles: Self-Realization Fellowship, 1973.

SCIENCE AND MATHEMATICS

AREHART-TREICHEL, JOAN. "The Mind-Body Link," *Science News*, 108, no. 25/26 (December 1, 1975), 394–95.

BARAVALLE, HERMAN. *Geometric Drawing and the Waldorf Plan*. Spring Valley, N.Y.: Anthroposophic Press (Rudolf Steiner —Waldorf Education).

————. *Introduction to Astronomy in the Waldorf School*. Spring Valley, N.Y.: Anthroposophic Press (Rudolf Steiner—Waldorf Education).

————. *Introduction to Physics in the Waldorf School*. Spring Valley, N.Y.: Anthroposophic Press (Rudolf Steiner—Waldorf Education).

————. *The Teaching of Arithmetic and The Waldorf Plan*. Spring Valley, N.Y.: Anthroposophic Press (Rudolf Steiner —Waldorf Education).

BLATT, F. J. "Nerve Impulses in Plants," *Physics Teacher*, 12, no. 8 (November 1974), 455–64.

FRANKLIN, WILBUR. "The Role of Paraphysics in Physics Education," in *Education in Parapsychology*, ed. Betty Shapin and Lisette Coly. New York: Parapsychology Foundation, 1976.

FROLICH, MARGARET. *Form Designing*. Spring Valley, N.Y.: Anthroposophic Press (Rudolf Steiner—Waldorf Education).

GREEN, ELMER, and ALYCE GREEN. "The Ins and Outs of Mind-Body Energy," *Science Year, 1974: World Book Science Annual*. Chicago: Field Enterprises Educational Corp. In T. Roberts, ed., *Four Psychologies Applied to Education: Freudian, Behavioral, Humanistic, Transpersonal*. New York: John Wiley & Sons, 1975.

HAWKHILL ASSOCIATES. *Spaceship Earth.* Black Earth, Wisc.: Hawkhill Associates, 1973. Six sound cassettes and filmstrips providing a oneness approach to space-science-ecology. Beautifully inspiring as well as instructive.

KETTLEKAMP, LARRY. *Astrology. Wisdom of the Stars.* New York: William Morrow and Co., 1973. Grades 4-6.

KING, MARJORIE. "Individualized Instruction in Continuation High School: Brainwave Biofeedback as a Science Lesson." Paper prepared for presentation at the First Area Convention, National Science Teachers Association, December 2, 1972, San Diego.

KOESTLER, ARTHUR. "The Word and the Vision," from *The Act of Creation,* pp. 169–73. New York: Dell Publishing Co., 1967. Also in T. Roberts, ed., *Four Psychologies Applied to Education: Freudian, Behavioral, Humanistic, Transpersonal.* New York: John Wiley & Sons, 1975.

LAMB, J. E., "Space Biology: Bringing the Far Out into Focus," *Science Teacher,* 43 (September 1976), 19–21.

LOASE, J. F. "Extrasensory Probability," *Mathematics Teacher,* 69, (February 1976), 116–18.

LUCE, GAY GAER. *Body Time.* New York: Bantam, 1971. Sections on body rhythms of children, pp. 102–15.

McCONNELL, R. A. "ESP and Credibility in Science," *The American Psychologist,* 24, no. 5 (1969), 531–38.

———. "Parapsychology vs. the Occult," *Science Teacher,* 40, no. 2 (February 1973), 13.

McPHAIL, HARTWELL. "Biorhythm." ERIC, ED–115–592.

NICHOLSON, SHIRLEY J. *Nature's Merry-Go-Round.* Quest book for Children. Wheaton, Ill.: Theosophical Publishing House, 1969. A transpersonal book of science experiments (cycles of life, etc)

RAYMO, CHESTER. "Science as Play," *Science Education*, 57, no. 3 (July–September 1973), 279–89.

SAMPLES, ROBERT E. "Get Out and Learn," *Earth Science Education Project Newsletter*, No. 1, September 1970.

———. "Notes on Teaching Science," *Science and Children*, 5, no. 6 (March 1968), 28–30.

SELYE, HANS. *From Dream to Discovery, On Being a Scientist*, p. 47. New York: McGraw-Hill, 1975.

Social Science Education Consortium. *Proceedings of the Invitational Conference "Ways of Knowing: Is Science on the Defensive?"* June 13–14, 1975, University of Denver. ChESS, 855 Broadway, Boulder, Colo. Forthcoming.

SELF-CONCEPT, VALUES, AND PSYCHOSYNTHESIS

ASSAGIOLI, ROBERTO. "The Education of Gifted and Super-Gifted Children." Psychosynthesis Research Foundation, New York, 1960.

———. "Smiling Wisdom." Issue no. 4, Psychosynthesis Research Foundation, New York.

———. "The Technique of Evocative Words" (with set of cards). Issue no. 25, Psychosynthesis Research Foundation, New York.

———. "Life as a Game and State Performance (Role-Playing) Cheerfulness (A Psychosynthetic Technique)." Issue no. 33, Psychosynthesis Research Foundation, New York, 1971.

BROWN, GEORGE ISAAC. "I Have Things To Tell," Psychosynthesis Research Foundation, Report No. 4, New York.

Canadian Institute of Psychosynthesis, Inc., 3496 Ave. Marlowe,

260 Montreal, Quebec, H4A–3L7. (1) "Exercises on the Subpersonalities." (2) "The Ideal Model." (3) "The Evening Review." (4) "On Keeping a Psychological Notebook or Log." (5) "Publication List."

CANFIELD, JACK. "Psychosynthesis and Education," in *Humanistic Education Yearbook—1975*, ed. J. Ballard and T. Timmerman. Also available separately. Institute for Humanistic and Transpersonal Education, P.O. Box 575, Amherst, Mass., 1976.

———— and HAROLD WELLS. *100 Ways to Raise Self-Concept in the Classroom.* Englewood Cliffs, N.J.: Prentice-Hall, 1976.

CRAMPTON, MARTHA. "Some Applications of Psychosynthesis in the Educational Field." Speech before the Psychosynthesis Seminars 1971–1972 Series. Psychosynthesis Research Foundation, New York. In T. Roberts, ed., *Four Psychologies Applied to Education: Freudian, Behavioral, Humanistic, Transpersonal.* New York: John Wiley & Sons, 1975.

DREWS, E. M. "The Four Faces of Able Adolescents." Psychosynthesis Research Foundation, Report No. 9.

JOHNSON, RICHARD K., and ROBERT G. MEYER. "The Locus of Control Construct in EEG Alpha Feedback," *Journal of Consulting and Clinical Psychology*, 42, no. 6 (December 1974), 913.

KRIPPNER, STANLEY, and R. BLICKENSTAFF. "The Development of Self-Concept as Part of an Arts Workshop for the Gifted," *Gifted Child Quarterly*, 14, no. 3 (1970), 163–66.

MASLOW, ABRAHAM. *Toward a psychology of being.* New York: Van Nostrand Reinhold, 1968.

MASTRIANO, DONALD J. *The Design, Implementation, and Evaluation of a Workshop in Self-Identification as Taught in Psychosynthesis.* Unpublished Doctoral Dissertation, University of Massachusetts, 1973.

THOMAS, HOBART F. "Education for Self-Awareness." Psychosynthesis Research Foundation, Issue No. 20, New York.

SPECIAL EDUCATION

Angie Hall Hospital for Learning Disabilities. "Alpha Biofeedback Training as a Behavior Modifier in Hyperkinetic Children with Learning Disabilities." Mimeo. Beaumont, Tex., 1972.

Brain/Mind Bulletin. "Hyperkinetic Syndrome Improved by Biofeedback of Sensorimotor EEG," 1, no. 21A (September 20, 1976), 1, 3.

CLEMENT, PAUL W. "Elimination of Sleepwalking in a Seven Year Old Boy," *Journal of Consulting and Clinical Psychology*, 34, no. 1 (February 1970), 22–26.

CONLEY, DANIEL P., RICHARD BESSERMAN, and JOSEPH F. KIFSCHVINK. "Electromyography (EMG) Biofeedback on Hyperkinetic Children," *The Journal of Bio-feedback*, 2, no. 1 (Spring–Summer 1974), 24ff.

DIAMOND, SEYMOUR, and MARY FRANKLIN. "Biofeedback: Choice of Treatment in Childhood Migraine." Paper presented at the Seventh Annual Meeting of the Biofeedback Research Society, Colorado Springs, February 27–March 2, 1976. Reprint available from Biofeedback Research Society.

FERGUSON, P. C., "Transcendental Meditation and Its Potential Application in the Field of Special Education," *Journal of Special Education*, 10 (Summer 1976), 211–20.

FINLEY, WILLIAM W., *et al.* "Frontal EMG Biofeedback Training of Cerebral Palsy Children." Paper presented at the Seventh Annual Meeting of the Biofeedback Research Society, Colorado Springs, February 27–March 2, 1976. Reprint available from Biofeedback Research Society.

GREGORY, HUGO H. "An Assessment of the Results of Stuttering Therapy," ERIC, ED–043–178, September 1969.

GUNTER, ISABEL. *For the Parents of a Mongoloid Child.* Spring Valley, N.Y.: Anthroposophic Press (Rudolf Steiner—Waldorf Education).

HAIGHT, MARYELLEN J., *et al.* "The Response of Hyperkinesis to EMG Biofeedback." Paper presented at the Seventh Annual Meeting of the Biofeedback Research Society, Colorado Springs, February 27–March 2, 1976. Reprint available from Biofeedback Research Society.

HANNA, RICHMOND, *et al.* "A Biofeedback Treatment for Stuttering," *Journal of Speech and Hearing Disorders,* 40, no. 2 (May 1972), 270–73.

HARDYCK, C., and L. PETRINOVICH. "Treatment of Subvocal Speech During Reading," *Journal of Reading,* 12, no. 5 (1969), 361–68.

JAMPOLSKY, GERALD G., and MARYELLEN J. HAIGHT. "A Pilot Study of ESP in Hyperkinetic Children," The CHILD Center Annex, Tiburon, Calif. Undated.

KOENIG, KARL. *The Handicapped Child.* Spring Valley, N.Y.: Anthroposophic Press (Rudolf Steiner—Waldorf Education), 1973.

LUBAR, JOEL F., and MARGARET N. SHOUSE. "EEG and Behavioral Changes in a Hyperkinetic Child Concurrent with Training of the Sensorimotor Rhythm (SMR): A Preliminary Report," *Biofeedback and Self-Regulation,* 1, no. 3 (September 1976), 293–306.

NORDOFF, PAUL, and CLIVE ROBBINS. *Music Therapy for Handicapped Children.* Spring Valley, N.Y.: Anthroposophic Press (Rudolf Steiner—Waldorf Education).

O'MALLEY, J. E., and C. K. COMERS. "The Effect of Unilateral

Alpha Training on Visual-Evoked Response in a Dyslexic Adolescent," *Psychophysiology*, 9 (1972), 467.

O'NEIL, GISELA THOMAS. "Reading Disability: A Product of the Age," *Education as an Art*, Fall/Winter 1972-73, pp. 1-27. In Earl J. Ogletree, *The Socially Disadvantaged*. MSS Information Corp., New York, 1974.

PARSKY, LARRY, and JAMES D. PAPSDORF. "EMG Biofeedback Suppression of Subvocalization in Reading Disabled Grade VI Students." Paper presented at the Seventh Annual Meeting of the Biofeedback Research Society, Colorado Springs, February 27-March 2, 1976. Reprint available from Biofeedback Research Society.

SHOUSE, MARGARET N., and JOEL F. LUBAR. "Management of the Hyperkinetic Syndrome in Children Concurrent With Sensorimotor Rhythm Biofeedback Training." Paper presented at the Seventh Anual Meeting of the Biofeedback Research Society, Colorado Springs, February 27-March 2, 1976. Reprint available from Biofeedback Research Society.

SINGER, D. G., and M. L. LENAHAN. "Imagination Content in Dreams of Deaf Children," *American Annals of the Deaf*, 121 (February 1976), 44-48.

WAMBOLD, C. L., and C. HAYDEN. "Training Cognitive Strategies in the Mildly Retarded: An Applied Approach," *Education and Training of the Mentally Retarded*, 10 (October 1975), 132-37.

WEIKS, THOMAS. *Children in Need of Special Care*. Spring Valley, N.Y.: Anthroposophic Press (Rudolf Steiner—Waldorf Education).

WIEDEMANN, HANS MULLER. "Social Development in Handicapped Children," *The Cresset*, 11, no. 1 (1964), 15-26. Reprinted in Earl J. Ogletree, ed. *The Socially Disadvantaged*, Vol. II. MSS Information Corporation, New York, 1974.

WORD, P., and V. ROZYNKO. "Behavior Therapy of an Eleven-

Year-Old Girl with Reading Problems-Desensitization," *Journal of Learning Disabilities,* 7 (November 1974), 551-54.

ZWAIG, MARILYN S. "A Successful Camp Experience for the LD Child," *Academic Therapy,* 9, no. 6 (Summer 1974), 445-49.

———. "The Effect of Yoga on Atypical Children," *Sivanandra Ashram Yoga Camp Bulletin,* 1974, pp. 21-22.

SUGGESTION AND SUGGESTOLOGY

ANDREWS, A., *et al.* "Report of the Canadian Team on Their Stay at the Institute of Suggestology in Sofia." (To the Bureau of Languages, Canadian Ministry of Education, December 20, 1972.) Private Manuscript translated from the French by *Mankind Research Foundation, Inc.,* Washington, D.C.

BALEVSKY, P. "EEG Changes in the Process of Memorization under Ordinary and Suggestive Conditions," *Suggestology and Suggestopaedia,* 1, no. 1 (1975), 26-36.

BANCROFT, W. JANE. "Progressives and Pedagoges in the USSR," *Educational Courier,* December-January 1971, pp. 8-9.

———. "The Lozanov Language Class," *Journal of Suggestive-Accelerative Learning and Teaching,* 1, no. 1 (Spring 1976), 48.

———. "The Psychology of Suggestopedia: Or Learning Without Stress," *Educational Courier,* 42, no. 4 (February 1972), 16-19.

———. "Foreign Language Teaching in Bulgaria," *Canadian Modern Language Review,* March 1972, pp. 9-13.

———. "Education for the Future: Or the Lozanof System Revisited," *Educational Courier,* 43, no. 8 (June 1973), 11-13.

BENITEZ-BORDON, R., and D. P. McCLURE. "Toward a Theory for Research of Learning in an Altered State of Consciousness," unpublished monograph, University of Iowa, 1974.

————, and DONALD H. SCHUSTER. "Foreign Language Learning via the Lozanov Method: Pilot Studies," *Journal of Suggestive-Accelerative Learning and Teaching*, 1, no. 1 (Spring 1976), 3–15.

————. "The Effects of Suggestive Learning Climate, Synchronized Breathing and Music on the Learning and Retention of Spanish Words," *Journal of Suggestive-Accelerative Learning and Teaching*, 1, no. 1 (Spring 1976), 27–40.

BIGGERS, JULIAN L., and MATHIAS E. STRICHERZ. "Relaxation and Suggestion in a Recognition Task," *Journal of Suggestive-Accelerative Learning and Teaching*, 1, no. 2 (Summer 1976), 100–106.

Brain/Mind Bulletin. "Educators, Researchers Organize: Suggestology to be Explored in U.S.," 1, no. 6 (January 19, 1976), 1–2.

————. "State of Iowa Finances Suggestology Training," 1, no. 19 (August 16, 1976), 3.

————. "Suggestology, not hypnosis," 1, no. 8 (March 1, 1976), 3.

————. "Suggestology-Based Methods Explored at Des Moines Workshop," 1, no. 11 (April 19, 1976), 1–3.

Canadian Government Printing Office. *A Teaching Experience with the Suggestopaedic Method*. Order No. SC82–6/1975. Att.: J. Tourigny, 171 Slater St., Ottawa, Ontario, Canada, KIA 059.

CARSON, Jo. "Learning Without Pain—Doctor Explains Suggestology," *Globe and Mail*, Toronto, March 4, 1971.

CASKEY, OWEN L. *A Suggestopedia Primer*. Lubbock: Texas Technological University, 1975.

————, and MURIEL L. FLAKE. *Essentials of Suggestopedia: A Primer for Practitioners*. ERIC, ED-119-063, 1976.

——. *Suggestive—Accelerative Learning: Adaptations of the Lozanov Method.* Des Moines: SALT, 1976.

DONK, LEONARD J., *et al.* "The Comparison of Three Suggestion Techniques for Increasing Reading Efficiency Utilizing a Counterbalanced Research Paradigm," *The International Journal of Clinical and Experimental Hypnosis,* 18, no. 2 (April 1970), 126–33.

GETTERT, TWYLA J. "The First International Working Conference and Symposium on Suggestive-Accelerative Learning and Teaching and Suggestology, Des Moines, Iowa, March 29-April 2, 1976," *Journal of Suggestive-Accelerative Learning and Teaching,* 1, no. 2 (Summer 1976), 137–41.

GRITTON, CHARLES E., and RAY BENITEZ-BORDON, "Americanizing Suggestopaedia: A Preliminary Trial in a U.S. Classroom," *Journal of Suggestive-Accelerative Learning and Teaching,* 1, no. 2 (Summer 1976), 83–94.

HARMIN, MERRIL. "Est and Education," *Journal of Humanistic and Transpersonal Education,* 1, no. 1, forthcoming 1977.

HELD, DEAN. "Suggestive-Accelerative Learning and Teaching: An Experiment with Elements of an Altered States Approach in Reading," *Journal of Suggestive-Accelerative Learning and Teaching,* 1, no. 2 (Summer 1976), 131–36.

INSTITUTE FOR HUMANISTIC AND TRANSPERSONAL EDUCATION, "S.A.L.T. Suggestive-Accelerative Learning and Teaching," *Newsletter,* no. 1 (October 1976), p. 4.

KEMLER, D. G., and P. W. JUSCZYK. "Developmental Study of Facilitation by Mnemonic Instruction," *Journal of Experimental Child Psychology,* 20 (December 1975), 400–410.

KLINE, PETER. "The Sandy Spring Experiment: Applying Relaxation Techniques to Education," *Journal of Suggestive-Accelerative Learning and Teaching,* 1, no. 1 (Spring 1976), 16–26.

LOZANOV, G. "The Nature and History of the Suggestopaedic System of Teaching Foreign Languages and its Experimental

Prospects," *Suggestology and Suggestopaedia*, 1, no. 1 (1975), 5–15.

LOZANOV, GEORGI. *Suggestologiya*. Sofia, Bulgaria: Izdatelstvo Nauka i Iskustvo, 1971. English version in press, Gordon and Breach, 1976.

———. "Suggestopedia," *Zemedelsko Znami*, Sofia, Bulgaria, December 9, 1965.

———. *Suggestology and Suggestopaedy*. Sofia, Bulgaria: Nauka Press, 1971. English edition in preparation.

NATAN, T., and T. TASHEV. "Suggestion to Aid Teachers and Doctors," *Bulgaria Today*, 9 (1966), 24–27.

PHILIPOV, E. *Suggestology: The Use of Suggestion in Learning and Hypermnesia*, unpublished dissertation. U.S. International University, San Diego, 1975. Ann Arbor, Mich., University Microfilm 75-20255.

POLLACK, CECELIA. "Educational Experiment: Therapeutic Pedagogy," *Journal of Suggestive-Accelerative Learning and Teaching*, 1, no. 2 (Summer 1976), 95–99.

PRITCHARD, ALLYN, and JEAN TAYLOR. "Adapting the Lozanov Method for Remedial Reading Instruction," *Journal of Suggestive-Accelerative Learning and Teaching*, 1, no. 2 (Summer 1976), 107–15.

———. "An Altered States Approach to Remedial Reading Instruction." Mimeographed. Georgia State Department of Instruction, State Office Building, Atlanta, undated.

RUBIN, F. *Current Research in Hypnopaedia*. New York: Elsevier, 1968.

SALT. "Suggestive, Accelerative Learning and Teaching," *Classroom Manual*. Des Moines, Iowa.

SCHUSTER, DONALD H. "A Preliminary Evaluation of the Suggestive-Accelerative Lozanov Method in Teaching Beginning Spanish," *Journal of Suggestive-Accelerative Learning and Teaching*, 1, no. 1 (Spring 1976), 41–47.

————. "The Effects of the Alpha Mental State, Indirect Suggestion, and Associative Mental Activity on Learning Rare English Words," *Journal of Suggestive-Accelerative Learning and Teaching*, 1, no. 2 (Summer 1976), 116–23.

————, MARK STAVISH, and MARGARET BURCHINAL. "The Effects of Imaging Ability, Prepared Images and Sex of Subject on Learning English Words," *Journal of Suggestive-Accelerative Learning and Teaching*, 1, no. 2 (Summer 1976), 124–30.

————, RAY BENITEZ-BORDON, and CHARLES A. GRITTON. *Suggestive, Accelerative Learning and Teaching: A Manual of Classroom Procedures Based on the Lozanov Method.* (SALT) Society for Suggestive-Accelerative Learning and Teaching, 2740 Richmond Ave., Des Moines, Iowa. 1976. Bibliography.

SOCIETY FOR SUGGESTIVE-ACCELERATIVE LEARNING AND TEACHING. "S.A.L.T. in the Classroom," *Newsletter,* August-September 1976. Third-grade teacher uses suggestology to teach spelling.

————. "University of Wisconsin-Superior S.A.L.T. News and Views," *Newsletter,* 1, no. 5 (August-September 1976), 2.

————. "S.A.L.T. Teachers Trained at Iowa State University," *Newsletter,* 1, no. 5 (August-September 1976), 1.

————. "Resources Guide to S.A.L.T.," *Newsletter,* 1, no. 5 (August-September 1976), 3 & 4.

Suggestive-Accelerative Learning and Teaching, Journal of, "A Professional Society Formed in Iowa," 1, no. 1 (Spring 1976), 75–77.

TRUCE, G. "Suggestibility and Learning," *Intellect,* 102 (March 1975), 350–51.

TURKEVICH, LUDMILLA B. "Suggestology," *Russian Language Journal,* 26 (Spring-Fall 1972), 81–91, 94–95.

WESTHEIMER, BENJAMIN S. "Experiencing Education with *est,*" in *Four Psychologies Applied to Education: Freudian, Behavioral, Humanistic, Transpersonal,* ed. T. Roberts. New York: John Wiley & Sons, 1975.

SURVEYS AND MULTI-TOPIC SOURCES

CANFIELD, JACK. *A Basic Do-It-Yourself Background Kit for Transpersonal Education.* New England Center for Humanistic and Transpersonal Education. P.O. Box 575, Amherst, Mass., 01002. 35¢

———. *A Guide to Resources in Humanistic and Transpersonal Education.* Forthcoming 1977.

CLARK, FRANCES V. "Rediscovering Transpersonal Education," *Journal of Transpersonal Psychology,* 6, no. 1 (1974), 1–7.

CORDOZO, PETER, and TED MENTEN. *The Whole Kids Catalog.* New York: Bantam, 1975.

DANIELS, VICTOR, and LAURENCE J. HOROWITZ. *Being and Caring.* San Francisco: San Francisco Book Company (Distributed by Simon and Schuster, N.Y.), 1976.

East-West Journal. "Toward A Higher Education," Vol. 4, no. 8, September 1974. Entire issue is devoted to spiritual and transpersonal education.

FERGUSON, MARILYN. "Revolution in the Cradle" and "Trance Learning and Memory Molecules," in *The Brain Revolution.* New York: Bantam Books, 1975.

GREEN, ALYCE, ELMER E. GREEN, and E. DALE WALTERS. "Brainwave Training, Imagery, Creativity, and Integrative Experiences." Paper read at The Biofeedback Research Society Conference, February 1974. Research Department, The Menninger Foundation, Topeka.

HARRISON, ALTON, and DIANN MUSIAL. *Transpersonal Education: Altered States of Awareness Applied to Classroom Instruction.* (working title) Santa Monica, Calif.: Goodyear Publishing Co., 1977.

HENDRICKS, GAY, and JAMES FADIMAN. *Transpersonal Education: A Curriculum of Feeling and Being.* Englewood Cliffs, N.J.: Prentice-Hall, 1976.

————, and RUSSEL WILLS. *The Centering Book: Awareness Activities for Children, Parents, and Teachers.* Englewood Cliffs, N.J.: Prentice-Hall, 1975.

————. "Feel–Good Activities for Parents and Young Children," *Parents' Magazine,* September 1975.

HOUSTON, JEAN. "The Psychenaut Program: An Exploration into Some Human Potentials," *Journal of Creative Behavior,* 7, no. 4, 253–78, Fourth Quarter, 1973b.

————. "Putting the First Man on Earth," *Saturday Review,* February 22, 1975, 28–32, 53.

Institute for Humanistic and Transpersonal Education. "Transpersonal Ed Network," *Newsletter,* no. 1 (October 1976), pp. 13 & 14.

IRWIN, SAMUEL, REXINE M. HAYES, and LEE R. FRUNDEN. "Education for Living: Awareness and Creative Choice (Alternative to Drugs)," *Journal of Psychedelic Drugs,* 7, no. 1 (January–March 1975), 49–57.

KRIPPNER, STANLEY, *et al.* "The Creative Person and Non-ordinary Reality," *Gifted Child Quarterly,* 16, no. 3 (February 1972), 203–28, 234.

LaCHAPELLE, DOLORES, and JANET BOURQUE. *Earth Festivals: Seasonal Celebrations for Everyone Young and Old.* Finn Hill Arts, P.O. Box 542, Silverton, Colo. 81433. 1976.

McCORMICK, MAURICE D. "Ways of Growth" (Chapter 13); "How to Meditate: Meditation and Education" (Chapter 14); "Love" (Chapter 15); "Love, Happiness, and Higher Consciousness" (Chapter 16); *An Invitation to Grow: Humanistic and Transpersonal Activities for Interpersonal Effectiveness and Personal Growth.* RF Publishing Co., Distributed by University Press of America, Washington, D.C., 1976.

MOFFETT, JAMES. "A Talk With James Moffett," interviewed by David Sohn, *Media and Methods*, 11, no. 6 (February 1975), 22–24, 50–61.

OTTO, HERBERT A. "New Light on the Human Potential," *Childhood Education*, 47, no. 1, 2.

PRIVETTE, GAYLE. "Transcendent Functioning: The Full Use of Potentialities." In Herbert Otto and John Mann, eds., *Ways of Growth: Approaches to Expanding Awareness*. New York: Grossman, 1968.

Psychosynthesis Research Foundation. Psychosynthesis in Education. Issue No. 2, New York.

RING, KENNETH. *Ken Ring's Annotated Reading List*. Association for Transpersonal Psychology, Palo Alto, Calif., 1975.

ROBERTS, THOMAS B. "Transpersonal: The New Educational Psychology," *Phi Delta Kappan*, November 1974, pp. 191–93.

———. *Transpersonal: The New Educational Psychology*, ERIC, ED–099–252, April 1975a

———., ed. "Transpersonal Psychology Applied to Education." Section IV of *Four Psychologies Applied to Education: Freudian, Behavioral, Humanistic, Transpersonal*, pp. 392–550. New York: 1975b. John Wiley & Sons.

———. "Transpersonal Psychology in Education: Bibliography and Resource Guide," Amherst, Mass.: The New England Center (P.O. Box 575), 1975.

———. "Transpersonal: A Research Agenda for the Threshold of the Twenty-First Century," *Simulations & Games*, forthcoming 1977.

———. "Transpersonal Education: A Personal View," *Journal of Humanistic and Transpersonal Education*, 1, no. 1, forthcoming 1977.

———, and FRANCES V. CLARK. *Transpersonal Psychology in Education*, Fastback Pamphlet Series, #53, Phi Delta Kappa Educational Foundation, Bloomington, Ind., April 1975c. Also ERIC, ED–107–626, 1975c.

———, "Transpersonal Psychology in Education," in *Transpersonal Education: A Curriculum for Feeling and Being*, ed. Gay Hendricks and James Fadiman. Englewood Cliffs, N.J.: Prentice-Hall, Inc., 1976.

SAMPLES, ROBERT E. *Opening: A Primer for Self-Actualization*. Menlo Park, Calif.: Addison-Wesley, 1973.

Saturday Review, February 22, 1975. Entire issue devoted to transpersonal psychology and related topics.

SEXTON, T., and D. POLING. *Can Intelligence Be Taught?* (Monograph) Phi Delta Kappa Educational Foundation Fastback Series #29. Bloomington, Ind., 1973.

Synthesis. Psychosynthesis Workbook, 1, no. 1 (1974), 1–74.

———. Psychosynthesis Workbook, 1, no. 2 (1975), 49–118.

TART, CHARLES T., ed. *Transpersonal Psychologies*. New York: Harper & Row, 1975. Paperback, New York: Harper & Row, 1977.

WALLECHINSKY, DAVID, and IRVING WALLACE. *The People's Almanac*. Garden City, N.Y.: Doubleday, 1975. Mostly socially and politically oriented, but with chapters on psychics, religion, death, the unknown, and mysterious happenings.

TEACHERS' AND COUNSELORS' NEW ROLES

BLOFELD, JOHN. "Ways of Teaching," in *Transpersonal Education: A Curriculum for Feeling and Being*. ed. Gay Hendricks and James Fadiman. Englewood Cliffs, N.J.: Prentice-Hall, Inc., 1976.

BOYD, DOUG. "On gurus," (pp. 289–294). *Swami*. New York: Random House, 1976.

BROWN, DEAN. *Learning and Teaching.* Los Gatos, Calif., Lamplighters Roadway Press, 1974.

CASTANEDA, CARLOS. *Introduction to Journey to Ixtlan: Two Lessons of Don Juan.* New York: Touchstone/Simon and Schuster, 1972.

KENNETT, JIYU (ROSHI), SWAMI RADHA, and ROBERT FRAGER. "How to Be a Transpersonal Teacher Without Becoming a Guru," *Journal of Transpersonal Psychology,* 7, no. 1, (1975), 48–65.

LEFORT, RAFAEL. "An Interview with One of Gurdjieff's Teachers," in *Transpersonal Education: A Curriculum for Feeling and Being,* ed. Gay Hendricks and James Fadiman. Englewood Cliffs, N.J.: Prentice-Hall, Inc., 1976.

MORRIS, ROBERT L., "The Responsibilities of Instructors in Parapsychology," in *Education in Parapsychology,* ed. Betty Shapin and Lisette Coly. New York: Parapsychology Foundation, 1976.

THE MOTHER, et al. *The True Teacher,* ed. N. Dowsett and S. R. Jayaswal. Mt. Tremper, N.Y.: Matagiri.

PAYNE, J. S. "Teaching Teachers and Teaching Mind Readers," *Phi Delta Kappan,* 53 (February 1972), 375–76.

PETERS, FRITZ. "Gurdjieff as Elementary Teacher," in *Transpersonal Education: A Curriculum for Feeling and Being,* ed. Gay Hendricks and James Fadiman. Englewood Cliffs, N.J.: Prentice-Hall, Inc., 1976.

RAM DASS, BABA. "One Pointedness of Mind and Teachers as Conveyers of the Universe," *The Only Dance There Is,* pp. 93–99. New York: Anchor-Doubleday, 1974.

ROBERTS, DAYTON Y. *Personalizing Learning Processes.* Paper presented at the annual meeting of the American Association of Community and Junior Colleges, Seattle, Wash., April 13–16, 1975. ERIC, ED–115–322. Jungian types.

Salamander Publications. *The Teacher: Eleven Aspects of the Guru Rinpoche*, Sausalito, Calif., 1972.

TRUNGPA, CHOGYAM. *Born in Tibet*. Baltimore: Penguin Metaphysical Library, 1971. Account of early training of a Tibetan lama.

WEINHOLD, BARRY K. "Transpersonal Communication in the Classroom," in *Transpersonal Education: A Curriculum for Feeling and Being*, ed. Gay Hendricks and James Fadiman. Englewood Cliffs, N.J.: Prentice-Hall, Inc., 1976.

CATALOGS

Academy of Parapsychology and Medicine, *Publication List*, 314 Second Street, Los Altos, Calif. 94022.

Aesthetic Research Center of Canada, *Catalog*, P.O. Box 3044, Vancouver, B.C., Canada, V6B 3X5.

American Society for Psychical Research, *Courses and Other Study Opportunities in Parapsychology*, November 1974 (revised periodically), 5 West 73rd Street, New York, N.Y. 10023. $2.00.

Anthroposophic Press, *Catalog*, Threefold Farm, Hungry Hollow Road, Spring Valley, N.Y. 10977.

Banyan Books, *More Light!* (Booklist), Summer 1975 Supplement features special section on books for children, 2715 West Fourth Avenue, Vancouver, B.C., Canada V6K 1P9.

Big Sur Recordings, *Catalog*, 2015 Bridgeway, Sausalito, Calif. 94965.

BioMonitoring Application, Inc., *Catalog*, Cassette tapes, 270 Madison Avenue, New York, N.Y. 10016.

Brain Information Service, *Publications List,* UCLA, Center for the Health Sciences, Los Angeles, Calif. 90024.

Bruce, Raymond, Ltd., *Audio/Visual Catalogue No. 1,* Autumn 1975, 2264 Lakeshore Boulevard, West Toronto, Ontario, Canada, M8V, 1A9. USA agent: USCAN, 528 North Michigan Avenue, Chicago, Ill. 60611.

Edmund Scientific Co., *Catalog,* 402 Edscorp Building, Barrington, N.J. 08007. Equipment for Kirlian photography, ESP, parapsychological experiments, etc.

Esalen Institute, *Catalog,* Big Sur, Calif. 93920.

Hartley Productions, *Films for the New Age,* Cat Rock Road, Cos Cob, Conn. 06087. Excellent.

Mandala, *Catalog,* Box 796, Amherst, Mass. 01002. Booklist.

Multi-Media Productions, Inc., *Catalog,* P.O. Box 5097, Stanford, Calif. 94305. Issued periodically. See especially the sound filmstrips: "Auroville: Global Community for a Future World"; "Jungian Symbols: A Door to Self-Awareness", "Can Eastern Thought Help the West?"; "Hinduism"; "Buddhism"; "Christianity"; "Introduction to Parapsychology—Telepathy."

Pacifica Foundation, *Pacifica Tape Library Catalog,* 5316 Venice, Los Angeles, Calif. 90019.

Self-Management Tapes, *Catalog,* Tape cassettes, 1534 Oakstream, Houston, Texas. 77043.

Shambala Review, 2045 Francisco Street, San Francisco, Calif.

Techter, David. List of slides on psychic, parapsychological, and religious topics. Duplicated to order. P.O. Box 362, Highland Park, Ill. 60035.

YES! Inc., *Books for Inner Development,* Booklist, 1039 31st Street, N.W., Washington, D.C. 20007. Large, interesting, annotated bibliography.

ORGANIZATIONS

American Alliance for Health, Physical Education, and Recreation, PEPI Project, 1201 16th Street, N.W., Washington, D.C. 20036.

American Association for the Advancement of Tension Control, P.O. Box 7512, Roanoke, Va. 24019.

American Association of Biofeedback Clinicians, 2424 Dempster Street, Des Plaines, Ill. 60016.

American Metapsychiatric Association, 1800 Northeast 114th Street, Miami, Florida 33181.

American Society for Psychical Research, 5 West 73rd Street, New York, N.Y. 10023.

Association for Holistic Health, Box 23231, San Diego, Calif. 92123.

Association for Research and Enlightenment, P.O. Box 595, Virginia Beach, Va. 23451. Research on work of Edgar Cayce.

Association for Transpersonal Psychology, P.O. Box 3049, Stanford, Calif. 94305.

Biofeedback Research Society, University of Colorado Medical Center, Room C268, 4200 East Ninth Avenue, Denver, Col. 80220.

Bucke, (R.M.) Memorial Society, 1266 Pine Avenue West, Montreal, Canada.

California Institute of Transpersonal Psychology, P.O. Box 2364, Stanford, Calif. 94305.

Canadian Academy of Psychotronics, Suite, 803, 43 Eglinton Avenue East, Toronto, Canada, M4P 1A2.

Canadian Institute of Psychosynthesis, 3496 Avenue Marlowe, Montreal, Quebec, Canada, H4A 3L7.

Center for Integral Medicine, 465 North Roxbury Drive, Beverly Hills, Calif. 90210.

Council of Nurse Healers, c/o Dolores Krieger, 70 Shelly Avenue, Port Chester, N.Y. 10573. Or: Effie Chow, 33 Ora Way, San Francisco, Calif. 94131.

East West Academy of Healing Arts, 33 Ora Way, San Francisco, Calif. 94131.

Essentia, P.O. Box 129, Tiburon, Calif. 94920.

Foundation for ParaSensory Investigation, 1 West 81st Street, Suite 5D, New York, N.Y. 10024.

Foundation for Research on the Nature of Man, 402 Buchanan, Durham, N.C. 27708. J. B. Rhine's parapsychological research center.

Human Dimensions Institute, Rosary Hill College, 4380 Main Street, Buffalo, N.Y. 14226.

Humanistic Parapsychology Network, Jerry Muehe, Box 655, Cotati, Calif. 94928.

Information Services for Psi Education, Mrs. J. E. Nester, ASPR, 5 West 73rd Street, New York, N.Y. 10024.

Institute for Consciousness and Music, Room 104, 31 Allegheny Avenue, Towson, Md. 21204.

Institute for the Study of Human Knowledge, P.O. Box 2045, Stanford, Calif. 94305.

Institute for the Study of Humanistic Medicine, 3847 Twenty-First Street, San Francisco, Calif. 94114.

Institute of Noetic Sciences, 530 Oak Grove Avenue, Suite 201, Menlo Park, Calif. 94025.

International Institute of Integral Human Sciences, Box 1387, Station H, Montreal, P.Q., Canada, H3G 2N3.

Maharishi International University, Fairfield, Iowa 52556.

Mankind Research Unlimited, 1143 New Hampshire Avenue, N.W., Washington, D.C. 20073. Suggestology.

National Council on Wholistic Therapeutics in Medicine, Box H. Brooklyn, N.Y. 11202.

Noetics Education Association, c/o Diane Brown, P.O. Box 784, Orinda, Calif. 94563.

Parapsychology Foundation, Inc., 29 West 57th Street, New York, N.Y. 10019.

Planetary Citizens (an association), 777 UN Plaza, New York, N.Y. 10017.

Psychical Research Foundation, Duke Station, Durham, N.C. 27706. Research on life beyond death.

Rudolf Steiner Information Center, 211 Madison Avenue, New York, N.Y. 10016.

Society for Psychical Research, 1 Adam and Eve Mews, London W8 6UQ, England.

Spiritual Frontiers Fellowship, 800 Custer Avenue, Evanston, Ill. 60202.

Suggestopaedia Canada, Gabriel Racle, Director, Room 419, 1725 Woodward Drive, Aselford-Martin Building, Ottawa, Ontario, Canada K1A 0M7.

Theosophical Society in America, P.O. Box 270, Wheaton, Ill. 60187.

Touch for Health, Box 751C, Pasadena, Calif. 91104. Applied Kinesiology.

Transpersonal Education Network, Institute for Humanistic and Transpersonal Education, Box 575, Amherst, Mass. 01002.

Transpersonal Psychology Program, c/o Hugh Redmond (Director), Johnston College, University of Redlands, Redlands, Calif. 92373.

Waldorf Institute for Liberal Education, Adelphi University, Garden City, N.Y. 11530.

Well Being (a network for spiritual journeyors), P.O. Box 887, San Anselmo, Calif. 94960.

Yoga Teachers' Association, Box 11476, Chicago, Ill. 60611.

PERIODICALS

Education Index. Useful descriptors:
    biological control systems
    brain
    consciousness
    dreams
    extrasensory perception
    fantasy
    hypnosis
    images and imagery
    meditation
    psychical research
    relaxation
    subconsciousness
    trance

ERIC (Education Resources Information Center), Useful descriptors for *Current Index to Journals in Education* (always the first place to search) and for *Research in Education:*
    biofeedback
    cerebral dominance
    educational psychology
    extrasensory perception
    fantasy
    feedback
    hypnosis
    imagery
    imagination
    lateral dominance
    mysticism
    mythology
    progressive relaxation
    psychiatry
    psychological characteristics

psychological studies
psychophysiology
psychotherapy

American Journal of Clinical Hypnosis, 800 Washington Avenue, S.E., Minneapolis, Minn.

Biofeedback and Self-Control (annual), Aldine Publishing Co., Chicago, Ill. 1970+.

Biofeedback and Self-Regulation. Included in membership in the Biofeedback Research Society. Available separately from Plenum Publishers, New York. ($15.00).

Biofeedback Network, E. W. (Dub) Rakestraw, Editor, 103 South Grove, Greensburg, Kan. 67054. $5.00/year.

Brain/Mind Bulletin, P.O. Box 42211, Los Angeles, Calif. 90042. Excellent semi-monthly newsletter.

Confluent Education Journal, CEDARC, P.O. Box 30128, Santa Barbara, CA 93105.

Consciousness and Culture Review, The International Transdisciplinary Journal of the Human Sciences, Department of Philosophy, Iowa State University, Ames, Iowa 50011.

Dreams and Inner Spaces, Edendale, P.O. Box 26556, Los Angeles, Calif. 90026.

East-West Journal, 233 Harvard Street, Brookline, Mass. 02146.

Energy and Character: Journal of Bioenergetic Research, David Boadella, Editor, Abbotsbury, Weymouth, Dorset, U.K. Emphasis on Reich, Lowen, and energy fields.

Essentiasheet, P.O. Box 129, Tiburon, Calif. 94920.

Fields Within Fields, Within Fields, World Institute Council, 777 United Nations Plaza, New York, N.Y. 10017.

Human Dimensions, Rosary Hill College, Buffalo, N.Y. 14226.

Journal for the Study of Consciousness (ceased publication). Philadelphia, 1968–1972.

Journal of Altered States of Consciousness. Baywood Publishing Co., Farmingdale, N.Y. 11735.

Journal of American Society for Psychical Research. 5 West 73rd Street, New York, N.Y. 10023.

Journal of Biofeedback. Biofeedback Technology, Inc., Publications Division, 10602–A Trask Avenue, Garden Grove, Calif. 92643.

Journal of Creative Behavior. State University College at Buffalo, 1300 Elmwood Avenue, Buffalo, N.Y. 14222.

Journal of Humanistic and Transpersonal Education, P.O. Box 575, Amherst, Mass. 01002.

Journal of Humanistic Psychology. 325 Ninth Street, San Francisco, Calif. 94103.

Journal of Parapsychology. College Station, Durham, N.C. 27708.

Journal of Society for Psychical Research. 1 Adam and Eve Mews, London W8 6UQ, England.

Journal of Suggestive-Accelerative Learning and Teaching. Box 927, Des Moines, Iowa 50306.

Journal of Transpersonal Psychology. P.O. Box 4437, Stanford, Calif. 94305.

Mnemonic (The Mushroom Newsletter: Ethno-Mycological Origins of Noetic-Intuitive Consciousness), P.O. Box 30039, St. Paul, Minn. 55175.

New Age Journal, 145 Portland Street, Cambridge, Mass.

New Games Newsletter, Box 7901, San Francisco, Calif. 94120. The new physical education.

New Horizons. P.O. Box 427, Station F, Toronto, Ontario, Canada, M4Y 2L8.

New Realities. Bolen Co., 680 Beach Street, San Francisco, Calif. 94109.

Parapsychology Review, 29 West 57th Street, New York, N.Y. 10019.

Personal Growth. P.O. Box 1254, Berkeley, Calif. 94701.

Psychedelic Review. 290 Seventh Street, San Francisco, Calif. 94103.

Psychoenergetic Systems. Gordon & Breach, One Park Ave., New York, N.Y. 10016.

Religious Education. 409 Prospect Street, New Haven, Conn. 06510.

Rising Mind. 2186 Meadowgate Way, San Jose, Calif. 95132.

Somatics. 1516 Grant Avenue, Suite 220, Novato, Calif. 94947. A Magazine-Journal of the Bodily Arts and Sciences.

Suggestology and Suggestopedia, Box 927, Iowa City, Iowa 52240.

Sundance Community Dream Journal. A.R.E., P.O. Box 595, Virginia Beach, Va. 23451.

Symbology, International Journal of. Psychology Department, Georgia State University, Atlanta.

Synthesis. 830 Woodside Road, Redwood City, Calif. 94061.

"Psychosynthesis Workbook." A regular feature with practical ideas and techniques for enhancing one's personal development and integration.

Theta (a periodical having to do with survival after death). Psychical Research Foundation, Box 6116, Duke Station, Durham, N.C. 27706.

X. X Press, P.O. Box 2237, Boulder, Colo. 80306. X, a bridge between the known and unknown in art, science, and literature. Forthcoming 1977.

Yoga Journal. California Yoga Teachers Association, 1736 Ninth Avenue, San Francisco, Calif. 94114.

Zetetics. c/o Marcello Truzzie, Sociology Department, Eastern Michigan University, Ypsilanti, Mich. 48197. Journal dedicated to exposing parapsychology research.